Peter Kemp (Ed.)

History in Education

Proceedings from the Conference *History in Education*

Held at the Danish University of Education
24-25 March, 2004

The Present Publication is Financially Supported by
Korea Research Foundation
and the Danish University of Education

Danish University of Education Press

History in Education

Author: Peter Kemp (Ed.)

Proceedings from the Conference History in Education
Held at the Danish University of Education 24-25 March, 2004

The Present Publication is Financially Supported by Korea Research Foundation and the Danish University of Education

Published by Danish University of Education Press
The Danish University of Education
54, Emdrupvej
DK– 2400 Copenhagen NV
www.dpu.dk/forlag

Typeset and Cover: Pitney Bowes Management Services – DPU
Cover Illustration: Armageddon, 2000,
Bandung, Indonesia. Polyester resin, 48x40x70 cm
Print: IKON Document Services

1. edition
ISBN 87-7684-006-9

How to buy:
National Library of Education
101, Emdrupvej, DK – 2400 Copenhagen NV
www.dpb.dpu.dk
bogsalg@dpu.dk
T: +45 8888 9360
F: +45 8888 9394

Contents

Preface

This book is the result of an international conference in Copenhagen in March 2004 on the theme *History in Education* organized by the *International Federation of Philosophical Societies* (FISP – Fédération Internationale de Sociétés de Philosophie) together with the *Korean Philosophical Association* and the *Danish University of Education*. As members of the Steering Committee of FISP, philosophers from all over the world met with philosophers and historians from the Danish University of Education in order to discuss the importance of history for the cultivation (Bildung) or formation of ourselves.

Until recently the opinion shared by many people was that learning history had lost all significance for personal and social life. It was argued that rapid technological changes meant that we could no longer learn anything from our past, and our technological mastery of the world meant that there was no need to imagine a historical process that could make our world essentially better.

In fact, two visions of history seemed obsolete: The vision of a time in the past of deep contemplation of the human condition, which could help us understand our life in the present, and the vision of a time in the future when we might experience a radical new order of things, which could give our life today direction or a goal.

The first vision of history includes both what Nietzsche in his "On the Advantage and Disadvantage of History for Life" calls *antiquarian* history, which "helps people to persist in what a well-established tradition rooted in familiar soil offers as habitual and worthy of reverence" and what the same philosopher calls *monumental* history, which concerns active people in search of "models, teachers and comforters [they] cannot find among [their] contemporaries".

In Denmark a recent television series about a group of Danes living in the fifties enjoyed enormous popularity. The series, called *Krøniken* (*The Chronicle*), was not very dramatic and featured no real deep psychological conflicts - in fact, it was rather banal and sometimes involuntarily comical - but it reinforced viewers' feelings of being part of a shared history and of identifying with their own past, the past of their parents, their grandparents and great-grandparents etc. This television show proves that antiquarian history is by no means dead in the minds of ordinary people.

Monumental history also thrives today, as seen in particular in readers' fascination with biographies of great personalities of the past. In Denmark, for instance, the biography of the Danish prime minister of the sixties, Jens Otto Krag, has aroused a great deal of interest. I therefore do not see any grounds for declaring that monumental history is dead either.

History can, however, also be conceived of as what I would call prophetic history. This corresponds to what Nietzsche calls critical history, which breaks with the present in order to realize a goal in the future.

This idea of history was declared dead by the American philosopher Francis Fukuyama in his best-seller *The End of History and the Last Man*, which appeared in 1992. He claimed at the time that technological and economic development had created the conditions of liberal democracies that could render superfluous the wars that until then had made history one long battle for recognition until finally the victor emerged as a superpower. Great wars and violent revolutions were no longer necessary; the human being became "the last man" who, according to Nietzsche, is satisfied with his quiet little existence and feels no need to change the world and make world history.

Today Fukuyama has given up his own claim about the end of history because new gene technologies have made radical changes of human beings possible, thereby opening up the horizon to a post-human future - a radical change of history abhorrent to Fukuyama. In other words, world history, according to

Fukuyama, has reemerged thanks to a fight to protect humankind against its own destruction through the use of excessively violent biotechnology.

I see, however, a more radical return of prophetic history: The challenge to humankind from terrorism. Before September 11, 2001 an American citizen such as Fukuyama could believe that peace for the United States was secured forever. But after this event the American president declared a worldwide war on terrorism, meaning that from then on the whole world was in danger and we can today only hope for a better future.

The political wisdom of that war may be questioned in that a war against the misery in the world today may have been more effective in limiting terrorism, but the vision of history is still prophetic. It is the vision of a better world, for which people must fight in order to protect their daily lives from the terrorism that increasingly poses a threat towards them.

Thus, what we discover today is that the sense of history has not disappeared from our minds but is present in our social and political understanding of ourselves, both as a vision of a past that can teach us something about how to overcome difficulties thanks to hard-earned experiences acquired in suffering and hope, and also a vision of a future that passes down a peaceful world to our descendants, a world without wars and terrorism, without exploitation of resources and pollution of nature.

It is probably inevitable that this sense of history will become the guiding perspective of all education from nursery school to university if we want to survive in the dangerous world we live in today, and it must therefore be the task of philosophers of our time to reflect on and explain the meaning and indispensability of this sense of history for the moral and political formation of ourselves.

In this book philosophers and historians take this task seriously.

Peter Kemp
President of FISP

'History' of the Present regarded as the Past of the Future

Lars-Henrik Schmidt

As Friedrich Nietzsche mentioned in one of his early writings: "Zu allem Handeln gehört Vergessen" ["to all action belongs oblivion"].[1] It is my conviction as a historian of ideas by profession that most of us do not want to forget, to repulse or to deny, but the sense of history is something apart from this. It is an educational problem – i.e. a problem for the educational system

History may have come to an end – as it has been claimed in popular writings[2] - perhaps even be dead, but the philosophy of history is alive and kicking once again. The question is whether or not educationalists should look for a new way of training historical consciousness.

In my presentation I shall try to argue that 'history in education' will lead to the return of the philosophy of history – not of history as an academic discipline or of the didactics of history as an academic discipline. It will of course be a very different philosophy of history than the one we know from the philosophic tradition. It will not be a philosophy based on rationalization after the fact, but rather a sort of "philosophy of hope". Not as a principle of hope, as in Ernst Bloch or the late Jean Paul Sartre, but simply as an insistence on the *openness* of the world. When history becomes embedded in education, a new chord is struck. History has a future. I doubt, no doubt. I shall try to explain a perspective on the opening.

The question is how we should thematize 'history' in education anew. There is no crisis in relation to the significance of historical consciousness.

---

1   Friedrich Nietzsche: *Vom Nutzen und Nachteil der Historie für das Leben*; Werke I FaM 1962 (1874), p. 213.

2   See Fukuyama, Francis: *The End of History and the last Man*. New York, 1992.

In the second half of the 19th century, Nietzsche talked of the development of a "historic sense" [3]; I have since tried to translate this into a competence in "historical imagination"[4]. This is the angle I will be taking today. Nietzsche was concerned about the excess of history – he even spoke of the "historical malady",[5] and for this we must find an appropriate remedy;[6] we are concerned about a deficit of history nowadays, so our tonic must be to adhere to the historical perspective in a world in which only a small minority knows when the television was invented – a medium which these days is the mainstay of universalization to such a degree that we forget that it was the telegraph that brought us together. The mobile phone is a modern telegraph; the Internet is still a physical connection between computers – but for how long? A new technology opens new doors, it creates a new intimacy, but it does not connect us with our history, unless we wish to look upon our access to new experiences, to plastic illustration as a goal in itself. Access to knowledge and connected knowledge are not of the same breed. Our time valorises access just as we prefer to exercise our freedom as the freedom to choose, as voluntariness. Is it possible to choose one's history? No, probably not – others have views on the gospels – but we retell ourselves and thereby come into being. We have a freedom to be in the world. We are no longer "thrown into the world" as Heidegger emphasizes, nor are we only capable of "creating something in the world" as Arendt would say.

The modern human being can edit his world. This is possible because things are only things to the extent to which this is documented. We have now spent five hundred years internalizing observation. Now we need to understand that we are always already "in the spotlight": "Show me your best"!

It must seem to the majority of educators that 'history' is regarded as an unavoidable subject in our educations. In Denmark we put it this way: "It shall be the aim of the teaching in the subject of history to strengthen the students' awareness of history and identity and to increase their desire and motivation for active participation in a democratic society. This is done by furthering their insight into the fact that man is created by history as well as creating history."

---

3   Friedrich Nietzsche: *Vom Nutzen und Nachteil der Historie für das Leben*; Werke I FaM 1962 (1874), p. 213

4   See, for instance, *Magtens fysik*; Kbh. 2000 (1979), p. 9ff.

5   Op.cit. p. 281

6   In Nietzsche the remedy is called "das Unhistorische und das Überhistorische" (the ahistorical and the transhistorical), ibid.

This formulation is taken from the "Order on the Aims of Teaching" for the Danish primary and lower secondary school[7]. At one time history was the narrative of exemplary exploits and an invitation to continuity. It was crucial to be exemplary, i.e. a model for imitation, like the Holy Francis of Assisi or even Jesus. In our cultural sphere imitation has been the decisive theme – and thereby also the selective or 'exclusive' theme, as an ideal or as a contrast. It has been an educational narrative, a moral narrative. The science of history, history as an academic discipline has consistently destroyed this dimension. The training of the critical gaze has dominated over fascination.

We should not decide between these two viewpoints; rather, a new theme should be adopted: what does this insight give you in the way of hopes?

We presume that through historical experience, teaching and learning, pupils can develop insight into people's lives and living conditions throughout time, and understand their own culture, other people's cultures and the interaction between man and nature.

They must understand the interaction between the past, the present and the future – i.e. they must develop an understanding of the dimension of time, which will pave the way to an experience of the relationship between continuity and change.

I

Formulations such as these are initially harmless.

A distinctive notion prevails that there is a connection between an awareness of history, identity and civic participation – participation is especially crucial in Danish pedagogy. The demand for participation is echoed on many different levels of education and has its roots in a long Danish tradition for 'public enlightenment' (folkeoplysning). In Denmark, 'folkeoplysning' (one might say giving birth to a nation), including adult education, has always – not least thanks to Grundtvig, a true philosopher of history – played first fiddle in the orchestra of education.

The formulation that we are created by history as well as creating history is *ceteris paribus* a metaphysical problem. It is reliable, almost nonchalant, but it touches on a very large theme. Taking a position on the question of history in

---

7   Undervisningsministeriet: *Formål og centrale kundskabs- & færdighedsområder*, Kbh. 1994, p. 25f.. Similar formulations in relation to other levels in our educational system can be found elsewhere.

education is hardly a question of the position of the subject of history in our present-day curricula. It is not a question of whether or not history should be included in our curricula, but rather a question of the purpose of including it in our curricula – how is it useful? As such, it may be considered a didactic question, but above all it is a philosophical question, which brings to mind not least Hegel's contemplations in the introduction to the "Vorlesungen über die Philosophie der Geschichte" (1822-1832) [8] on the relationship between "Geschichte" and "Historie" (an organised narrative of historical events and history as a form of recording events respectively). The metaphysical dilemma of whether we are created by history and/or creating history and the connection between these perspectives has not, however, been elucidated as yet. The formulation of the problem echoes Karl Marx's formulation of 1845 that circumstances create human beings inasmuch as they create the circumstances. [9] We are not only dealing with how we got here, but also with where we are going. The questions that the subject of history addresses must therefore be: who are we, where are we going and what prevents us from getting there?

'History in education' in my opinion means something very simple: How do we communicate to pupils the fact that they are living in a modern world, a world not born yesterday but which nonetheless is on its way to somewhere else. What does this mean? It means that the present is the past of the future; it is not enough to regard the matter as if we are products of a past, that we are standing on the shoulders of our ancestors and that we are duty bound to be grateful to them in one way or another – which of course is a crucial educational and anthropologic task – and it is this point which is my first thesis.

History will no longer be the knowledge of how things used to be, knowledge of events and occurrences, but a historical consciousness of or perhaps, rather, an awareness of the fact that things could have been different, *will* be different and that others will have another interpretation. This is the practical dimension in Aristotle and the principle of freedom in Kant. Historical consciousness is rooted in the fact that things could have been different – but they were not.

---

8   Cf. G.W.F. Hegel: *Vorlesungen über die Philosophie der Geschichte* i Werke 12; FaM, 1970. One might add that the first edition of Hegel's introduction (1822, 1828) was entitled "Die Behandlungsarten der Geschichte" (ways of dealing with history), and the second edition (1830) was simply entitled "Die philosophische Weltgeschichte" (the philosophical history of the world). Hegel is interested in 'Geschichte' and refers to his views on 'die Historiker vom Fach' (academic historians) (ibid.) P 22f), who have an altogether different approach – i.e., a pragmatic approach.

9   Karl Marx: *Die deutsche Ideologie*, in Marx-Engels Werke (Berlin 1953ff) B. 3 p. 38

In the following I shall not dwell on developments in the academic discipline of history, but rather at stations in the modern milestones of the philosophy of history. My second thesis is that the philosophy of history became the stronghold of metaphysics in the modern world.

The history of the world will be seen as globalization. Today this is borne by completely new technologies. The monuments of the past appear in a different light than the documents of the present. We experience too much. This was Nietzsche's proviso in relation to what he termed the "historical malady". Today we must understand the historical malady to be the malady of globalisation and we might appropriately speak of "the use and abuse of information" instead of speaking, as Nietzsche does, "vom Nutzen und Nachteil der Historie für das Leben". [10] It is crucial that we do not use history in our century to serve life, but rather to serve *understanding*.

My third thesis is that history as a subject should in future not be a subject area that addresses the past, but rather one turned towards the future – and here I switch from Geschichte to history – and the way to do this is to include the dimension of a diagnostics of our age, which I will try to contribute to on this occasion.

As I have already suggested, 'history' should not be used in teaching to understand who you are and who we are, but who we are and where we want to go and why. We must maintain that we are "animals governed by reason".[11] We must understand that there is no transcendental yardstick and the openness to chance – the chance that Hegel wanted to master in a deferred manner by moving from history as an academic subject to the philosophy of history[12] – places us in a different position in the world than previous generations. It is fated that some agents are more powerful than others. It is not fate that decides, but our fate is that some people can decide more than others. This is what is expressed in the pragmatics of globalization. At the same time, the vulnerability of the non-transcendental universalisation is expressed when a person is willing to sacrifice his or her life intending to sacrifice the lives of others and thereby ontological security of every bodies everyday life.

History has become hypothetical in our everyday life and this is why we need to study more closely its hypothetical nature. In the second half of the 18th

---

10 Werke I, 1962, p. ff.

11 See Schmidt, Lars-Henrik: *Diagnosis II. Socialanalytiske fatninger.* København, 1999, p. 22.

12 Op. cit., p. 22

century in France, Jean-Jacques Rousseau's contemplations, as always, still affect the modern world.

II

If we are to reintroduce some kind of philosophy of history we should – in the same spirit – reflect a little on the birth of it as well as the critique of it in order not to be overwhelmed by the fact that the educational system once again considers historical conditions.

It would not be correct to claim that Rousseau invented the philosophy of history, but he does constellate – even gives birth to – the modern Western philosophy of history as something other than history as an academic discipline.

The Enlightenment philosophy of his contemporaries culminated with Kant and Condorcet, who, respectively, were preoccupied with progress towards something better or the promise of something better than the present[13], but Rousseau believed and stated that civilization was characterized by the loss of freedom and the growth of dependence. However, whether one perceives progress in changeability as merely a form or as a norm, it is Rousseau's connection with a specific pedagogy and a specific anthropology that creates a new caesura and 'problématique'.

He reasons on the basis of an intertwinement of three systems that derive mutual energy from each other. These systems are first, the transition of society from a natural state to a civil state; second, civilization's clash with the natural state existing in the colonies, which we can read about in contemporary travel tales, and third, the transition of the child from a natural state to an adult civil state. These three very different transitions are merged into one and the same development, a so-called progress that depraves the natural state. Rousseau does not write history, but rather what he calls 'hypothetical history'. [14] The natural, the natural state as a fictitious state – which he undertakes to construct – is placed in relation to and borrows energy from what it once was (1) what is out there (2) and what is inside, that is, the childishness and immediacy that has been lost. On the strength of the fictitious history, the political, the anthropological and the educational come together as one. This is called the

---

13 See Lars-Henrik Schmidt: *Immediacy Lost*; Kbh. 1986, p. 67ff.

14 Jean Jacques Rousseau: *Discours sur inegalité parmi les hommes*, In Œuvres complètes v. III, p. 127

natural state and it is populated by 'l'homme en général'. Our civilisatory endeavours must consist in replacing this loss with another nature.

In my opinion the foundations are hereby laid for understanding why we still need 'history in education'.

However, it was clear to Rousseau that we shouldn't bring 'l'homme en général' into being, but when the problem was translated into German, more specifically in Kant, the goal is so to speak to bring 'der Mensch' into being. Suddenly we are also people in public ("Allgemeinheit") and not chained, dependent people in general. From the perspective of the history of ideas, we can say that Kant pragmatises anthropology (he speaks, for example, of the physical appearance of different races etc.) and pedagogy, in which he is inspired by his philosophy of progress with stages of self-control. [15] The dimensions are included, but he concentrates on the transcendental subject and still manages to sustain the paradigm of historical philosophy and to favour parallelism. Not with empiricism in mind, but rather with world history in mind.

What has happened? We now have a subject without a childhood. The transcendental subject has no childhood. This is crucial and what is of interest in Kant's analysis of Genesis is that Adam is "born" an adult. [16] The point is that Kant does not abandon but rather revives the parallelism that is the mark of the modern philosophy of history – in my view.

It is Kant's insight into the transcendental subject's constitutions and dispositions that allow him to judge history. Because Kant believes that he knows the humanity of humans he also believes that he knows what shall be realized in human history. It is this fallacy that determines Kant's parallelism. Elsewhere I have called this 'the pragmatic fallacy'. [17]

Through this characterization I want, of course, to allude to 'the naturalistic fallacy' that Hume pointed to already in 1739[18] – but was explicated by G.E. Moore. But now it is not a question of moving from description to prescription, from 'is' to 'should be', but rather of the transition from ability to obligation, which suspends the question of volition.

Because Kant believes that he knows the humanity of humans, he thinks that the purpose of human history is realization in the form of the history of

---

15 See Kant, Immanuel: *Werke, B. XI og XII*. Frankfurt, 1977.

16 See Kant, Immanuel: *Werke*. Frankfurt, 1977.

17 See Lars-Henrik Schmidt: *Diagnosis I*; Copenhagen, 1999, p. 166ff.

18 See David Hume: *A Treatise of Human Nature*, Book 3, London, 1974, p. 177f.

humanity. A possibility (an ability) must be realized (an obligation). But this begs the question of whether this is what we want (volition).

Educators who think in this way must imagine that they have a significant role to play. Teaching history is about being able to find out whether we want to do what we can do. Kant's formulations may seem outdated to a modern educator, but the figure is entirely the same as the one we meet in Jürgen Habermas today, who, as far as I can see, claims that because "Verständigung" is possible, since we understand the universal pragmatics of language, then we must opt for democracy. [19] What we are witnessing is that the philosophy of history is no longer connected with the professional identity of historians, that is, those who tell stories about facticity.

This is precisely Hegel's reason for distinguishing between different views on history, to wit, original history, reflective history and philosophic history. [20] He distances himself from pragmatic history, which is part of reflective history because it asks, "what exactly is the use to us?" but has no illusions about the original narrative form. Philosophic history, the history of the philosophic world insists on finding reason in history. The idea is that reason governs history and thus that the course of world history has been reasonable. [21] It is a question of keeping chance in check, and "wer die Welt vernünftig ansieht, den sieht sie auch vernünftig an [to him who looks at the world rationally the world looks rationally back]" says Hegel. [22]

It is often asserted that Karl Marx was a left-wing Hegelian, but in my view he was much closer to Kantian than Hegelian parallelism. Karl Marx' originality lies not in his insistence on the world spirit but in his insistence on including real history once again, that is, on transforming the philosophy of history into a theory about history. This impressive experiment has its limitations.

"The educator must himself be educated" as has already been stated in Feuerbach's theses. [23] The originality of the young Marx lies in his emphasis on *historicity*; he made his point by referring to the *factum brutum* of the existence of the Chinese cherry tree in Europe – but insists on an older form of historicity than that found in German idealism. His critique was directed at both the old

19 See Jürgen Habermas, "Was heisst Universalpragmatik"?, in Apel (Hrsg: *Sprachakttheorie und tranzendentale Sprachpragmatik*, FaM 1976.

20 Hegel op.cit. p.543.

21 ibid. p. 20.

22 ibid. p. 23.

23 Karl Marx: "Die Feuerbachtesen" i MEW (Berlin 1953ff) B. 3. p. 6s.

and the young Hegelians and at the same time attacking the so-called 'objective historians' of his time (for the most part inspired by contemporary French historians) for regarding religious illusion as the driving force of history ("Geschichte"). He claims that Hegel's philosophy of history ("Geschichtsphilosophie") is the purest consequence of the way of writing history ("Geschichtschreibung"). He states that until his intervention, views on history ("Geschichtsauffassung") had neglected the real basis of history ("diese wirkliche Basis der Geschichte"), which he in 1845 claims to be the history of Communism ("die Geschichte des Kommunismus"). [24] His is thus to some extent obsessed with the idea of empirical reality, i.e. reality open to real positive science - what he terms "wirkliche Geschichte", which may be difficult to translate since this conception of history deals with human beings "wie sie *wirklich* sind, d. h. wie sie *wirken*".[25] By this statement Marx is unwillingly echoing Hegel, since Hegel stated that "was vernünftig ist, das ist wirklich, und was wirklich ist, das ist vernünftig".[26] I say unwillingly, since what Marx is out to do is to make way for something other than reason to be related to reality. What he terms Communism is not an ideal by which reality may be judged, it is not a "Zustand" (condition), it is rather the real *tendency* ("die *wirkliche* Bewegung").[27]

This is what Marx means by Communism. It is the critique of a history of philosophy and of academics from whose point of view history is regarded from without. They *write* history for an angle ("Massstab") outside history.[28] They do not deal with the real history that has no goal, no beginning and no end, but which is transforming nevertheless, and we are capable of analysing the tendencies in this transformation. Twenty years later Karl Marx opens *Das Kapital* by claming that we should concentrate on the laws themselves, which due to hard necessity are "Wirkenden und sich durchsetzenden Tendensen".[29] Even twenty years later, the focus is on the world market, the idea being that "der Mensch" does not exist, but that the world market via the civilizing influ-

---

24 See: *Die deutsche Ideologie* in MEW 3 op.cit. p. 39.

25 ibid. p. 25 ('How they really are, i.e. how they really work'. – A translation along these lines matches the Marxist tone, but probably not its intention.)

26 Hegel: *Grundlinien der Philosophie des Rechts*; Werke (op.cit.) B. 7 p. 24 (What is reasonable is real and what is real is reasonable.)

27 *Die deutsche Ideologie* op. cit. p, 35. From an academic philological view I might not translate – die wirkliche Bewegung" with 'real tendency' since 'tendency' only emerges is the writings of the later Karl Marx, but in my opinion, "die wirkliche Bewegung" was his first effort in this direction.

28 ibid. p. 39

29 *Das Kapital* MEW op.cit. B. 23 p. 12

ence of capital will realize what the philosophy of history thought of humanity. History is not the history of mankind but of the world market. I think this is called globalisation these days.

Today, from our perspective, what is crucial in Karl Marx is that he broke the parallelism upon which the philosophy of history rested in order to point out tendencies in the present age ("Gegenwart" in German). As a historian and a historical philosopher he is relatively trite, but he does introduce a new idea. The ends of history should not be found outside history and there is no parallelism to make this insider trade valid.

Marx concentrated his criticism saying that the outsider-view blurred the possibility of real history. His critique was concentrated on the history of philosophy – but he is very much a part of it.

Strangely enough, the point is echoed in Friedrich Nietzsche's philosophy, in which the philosophy of history is similarly abandoned for the benefit of specific *perspectives on history*, notably on both Geschichte and history. Whereas Marx's ideal as a German idealist was in what was to come – for his part, Communism, though not determined, not as an ideal, but nevertheless idealizing the process,[30] for Kant the rule of reason in the Reign of Ends; and for Hegel, absolute knowledge – Nietzsche's aim was to abandon a goal for history by dismantling his contemporaries' idealization of Antiquity. And the return of ideals. He was interested in another question: how do we deal with history, in what way, from what perspective? He is interested in the use and abuse of history. He is not talking about how different views on history reflect real human life but about understanding how it may serve life – i. e. to make it better, more fulfilling. Why else should we look to history if not to explore the possibilities of life? He is not interested in change in the same way as Marx. He has an

---

30 The evidence in Karl Marx's writing of an idea of a new stage in the history of mankind is well established and one has to admit that there is some evidence for the critique from e.g. Karl Popper against "historicisms" in The Poverty of Historicism (London 1957), but one often forgets his definition of Communism. At least, many followers following the discourse reintroduced the philosophy of history as a legitimation of the possibility of Communism. With the world market as reference he did state that the developed countries were showing the less developed countries a picture of their future. (See *Das Kapital* op. cit. p. 12) I am trying to state hat his ideas were not that well established or exclusive. Communism in Karl Marx was a question of not knowing where it would end, but also a hope for the possibility that human wealth would follow societal wealth – without parallelism. In neo-Marxist theory – for example, in Louis Althusser – the point is that history is a process without subject and end(s) but with a drive named *class struggle*. (See *Réponse à John Lewis*; Paris 1973, p. 98). Subjects in history and a subject of history are not to be disentangled.

aesthetical perspective rather than a revolutionary view and this is why he can make the shift from "Geschichte" to "Historie". By both criticising German idealism and being unaware of the underlying parallelism he creates a new setting.

But his stage is set: we must want something from history! Why else should we bother? It has to be of significance to us.

I believe that this is still the problem.

Sigmund Freud is an overlooked historical philosopher who reintroduced parallelism on new terms – specifically, between phylogenesis and ontogenesis: Heidegger transformed it into a question of the history of being and thus retained the metaphysical balance. Foucault wrote a different history, as neither 'Geschichte' nor 'Historie'.

It is all about bringing history closer to our age.

If we no longer can bring our age up to scratch, or "Passhöhe" (Hegel's expression, repeated by Marx in relation to the study of history when he claims that it is easier to study the developed body than the cells that make up its constitution) - our sight, viewpoint - then we must find a new form of connection between the philosophy of history and the professional identity of historians. And is that not exactly 'history in education'? It is in my perspective.

III:

Nietzsche is probably the most interesting figure, since he is capable of engaging with history and of making it seem as though it happened yesterday. That is to say, he introduces a perspective which simultaneously historicizes everything and opts for a 'historic sense'. At the same time, he warns us that too much history drains modern man of his *élan vital*. He can discuss 'the problem of Socrates'[31] as a prime example of a timely problem – all the while retaining a sense of history because philosophy is historical philosophising. [32] There are two reasons for this: A part of history resists history. This is what Nietzsche calls 'the transhistorical'[33] – again, the eternal recurrence of the problem of Socrates. This the tragic moment: something, in a split second, comes irrevocably into being. [34] Second, the idea that there are several ways of engaging with history,

31 See *Götzen-Dämmerung*; Werke II op.cit.

32 See *Menschliches Allzumenschliches*; Werke I op. cit.

33 See *Vom Nutzen und Nachteil der Historie für das Leben* i Werke I op. cit.

34 See Lars-Henrik Schmidt: *Tragik der Aufklärung*, Århus, 1990.

what we call a sense of history or perspectives, namely the sense of the monumental and the antiquated and a critical faculty.[35] These must be properly laid
down if we are to avoid the historic malady. We must have the strength to make
sense of history, that is to say, to avoid being overwhelmed by it. According to
Nietzsche, we desire to and we can shape history; and the present is the past of
the future, which is why we must understand the present in a future perspective by grasping the past.

This manifesto renders Nietzsche 'unzeitgemäss' [obsolete] – that is to say,
historical in his diagnosis of his age, the contemporary. History should lift us up
and serve our self-expression. We mustn't lose ourselves in history as an academic discipline or in infinite causal regress and we mustn't be fooled by the
history of philosophy's transcendentalist justifications of its purpose. Instead,
we ought to meet belligerence with historical sense, and this includes our curious alienation from ourselves as historical phenomena. There are no ideals,
antiquity is not an ideal – this was the young Nietzsche's crucial objection to
the idealisations of his age, and we won't even call that utopian, rendered by
the future. But we can sing of the future.

This manifesto constitutes a radical break with both the philosophy of history and with history as an academic discipline – but without turning up our
noses at them.

In Nietzsche, history has by no means come to an end, nor is it dead; we
haven't seen the last of it. 'Gott [God]' and 'Götzen [false gods, idols]' may be
dead, but since we are
wrapped in the world we will continue to interpret history in order to understand ourselves, to understand how we become who we are. It is not a question of 'what it means to us', which is what Hegel described as the pragmatic
form of reflective historiography. [36]

With Nietzsche, the parallelism between the formation of civilisation and
the formation of the individual has been broken. When Freud revives paralle-

---

35 *Vom Nutzen und Nachteil der Historie für das Leben* op. cit. Hegel talks about different modes of writing
history (the origin-oriented, the reflective and the philosophical mode (op. cit. P. 543)) whereas Nietzsche
talks about the sense, the feeling and the use and abuse regarding the handling of knowledge of history as
a condition.

36 Jf. Hegel op. cit., p. 17.

lism – as already hinted at – he does so on different terms. [37] The formation of man is no yardstick for history. We are not banished from history, nor are we its model.

If we try to express this in educational terms, we may say that the point of being a child is no longer to grow up, but precisely to be a child. We're living the ideal – it doesn't lie at the root, the base and it is not an aim.

After Nietzsche, we have to make do with understanding history differently.

This is why some of the best Nietzscheans (Weber, Simmel, Gehlen) became sociologists and anthropologists. These days we call them diagnosticians of the contemporary.

We cannot make sense of the world without a sense of history. History in education is less a question of how history should be part of the curriculum in our educational system, but rather a question of refining our sense of orientation, while at the same time making sure that we cannot just say what we please; in other words, discourses and the validity of discourses may be tested.

In the hermeneutic tradition of the 20th century, Gadamer[38] and Ricœur[39] are the most distinguished proponents of a new philosophy of history and dialectics as the unity of meaning and history. We might say that hermeneutics deceives and underscores historical consciousness. And yet it is Nietzscheans like Heidegger and Foucault who – each in their own way – have been even more radical. Heidegger writes on the history of being[40], Nietzsche writes on it in one single page,[41] and afterwards Richard Rorty has written about it – and thus in our current embeddedness we find new ways; Foucault writes on the history of the asylum and the prison, which addresses our age with hope for the future – not as hermeneutic understanding. In his last years, Foucault was, in fact, working on something he called the 'history of the present' or 'une ontologie de l'actualité'[42].

---

37 Freud spoke of "Netzwerk der Verursachungen" (*Der Mann Moses und die Monotheistische Religion*, in GW London 1953, B. XVI p. 215) but on the other hand it is first and foremost his reflections on 'Nachträglichkeit' (deferred action) that is of interest to a new philosophy of history. The sole point being that in psychoanalysis you do not treat the experiences of the patients but rather the deferred 'mis en scène' of these experiences and their recollection. The crux of the matter is that history has never ended – as long as there are tales about what has happened and still is happening.

38 See *Wahrheit und Methode*, 1960.

39 See *Temps et récit*, Paris, 1984.

40 See *Nietzsche I*, Pfullingen 1961 p. 489.

41 See *Götzendämmerung*; Werke II op. cit p. 963. Nietzsche is able to present a condensed version of Western metaphysics as the history of a mistake ("Wie die "wahre Welt" endlich zur Fabel wurde").

42 See *Dits et écrits. T. IV*, Paris 1994 p. 688.

Poetry, History and Philosophy: the message of Aristotle Poetics 9

David Evans

We who inhabit the intellectual environment, live in an egalitarian age. When I first entered academic life several decades ago, subjects were regularly disparaged – or at the very least graded as less serious by contrast with other more serious branches. Initially classical philology, mathematics, physics and, of course philosophy reigned supreme, from which lofty position they were able to look down with contempt on the study of one's native literature – English literature in my case; this latter profession was deprecated as little more demanding than the recreational reading of novels and poetry. Somehow this kind of study has acquired a better cachet over the last few decades. Later sociology was deplored as a statement – in impenetrable and pretentious jargon – of obvious truths about the patterns of human choice and behaviour. Then that study became respectable; and now the new bugbears are such fields as media studies or tourism studies.

The process appears to be one in which after a certain period of scepticism and disdain, a subject is welcomed into the academic community; but one condition of that acceptance may well be the selection of a new whipping-boy with which the respectability of the new entrant can be contrasted. An illusion of discriminating elitism is created; but instead the reality is that sooner or later, and pretty soon at that, anything goes.

These diverse value-judgements among studies are one of the numerous features of our current intellectual life whose origins lie in the ancient Greek philosophers; and as usual these origins repay scrutiny. The habit starts with Plato, and it finds clear expression in a discussion in his *Gorgias*. That work has as its subject the nature and value of skill in rhetoric; and after some critical examination of the claims about rhetoric made by its professor Gorgias, Socrates proposes the following assessment:

"As cookery stands in relation to medicine, so also stands rhetoric in relation to justice" (*Gorgias* 465c4-5).

This apparently bald judgement sits in the middle of a much more extensive schema which also includes physical training, law-making, cosmetics, sophistry, and much else.

This Socratic habit of thought whereby intellectual practices are ranked in cognate manner as to their subject-matter and hierarchically as to their importance in life, persisted in Plato's philosophy even after he moved on from practical questions to explicit reflection on the nature of knowledge. In Republic Book 7 he adumbrates a programme of study in which, as the first stage, five distinct mathematical studies are followed. These studies are differentiated by the particular things examined in each – numbers in arithmetic, two-dimensional shapes in geometry, and so on. Then there is progress to another study – dialectic – which is higher in the hierarchy than the mathematical studies.[1] It exceeds them in intellectual worth, just as medicine exceeds cookery in the evaluative map of *Gorgias*.

In other parts of *Republic* Plato brings this same analytical approach to bear on the subject and study of poetry. As is well known, Plato assigns a low value to such productivity, on grounds which embrace metaphysics, ethics and psychology.[2] On the metaphysical front, poetry (and much more art) is condemned because it seeks to represent things which are in fact no more than representations of further, even more real entities; poetry is at a third remove from reality. From the moral point of view, it fails because the way in which it portrays characters are not guaranteed to promote a concern to pursue the good life; indeed, judged by currently available poetic works, they are not even liable to promote it. In *Republic* Plato first argues for the censorship of poetry in education (Book 3) and then (Book 10) for its elimination.

That intellectual background in Plato's published philosophy is essential for our understanding of Aristotle's commentary on the nature and value of poetry in his *Poetics*. The key text which I shall consider begins: "Poetry is more philosophical and moral than history" (9, 1451b5-6). He explains what he means by saying that even if the works of Herodotus were recast into verse form, this would not make them poetical. It is not the form but the content that distin-

---

1   *Republic* 524-34.
2   C.Janaway, *Images of Excellence* (Oxford: Clarendon Press, 1995), pp.133-57.

guishes the two genres; history recounts what has actually happened, poetry the sort of thing that might happen. He then justifies the distinction by exploring its significance further. Poetry recounts what is universal, history what is particular.

> "The universal is that someone of a type should happen to say or do things of a type, in accordance with what is likely or inevitable; and poetry aims at this by imposing a name on these things. The particular is what Alcibiades did or had done to him" (1451b8-11).

Our task is to unpack this very dense text.

On first reflection its claims are unclear, if not actually implausible. Let us fasten attention on Herodotus and Alcibiades, who evidently exemplify the disparaged end of Aristotle's analysis and comparison. Herodotus wrote about the actions of powerful people – mostly in what was (for him) the recent past but also, in Book I, the more remote past. His cast of historical characters includes Priam, Helen and Io, as well as Croesus. Alcibiades was, for Aristotle, a historical figure of about six decades earlier. In temporal and also apparently in cultural terms, as Solon, Pisistratus and Cambyses stand to Herodotus, so also Alcibiades stands to Aristotle. Yet Alcibiades also figures as a character in Plato's *Symposium*. So he is both an actual historical figure and an object of creative artistry.

Now turn to the other side – the corpus of Greek literature, which was available to Aristotle. These writings relate the actions and sufferings of certain figures who lived mostly in the remote past. Theseus, Oedipus, Agamemnon and the like. But remote though these figures were, the Greeks did not regard them as essentially fictional; rather they were thought to be real people who lived real lives in the far past and continued in various ways to influence subsequent people and events. Moreover some tragedies deal with less remote times; the most signal example of this is Aeschylus' *Persai*, which portrayed events of only one generation earlier than that before which it was first performed.

So the actual cultural record seems to belie Aristotle's sharp separation of history and poetry. History spoke sometimes of ancient figures and sometimes of contemporaries; and so also did poetry, although admittedly the ancient predominate. Moreover the same people, whether ancient or modern, feature in the pages of writings from both genres. And why should we expect otherwise? The actions of Theseus, Darius or Alcibiades, we may well want to say, can and should be the subject both of historians and of poets. The former will treat of them in terms of their relation to the surrounding political, military and social context in which these individuals led their lives. – a context within which their own actions may be particularly significant. The poet, on the other hand, is less concerned with this context; instead he will likely locate the individual person within a wider network of personal relations. The emphases are different, but the subjects are the same. When Aristotle uses a distinction between the universal and the particular to characterise poetry by contrast to history, he seems to create too great a distance between them.

Immediately after the sentence, which I quoted just now, Aristotle justifies his assessment of the relative value of poetry and history in terms of types of thing which generalise over individuals. This language recalls the account which he gives of artistic skill in the *Metaphysics* and *Nicomachean Ethics*. In the *Ethics* Aristotle recognises a distinct intellectual virtue as appropriate to various skilled activities of the mind; these virtues are listed as wisdom, science, skill in living (practical skill), and artistry. Aristotle's main point here is to urge the avoidance of confusion between these skills and their virtues. But an implicit, less emphasised aspect of his commentary is that each of these intellectual virtues should be recognised for its independent merit. The obvious contrast case is that of Socrates and Plato, who regarded practical and artistic skill as valuable only insofar as they replicated wisdom – or, at least, that is how Aristotle interprets their positions.[3]

Although Aristotle finds value in these distinct forms of intellectual skill, the values are not equal. As the related discussion in *Metaphysics* A makes clear, there is scope for advance from the exercise of some of these skills to others. In this scheme artistry forms an intermediate stage in a progression that leads from empirical knack to science. Empirical skill, which is built out of the two human psychological faculties of perception and memory, treats individual cases in all their individuality. In *De Sophisticis Elenchis* Aristotle speaks of "pre-artistic" purveyors of dialectical and rhetorical arguments who could supply the need for footwear, not on the basis of the principles of the shoemaker but simply by making available a large variety of sizes and shapes of shoe.

What marks the advance from this kind of ability to genuine artistry is a grasp of the kinds or types under which the individuals fall. Hitherto these individuals are treated piecemeal; consideration of them is as separate as the

---

3   For further elaboration of the contributions of these texts, see my chapter 'Aristotle on *Techne*', in P. Chabot & G.Hottois (edd.), *Les Philosophes et la Technique* (Paris: Vrin, 2003), pp.37-47.

individuals themselves are. When we have art, we can and should regard them as representative of the type. That approach will better facilitate the explanation of why this particular individual is as it is; so attention to types advances causal explanation.

As Aristotle himself point out, this distinctive focus may render the artist less adept in his encounter with an individual:

> "The healer treats Callias or Socrates, who happens to be a human being, but he treats a human being only incidentally. For it is an individual who is to be cured. So someone who has general knowledge but through lack of experience is unacquainted with the individual, will often fail in his cures" (*Metaphysics* A1, 981a18-24).

Nonetheless artistic skill is superior to empirical knack because it deals in generalities and also seeks causal explanations of the changes it seeks to promote. Those features make such skill a suitable staging-post on the way towards achieving true scientific understanding of universal causal principles.

The comments in *Poetics 9* on the relative merits of poetry, history and philosophy are entirely consistent with these more detailed accounts in the *Metaphysics* and *Nicomachean Ethics*. The text in *Poetics 9* recalls and relies on this background of theorising about artistic skill and its peculiar merits. But to get a keener sense of Aristotle's point here it is helpful to ponder its dialectical relationship to Plato's categorisation and evaluation of these various intellectual activities. What was wrong with art, for Plato, lay with the ontological status of its objects and with the epistemological pretensions which were built upon a certain set of ideas about those objects.

As he expounds it in *Republic 10* there is only real Bed. If there were more than one, the very particularity of these plural items would undermine their claim to reality. So the obviously plural beds on which each of us sleeps at night are not real. How much less real, then, are the beds that authors might put into words, or painters put into pigment! The carpenter who fashions what is, on this account, an unreal bed, does not harbour metaphysical illusions about its status. That is an affliction which besets the artist, who does overestimate the degree of reality in his product. In fact the order of esteem between him and the craftsman should be reversed since the products of the latter, although not fully real, are still more so than those of the former.

None of this ontology impresses Aristotle; and accordingly he rejects the value-judgements that are based on it.

The things that exist, in the primary sense are particular substances; and universals are epistemologically valid only to the extent that they facilitate our understanding – including practical and productive understanding – of these individuals.[4] This sharp distinction between the conditions for successful onto-logy and epistemology enables Aristotle to elevate science to the highest posi-tion, even though it studies things at a level of abstraction far from the actual particular. More pertinently for our analysis it raises art to its secondary positi-on because it is concerned with the universal. The ontological considerations, which had dominated Plato's evaluation, fall away in Aristotle's account. He marks the distance by demoting history to third place, mired as it is in the particular. I maintain that the entire thought in the *Poetics 9* sentence needs to be read as a strongly anti-Platonic polemic. At least part of the motive for Ari-stotle's valuations of these various activities, lies in his desire to show how Plato's different valuations went so badly amiss.

If that line of thought casts light on the relationship, in Aristotle, between poetry and philosophy, there still remains a problem about history. Was Ari-stotle unaware of the work of Thucydides? He never mentions the historian by name or even indirect reference; this is something of a mystery in the transmis-sion of culture in the fifth- to third-century BC Greek world.[5] Even so, given that Thucydides claimed universal significance for his account of the particular events that made up the Peloponnesian War, we may press the question of how such a work of history can fit with Aristotle's assessment of history as such. The answer, I think, is that if Thucydides' claim is credible, his work is to be classed as poetry rather than history. He has been so classified by one modern commentator;[6] and remember that for Aristotle it is no bar to that assessment that Thucydides wrote in prose instead of verse. More importantly, he is dealing with the same reality – a world of particular individuals – as are the poets and the scientists. It is the degree of abstraction from such particularity that deter-mines how any skilled commentator on this world is to be classified.

I have given an account of the thoughts of Aristotle and Plato on poetry, concentrating on the contribution which experience of its products can make to truth and knowledge. According to my account Plato devalued this truth and Aristotle sought to rescue artistic truth from this lowly status. There is a con-

---

4   This point is well emphasised by S.Halliwell, in his chapter 'Aristotelian mimesis and human understan-ding', in Ø. Andersen & J .Haarberg (edd.), *Making Sense of Aristotle: essays in Poetics* (London: Duckworth, 2001), pp.87-107.

5   The comment of G.Else, *Aristotle's Poetics* (Harvard University, Press, 1957), p304 n.9, still seems valid.

6   F.M. Cornford, *Thucydides Mythistoricus* (London: Arnold, 1907); the theme of Aristotle's relation to Thucy-dides and other historians is also taken up in S.Hornblower, *Thucydides* (London: Duckworth, 1987).

temporary debate on these matters, and Aristotle's theory can usefully be viewed by reference to it. The discussion is stimulated by statements of the sort that might occur in fiction, including poetic fiction; so let us consider some of them:

"Sherlock Holmes lives at 221B, Baker St, in London."

"Oedipus is married to Jocasta, and ignorant of her identity as his mother."

or, more pertinently to our present Danish context,

"Hamlet, prince of Denmark, is suspicious of the current rulers Claudius and Gertrude."

Are these statements true? I have chosen them because in some sense they seem obviously true. Yet how can that be? There is, in actual fact, no subject for them to be true about; and even if there were, the property specified in the sentence would not be true of that person. David Lewis has addressed this problem through his favoured apparatus of modal logic.[7] He proposes an analysis of the truth in fiction which makes it reside in the proximity of the possible world in which the statement is literally and straightforwardly true, to the actual world in which it is false even if fictionally true.

Aristotle would have no truck with the possible worlds analysis. Yet he does anticipate Lewis' modal approach to fictional truth when he says that the poet follows "what is probable or necessary" in deciding what types of person may say or do. On this view we are interested in Oedipus or Hamlet not because they inhabit possible worlds different from but near to our own actual world. The point rather is that we in our actual world recognise the probability or necessity of people like them behaving in certain ways. Lewis reaches out to a possible world to find a modal counterpart to actual people. Aristotle takes actual people as his starting-point and uses modal categories (necessity and probability) to reach out to other scenarios in which real people act in an instructive way.

Both philosophers are concerned with the truth in art. The truthful poet will let his modally inspired insights guide his creative work. Aristotle's aim is to remove hindrances to this creativity that might arise from poor philosophy.

---

7 'Truth in Fiction' in D. Lewis, *Philosophical Papers* vol.1 (Oxford University Press, 1983), pp.261-80.

Philosophical Tradition and Education of Civilization History

Jieho Yao

(1) Civilization History, Philosophy and Education

The history is civilization history of mankind in essence. The civilization consists in that human beings realize their essential potency in practice and represents itself as an organic integration historically formed by economic-political structure and basic cultural ethos in their mutual penetrating and mutual influencing. Education is the crucial agent promoting evolution of human civilizations. Philosophy is embodiment of Zeitgeist (time spirit), theoretic core of culture and living soul of civilization. In the beginning of new century, enhancing the education of civilization history interrelated with philosophical tradition is of importance for peace and development of world today.

In the long-standing history, the nations in the world have created their distinct culture, traditions, beliefs and values and given birth to time-honored and colorful civilizations. The diversity is the essential trait of world civilizations. Diversity means difference, difference necessitates communication, and communication facilitates development, thus making our world more colorful. Making a comprehensive view on history, it is the mainstream of progress in human civilizations that various civilizations have been always enriched and developed in their harmonious communication and mutual studies. The ancient Chinese philosopher Confucius has the saying, "Harmony in diversity", which means that we should respect our differences and diversity, and seek harmonious coexistence through exchange with each other to fulfill mankind's common interests and values. Civilizations and cultures have both the characteristics of diversity and identity. This kind of identity is the dynamic identity residing in diversity. It implies two meanings: one is the identity of national culture in certain civilization; another is that the different traditions of civilizations and cultures realize certain complementarity and the goals as well as values of common progress in their rational communications.

The report of a UNESCO International Experts Group entitled as *The Multicultural Planet* points out:" the future of all humankind cannot be characterized by unity without diversity, or diversity without unity. It is a challenge to all contemporaries to build such a world, and above all, to the cultures that underpin their worldviews and values."[1] In the globalization of world today, it should be avoid to make multi- civilizations to converge an unique civilization and to make cultures homogenizing, we should maintain the existing diversity of world civilizations and cultures; on other hand, it is necessary to promote the dialogue among various civilizations, to increase their mutual understanding, close some gulfs, reconcile antagonism, oppose against "clash of civilizations", so as to actualize the identity of civilizations and cultures. The international society is paying high attention to a globalization of humanity based on both the diversity and identity of world civilizations. Following the former Chinese Premier Zhu Rongii's proposal at the Fourth ASEM Summit held in Copenhagen, Denmark in 2002, thc ASEM Conference on "Cultures and Civilizations: Diversity and Unity" attended by Ministers and eminent experts from 26 ASEM countries, was successfully held in Beijing in last December. The published "Chairman's Statement" emphasizes on the crucial function of education in advancing the dialogue between different civilizations. Therefore, from my point of view, the education of civilization history just is one of foundational channels for dialogues and mutual understanding of different civilizations so as to attain both diversity and identity of world civilizations.

The philosophical tradition is highest theoretic crystal of basic cultural ethos in certain tradition of civilization, and evolves itself with progress of related civilization. It is not cultural specimen in museum, not a number of fault planes inlaid with some fragments of ossified spiritual fossils. The philosophical tradition as an accumulation of cultural results created by a nation's history, is rather a dynamic crystal of national civilization, which displays itself as an evolutionary process in the long river of history and successively obtain new meanings from changing practice of life. H. G. Gadamer's philosophical hermeneutics maintains that tradition as confluence of prejudices kept by history, is the premise of human activity of understanding, and human beings

---

1   *The Multicultural Planet*, ed. by Ervin Laszlo, p.232, Chinese version, Beijing: Social Sciences Literature Publishing House, 2001.

also participate evolution of tradition through their creative understanding and interpretation. According to American philosopher Alasdair MacIntyre's theory of virtue, in order to overcome the crises of moral relativism and skepticism in modern social life, it is necessary to attach importance to studies on constructing traditions, absorb and carry forward the essence of Aristotle's tradition and probe into the issue of "rationality of modern practice" in an effort to reconstruct individual and social virtues. To grasp the philosophical tradition should become the important link of education of civilization history. Due to the variety of historical contexts and living styles, the nations in world have been creating various philosophical traditions in the process of civilization, which are of both difference and similarity and can be in convergence and communication each others, therefore, it is a representation of interculturaliarity, and in the education of civilization history, to deepen the understanding on diversity and identity of philosophical traditions is the important aspect of intercultural teaching and research, the significant means for respecting and benefiting diversity and identity of world civilizations.

(2) Doctrines of Confucius and Socrates: Identity and Difference

Here, taking an example, I might make a brief comparative studies on philosophical doctrines of Confucius and Socrates to explain that both Chinese and Western philosophical traditions have been of identity and particularity, and in view of the both philosophical doctrines have been profoundly influencing upon the diversity and identity of both Chinese and Western traditions of civilization, it demonstrates that both Chinese and Western traditions of civilization might be of complementarity and in convergence and communication each another.

Both China and Greece have the age-old and splendid traditions of culture, and the two great nations have respectively made important contributions to the world civilization. Both Confucius (551—479 B.C.) and Socrates (469—399 B.C.) living in the nearly same era founded the new — type of philosophies considering ethics as their core, which exerted a profound influence on the historical process of Chinese and Western civilizations. Both Confucius and Socrates lived in a troubled times, the slave society or the slave — owning system of city — state were on the decline, and the traditional ethic values were collapsing. The two masters are also great educators and practitioners of morality, according to the real social situations, they created a sort of sound philosophy on human being for the first time. The doctrine of Confucius initiated the Confucianist Civilization existing today, the philosophy of Socrates provided with the foundation of scientific reason and humanistic spirit for Western Civilization. The two masters' doctrines, though appeared in the different place and times, embodied a common era ethos of enlightening humanity and improving society, we might find out many similarities between them reflecting the identity of two traditions of philosophy and Civilization. Here, I only briefly discuss their three similar points as following:

1.Humanitarian principle of philosophy.
Confucius said "my doctrine is that of an all-pervading unity"(*Confucian Analects* 4.15)..[2] "Benevolence" (Ren) is the central category going through his philosophical and ethical doctrines. It denotes a human nature. Confucius expounded the essential meaning of benevolence:" it is to love all men" and "to overflow in love to all", (12.22,1.6) it means that goodness, kindness and fraternity should be the true humanity; on the other hand, benevolence contains the basic principle of being faithful to one's good nature and realizing reciprocity for others, as his dictums "What do not want done to yourself, do not do to others," "the benevolent man, wishing to be established himself, seeks also to establish others; wishing to be perfected himself, seeks also to perfect others", (4.15, 15.24, 6.30) it just implies a deep philosophical connotation of tolerance. "Benevolence", as a newest philosophical category at that time, is a find of human being, a self-consciousness concerning human good nature. Confucius affirmed that everyone should have the right of survival and dignity of personality, and should perfect himself and benefit others in the light of faithfulness and reciprocity. Benevolence is the innate and inherent essence of human beings and ought to be recognized and actualized only by men themselves, as the Master said "the practice of benevolence is from a man hinself, not from others". (12.1) The principle of "Golden Mean" is the methodology for attaining the benevolence. By the Mean (Zhong Yong) is denoted the fixed principle regulating all under heaven and the correct way of mediating to pursue the state of equilibrium and harmony.[3] It means to take hold of two extremes, determine median appropriateness or medium, and employed it in government

---

2   *Confucian Analects* 4.15
3   *The Doctrine of the Mean*, Chapter 1.What is this?

of people"[4].that is to see clearly the contraries or the opposites of contradiction, with examining the factual situation and using method of medium, to realize the appropriateness, balance and harmony between them, so as to benefit the people and accomplish the reasonable moral sentiment. He held that in practicing the rule of propriety, harmony is to be prized. However, in his opinion, the harmony is not equal to some absolute identity, but a complementary unity of diverse things, like a dish of good cuisine consists of various ingredients.

"Goodness" (agathon) is the highest philosophical category of Socrates as well as a humanistic principle of his ethics quite similar to Confucian "Benevolence". With regard to its ontological meaning, goodness predicates the "order" and" rule" appropriate to the nature of everything in the cosmos that human being is its center. In *Gorgias*, Socrates said "the heavens and earth, gods and men, are bound together by fellowship and friendship, and order and temperance and justice, and for this reason they call the sum of things the ordered ,universe"' (508A) The human nature inhering in goodness incarnates the love, friendship, kindness and benevolence, and reciprocity, which make the social life a harmonious integration. To do the good makes man acquire the true happiness and freedom. (*Memorabilia* 4.5.2-5) "Goodness" as his highest category of philosophy correlated to cultivating the humanity is of many similarities with Confucian doctrine of "benevolence". For instances, "Know thyself", Socrates expounded this well-known inscription at Delphi Temple, emphasized its meaning of "sophrosyne", the very essence of "sophrosyne" consists in the self-knowledge, for "Know thyself" and "sophrosyne" are the same. (*Charmides* 164D – 165B) The sophrosyne not only implies modesty, kindness, restraint of lust, but essentially means a kind of wisdom to know the nature of real men, to examine themselves. The sophrosyne as an human self-consciousness is crucial to man's becoming good. "Nothing too much", another inscription that the ancient "seven sages" dedicated the fruit of their wisdom to Appolo in Delphi temple. (*Protagoras* 343 A—B) In Socratic view, it is the meaning inhering in sophrosyne. The temperate man should control extravagant desires so as to normalize his behaviors, not to deviate the regular life to the extreme. If understanding it in broad sense, it is also a methodology of mediation to obtain the definitions of virtues appropriate to the moral realities by synthesizing the contrary visions and to practice virtues by reconciling the opposi-

---

4   *The Doctrine of the Mean*, Chapter 6.

te forces or extreme moral feelings to regularize social or individual life. Aristotle inherited and developed this idea later and considered "mean" as a cardinal principle of his methodology of practical philosophy.

In the general, Socrates, like Confucius, put man himself in the central position in the philosophical tradition in the earliest. At that times, the sophists advocated " Man is the measure of everything",, however, such an image of sensitive Man acts only relying on individual capricious sensations ,desires and opinions, and thus has no true value criterion of certainty. Socrates fostered a lofty figure of rational Man. Hegel reviewed that Socrates considered "the man in thinking" as the measure and that his nature consisted in the true and good.[5]

2. The rationalist epistemology and theory of morality.

Both the two masters hold that reason is the essence of soul or mind and persons must apply their wisdom i. e rational thinking in studies to cognize the universal essence of virtue and to enhance their moral accomplishments in practice of virtue. Their teachings radiate the glamours converging reason and morality.

According to Confucius, knowing is the primary function of everyone's mind. The principle of Confucian epistemology is "investigating things and carrying knowledge to the utmost extent" (*The Great Learning*). The ethical meaning of knowledge is "to know nature of man himself" (12. 22), namely, to understand the benevolence and virtues; Confucius said: "By nature, men are nearly alike; by practice, they get to be wide apart".(17.2) The human nature originally is the good, the difference of acquired better and worse characters is formed due to postnatal affections from some surroundings. Only the wise are free from perplexities in their lives, (9.29) therefore, cultivation of virtues must depend on studying knowledge and moral training in practice. If having nothing to do with studies of knowledge, anyone would never obtain the varieties of virtues, but infect malady and evil. Just like Socrates, Confucius also acknowledged that he was quite conscious of his ignorance, because he was not one who was born in Possession of knowledge. (7.20,9.8)

Socrates initiated the rationalist tradition of philosophy in the western Civilization. He advocated that reason was the essential part of soul, to love wisdom ought to be the natural character of human being, and acquirement of

---

5 G.W.F.Hegel: *The Lecture on History of Philosophy* in Chinese edition, Vol.2, 1957, p.62.

knowledge must mainly rely on rational thinking exploring into essence or cause of things. E. Zeller points out: forming the new idea of knowledge is the centre of Socratic philosophy.[6] Socrates set forth the basic proposition of his moral philosophy: Virtue consists in knowledge. Using his dialectics pervaded by the strong logical arguments, Socrates discussed the definitions of various virtues with others, the conclusions of those dialogues were always reduced to the fact that virtues stemmed from knowledge, wisdom and human nature of reason, therefore, virtues were teachable. Everyone should approach goodness by pursuing knowledge, practicing Virtues and erecting sound value of morality, it is the very true meaning and value of human life.

3. The ethical politics and social ideal of realizing humanity and universal harmony.

Both the two masters advocated that morality should become the foundation of politics, the rulers should be the sages or superiors, who governed states according to ethical principle and educated people with morality so as to build a harmonious and prosperous society benefiting the plain citizens.

Socrates emphasized that morality was the foundation of managing city-states, and the Athenian crisis of democracy lay in the degeneration of morality. In *Gorgias*, he discoursed that the primary task of politicians should be to improve -souls and cultivate good citizens, the tragedy of great politician Pericles at the end of his life was rooted in losing moral education, because he only made great efforts to provide ships , walls , dockyards and many other such things, but made the citizens idle and wilder, besides, the sophists' moral teachings arguing for hedonism and hegemony polluted souls and disseminated the false aim of life in the city –state. (515E — 519D) In *Menexenushe*, he expected wise and good governor and ruler to be selected either in democracy or in aristocracy, (238B—239A) Socrates loved Athens and Greece, and put forth the ideal of rejuvenating his native state: erecting goodness and virtues as the goal of government and citizen, Athens and all city-states must be able to resurrect their heroic posture to obtain prosperity, glory and happiness.

In Confucian view, the "benevolence" should be the interior principle of the reasonable and sane politics. If a ruler can confer benefits on people and assist all, it is the very benevolent politics of a sage. "The ruler who exercises government by means of morality, may be compared to the north polar star, which

---

6   E. Zeller: *Socrates and the Socratic Schools*, London, 1885, p. 89.

keeps its place and all the stars turn towards it"' (2.1) With regard to people, Confucius insisted to enrich them first and then to teach them, (13.9) namely, the mass education should accompany with the economic development. The ideal society Confucius longed for is the" Great unification" which universally actualizes the principle of benevolence named as" Great Dao". Confucian successors described the ideal of "Great unification: "when the Great Dao absolutely prevails, public spiritedness ruled all the world. The wise and able are selected to the public, and everyone enjoys the trust between friends and strengthens the harmony between people. Therefore, everyone feels attached not only with his own parents but also with those of other' and he loves not only his own children but also those of others", all the people have their suitable positions and enough wealth, they treat the states as great family, there is no any war, theft and evil, but the prosperity, peace, harmony and order out of self-consciousness' (*Record of Propriety*). Such a fine social ideal makes us recall Kant's "the idea for a universal history with a cosmopolitan intent" and his discourse on "perpetual peace". The social aim of first stage Confucius expected is "Xiao Kang", a comparatively well-off society, in which the wise and able rulers carry out benevolent policies, govern the state by propriety and moral education and make people enjoy a comfortable life. China today establishes its strategy goal of "constructing the 'xiao kang' society in all round", using Confucian term "Xiao Kang", but assign it new meaning adapted to contemporary China.

Due to the various historical backgrounds and cultural contexts, there are naturally some differences between Confucian and Socratic doctrines, which are the elements causing the differentiae between the traditions of Confucian civilization and Western civilization. First, Confucian doctrine attaches importance to the patriarchal hierarchy and consanguinity of family, a state is considered as an expanded family, the doctrine demands the superiors to first cultivate themselves and rtgulate their families, then to be able to rightly govern states and make whole empire tranquil and happy. Chinese traditional ethics strongly influenced by Confucianism has the characteristic of holism or community values based on the differentiation within consanguinity, familiarity and patriarchal system. However, in the times Socrates lived, the ancient Greek relation of clan was getting slight and the democratic life was vigorous in Athens, therefore, Socrates emphasized the public ethics and cultivating virtues of city-state without characteristic of central value of family. Second, the constructive method of Confucian philosophical doctrine could be reduced to interpreting the meanings of categories and some classical texts by intellectual insight or intuition unifying dialectical reason implied in *Book of Change*, may be, it could be called a method of classical hermeneutics in ancient China. Though the Mohist school and school of Naming-Argument created the Chinese doctrines of logic later on and the Indian logic was introduced to China in Tang dynasty (about seventh century), their influence on Chinese traditional mode of thinking was limited. That Socrates applied his "dialectics" to exploration into the definitions of virtues and discourses of other issues contains the strong thought of logical analysis. In *Metaphysics*, Aristotle points out:" For two things may be fairly ascribed by Socrates— inductive arguments and universal definition, both of which are concerned with the starting-point of science"; (1078b25—30) according to Aristotle's "Posterior Analytics", both of induction and definition as well as axiom afford the basic and original premises for constructing knowledge of demonstrative sciences. Aristotle developed greatly the logical thought accumulated by the previous philosophers, especially by Socrates, founded his systematic doctrine of logic, which sublimed the ancient Greek philosophers' reflection on human reason and became the key-link to set up the western tradition of analytic reason.

As sources of two great civilization tradition of China and the West, both Confucian and Socratic philosophical and ethic doctrines have both similarities and differences, it demonstrates that the philosophical and cultural traditions of every nations inhere both creative diversity and identity as well as complementarity between them. Thus they might increase greatly rational communications in line with the principle of mutual respect, harmony in diversity and cross-fertilization so as to pursue the common cultural prosperity and social progress. It will benefit for world peace and common development. Therefore, however, untenable is the allegation that in the post cold -war world today, clashes between different civilization including Confucian and Western ones are inevitable and will dominate the global politics in the future. It is worthy to be advocated to unfold studies on "philosophy and civilization" and to make further comparative studies on various philosophical traditions including their basic ideas such as ones of human being and human rights in the different civilization contexts.

(3)Teaching and Studies of Civilization History and Philosophical Tradition in China

The Chinese institutions of education and research in social sciences and humanities today attach importance to teaching and studies of world history for two reasons: First, to broaden people's horizon so as to understand the history and reality of diverse civilizations in the world and to absorb in fine fruits from them. It is beneficial to overall, coordinated and sustainable development of economy, society and culture in China today, to overall progress of society and overall development of human being including respect and protection of human rights written in the revised Constitution. Second, for increasing understanding and researching the various civilization traditions in the world so as to unfold the dialogue of different civilization and rational intercultural communication by education and other means. For example, the scholars in the Institute of Philosophy and other Institutes, Chinese Academy of Social Sciences wrote and published "A Series of World Civilization"(12 volumes),which respectively discourses 12 kinds of civilizations in the world including Ancient Civilization of West Asia and North Africa, Civilization of Confucianism, Indian Civilization, Jewish Civilization, Western European Civilization, Islam Civilization, Slavic Civilization, American Civilization, Canadian Civilization, Japanese Civilization, Civilization of Latin America, and Africa Black Civilization, which emphasizes that exchange and convergence of different civilizations would be beneficial to progress of history, only transforming conflict to reasonable communication would conform with the era tide of peace and development.

The Chinese philosophy circle also pays more attention to teaching and researching on various philosophical traditions in the world. It is related to the teaching and studies of civilization history. Chinese traditional philosophy itself occupies a considerable proportion in our teaching and research of philosophy. Its main contents consists in the historical evolution of Chinese traditional philosophy as the fruits of Chinese civilization history , which contains the origins and varieties of Confucianism, Taoism, Buddhism and other doctrines in the teaching and studies on general history of Chinese traditional philosophy. The teaching and studies concerned deepens also many special subjects such as philosophy in the pre-Jing Dynasty, the philosophy and study of Confucian classics in the Han Dynasty, metaphysics in the Wei and Jin periods, Chinese Buddhist philosophy, Neo-Confucianism in the Song and Ming Dynasties, modern Chinese philosophy, contemporary Neo-Confucianism, the philosophical thought of Chinese minorities, etc. This teaching and studies also expounds and probe to the place and role of Chinese traditional philosophy in the process of contemporary Chinese civilization, especially in reconstructing the Chinese system of cultural value for the enterprise of Chinese modernization. Confucianism is the main stream in Chinese traditional philosophy and has been broadly disseminating in the East Asian area. The relationship of Confucianism and some successful experiences of socio— economic development in this area is attracting widespread attention and much studies. No doubt, the Confucian ethical tradition does not necessarily constitute roadblocks to modernization, not in accordance with Max Weber's theme, it could be played its effective role in the contemporary social development. For instances: the values of national community is conducive to integrating the economic and social orders, stressing on that education and respecting knowledge and talents are the key of economic taking-off, the learning of mind and character can regulate persons' mentality and behavior to successfully respond various challenges, the theory of virtues is helpful to perfection of personality and establishment of harmonious moral order of society, and Confucian ethical relationship has been renewed in the oriental ethics of enterprise useful for improving the economic management system.

The Chinese intelligentsia has been making efforts to increase the communication with the external tradition of philosophy and culture. In the history, the most successful one is importing of Indian Buddhism and becoming of Chinese Buddhist philosophy. Early in the Ming dynasty of sixteenth —seventeenth century, the Chinese scholars began to introduce the ancient Aristotle's philosophy and Greek science. Now, Chinese philosophical circle's open introduction to and research in western philosophical tradition in recent two decades much exceed the past, attaching importance to both integral grasping evolutionary process from ancient Greek philosophy to modern European and American philosophy and following studies on new trends and new changes of contemporary western philosophy. *Complete Works of Plato* (4 volumes) and *Complete Works of Aristotle* (10 volumes)in Chinese edition has already been published, and appeared the more valuable results in researching history of Greek philosophy by period. The scholars in Institute of philosophy, Chinese Academy of Social sciences are writing voluminous *A History of Western Philosophy* (8 volumes) with their own studies characteristics. Cooperating with Søren Kierkegaard Research Center in Copenhagen University, my own Institute is translating and will publish *Kierkegaard Anthology.* Some Chinese Scholars are conducting studies on history of communication and comparative studies between Chinese and western philosophies, and also the ones between Chinese traditional philosophy and the philosophies of other oriental countries as well as Islamic-Arabic philosophy, and cultivating the graduates in the speciality concerned. These studies and teaching enable various philosophical traditions to learn from each other strong points and offset their respective weakness and enable Chinese scholars imbibe the fine fruits from external civilizations including the doctrines reflecting on process of western civilization in the western philosophies. All these are also embodiment of significance in the education of civilization history.

Should we Teach the History of Philosophy?
Or, Should we Teach History at All?

William L. McBride

If, as seems reasonable, a person's fundamental belief commitments may usually be judged by his or her actions, there should be little doubt as to where I stand on the first question that I have posed. When I teach my middle-level course on social and political philosophy, I devote the first two-thirds of it to historical figures, then try to cover the current literature and issues in the final third; the same ratio is reflected in my textbook on this topic. When I teach the philosophy of law, a comparatively recent sub-specialty within the field of philosophy, with Hegel usually being recognized as the first to identify it *eo nomine*, and with most available textbooks in my country concentrating on contemporary issues within an American or at best Anglo-American context, I nevertheless consider it essential to refer to Aristotle and Aquinas, Beccaria and Bentham, Kant, Hegel and Mill, and to try as much as possible to bring in discussions of other legal traditions. Even when I teach a graduate seminar on, say, contemporary issues or a twentieth-century figure such as Rawls, I am constantly making allusions to philosophers from the past. It is simply my way of conceiving of philosophy.

Furthermore, since my knowledge of non-Western philosophical traditions is exceedingly weak, I consider myself to that extent an invalid, a handicapped person – or, as politically correct language norms would have it, "philosophically challenged." In fact, of course, the history of philosophy is not a single thread but rather a number of different threads made of very different materials that are now coming increasingly to be interwoven. But I always try to make clear my conviction that the teaching of philosophy at its best should incorporate many, ideally all, of those threads, even if I myself am incapable of doing that.

This commitment to considering the history of philosophy as central to the discipline itself has been reinforced repeatedly in my personal experience. I have never forgotten a chance encounter with my undergraduate university's vice-president, who held a Doctorate in Government from Harvard, at a time when I was taking a course that concentrated on Plato's *Republic*. Somehow this fact came out in our conversation, at which point he said, without sounding as pretentious as it might sound in the retelling, that that was good, but that no one could consider him- or herself an educated person until he or she had read the *Republic* thoroughly and carefully at least three times. On another occasion, when as a young faculty member I was spending a spring semester on leave in England, I was at a weekend conference in the countryside at which I had the good fortune to converse at some length with Gilbert Ryle, then retired but still considered by many to be the *doyen* of British analytic philosophers. I was rather surprised, given my preconception that this school considered the history of philosophy to be of no importance, to hear Ryle strongly deplore the lack of historical training among so many analytic philosophers of the younger generation. One of Ryle's last publications, as it turned out, was his interesting and provocative work, *Plato's Progress*, a proof of his own ongoing interest in the history of philosophy.

A further reinforcement of these convictions, if any was needed, has been provided by a short retirement tribute to his Harvard colleague Burton Dreben that was written a few years ago by the late John Rawls, in a text to which someone just recently called my attention. There, Rawls says:

> We would often discuss historical texts, some of which I would be teaching at the time, and these conversations confirmed my ideas about how to proceed. Of course, I often taught the works of contemporary writers and presented my own views, yet Burt and I agreed that a knowledge of basic historical texts was essential..... In [teaching this way] I followed what Kant says in the *Critique of Pure Reason* at B866, namely, that philosophy is a mere idea of a possible science and nowhere exists *in concreto*: '[W]e cannot learn philosophy; for where is it, who is in possession of it, and how shall we recognize it? We can only learn to philosophize, that is, to exercise the talent of reason, in accordance with its universal principles, on certain actually existing attempts at philosophy, always, however, reserving the right of reason to investigate, to confirm, or to reject these principles in their very sources.'[1]

So for me to answer "Yes" to my initial question, "Should we teach the history of philosophy?" is simply to conform to the habits of my entire adulthood. Nevertheless, this answer is not without its severe dissenters, whose arguments de-

---

1   John Rawls, "Afterword: A Reminiscence," in *Future Pasts: The Analytic Tradition in Twentieth-Century Philosophy*, ed. J. Floyd and S. Shieh ((Oxford University Press, 2001), pp. 426 and 427.

serve consideration. It is a commonplace among some of my colleagues with an interest in historical figures in philosophy to make a distinction – exaggerated, in my opinion, but that is just my opinion – between those among them who are committed to a fully historical approach that regards these figures as children of their own intellectual times, and those who study them in order to extract from them, as it were, philosophical arguments and concepts of contemporary relevance without regard to their original contexts; several of my colleagues favor the latter approach. And some of the most highly regarded philosophers of the past appear essentially to have succeeded, if indeed that is the correct way of expressing it in light of what Kant says about philosophy as a mere idea of possible science, by breaking, or at least trying to break, as completely as possible with their intellectual ancestors. In fact, is not such a break the *sine qua non* of philosophical originality? Think of Descartes, Kant himself, Husserl, Wittgenstein, and so many others. The slogan, "*Faire table rase*", has been invoked repeatedly in the history of philosophy – although those who wish to be consistent in heeding it ought to be unaware, or ought at least to try to suppress awareness, of all its earlier invocations.

In short, if the purpose of philosophy is simply to seek out and formulate truths concerning any given region of reality, then what has been said by previous seekers is, strictly speaking, irrelevant to it – with the exception of one region, to which I shall return shortly. Perhaps no one has put this point better than Thomas Hobbes did, in the conclusion to his *Leviathan*, from which I would like to quote at some length:

> That I have neglected the ornament of quoting ancient poets, orators, and philosophers, contrary to the custom of late time, whether I have done well or ill in it, proceedeth from my judgment, grounded on many reasons. For first, all truth of doctrine dependeth either upon *reason*, or upon *Scripture*; both which give credit to many, but never receive it from any writer. Secondly, the matters in question are not of *fact*, but of *right*, wherein there is no place for *witnesses*. There is scarce any of those old writers, that contradicteth not sometimes both himself and others; which makes their testimonies insufficient. Fourthly, such opinions as are taken only upon credit of antiquity, are not intrinsically the judgment of those that cite them, but words that pass, like gaping, from mouth to mouth. Fifthly, it is many times with a fraudulent design that men stick their corrupt doctrine with the cloves of other men's wit. Sixthly, I find not that the ancients they cite, took it for an ornament, to do the like with those that wrote before them. Seventhly, it is an argument of indigestion, when Greek and Latin sentences unchewed come up again, as they use to do, unchanged. Lastly, though I

reverence those men of ancient time, that either have written truth perspicuously, or set us in a better way to find it out ourselves; yet to the antiquity itself I find nothing due. For if we will reverence the age, the present is the oldest.

I have thus invoked the venerable historical authority of Hobbes as my witness to support the claim that philosophers *qua* philosophers, truth-seekers, have no need of the history of philosophy. Or, as the Scholastics whom he despised used to say when invoking the authority of Aristotle, "*ipse dixit.*" But to be more consistent I should perhaps rather forget about Hobbes and all the rest and simply say, concerning this matter, "*res ipsa loquitur;*" what need have we of witnesses?

As should now be obvious, I can't help myself: the history of philosophy keeps intruding into my philosophical thinking. Either I am incorrigibly corrupt in this respect, or perhaps – heretical thought – the seeking and formulating of truths about given regions of reality should not be construed as philosophy's sole purpose. After all, we are dealing here, *contra* Hobbes, with a question of both right and fact: what philosophy's purpose or purposes are or may be is not something imposed from outside the ongoing practices of philosophers. In any case, there is, as I hinted earlier, one region of reality about which it is impossible for a philosopher attempting to deal with it to avoid engaging in historical considerations, and that, of course, is history itself.

However, should history itself be taught and studied? *Quaeritur.* Aristotle – who, paradoxically enough, has bequeathed us so much rich information both about his own times and about earlier history, including the history of pre-Socratic philosophy – famously discounted the relative importance of history in the passage that formed the basis of Professor Evans' paper. As he said: "διο και φιλοσοφωτερον και σπουδαιοτερον ποιησις ιστοριας εστιν. η μεν γαρ ποιησις μαλλον τα καθολου, η δ' ιστορια τα καθ' εκαστον λεγει." (*Poetics* 9, 451b)

Now, it is true that the devaluing of history is not generally regarded with favor either in intellectual circles or among the public at large. I myself associate such a devaluing attitude most closely with Henry Ford, who said "History is bunk," and to whose promotion of the mass production of automobiles we must attribute so many catastrophes and so much widespread misery over the past century of human history. The idea of suppressing the teaching of history in order to benefit society was developed in a more intellectually interesting way by the behavioral psychologist, B.F. Skinner, in his utopian novel, *Walden Two.* But it is certainly not, to repeat, a very widely held point of view; I need only mention, for instance, the considerable popularity, in my own country, of the History Channel on cable television. Nevertheless, I believe that the potential value of at least a selective suppression of history needs to be seriously considered. I shall now consider, in turn, two recent historical examples that seem to me to lend weight to this contention – examples of past history exerting a baneful influence on later times, or, in other words, of history undermining itself.

My first example is taken from the wars in former Yugoslavia during the decade of the 1990s. I was in that country on two separate occasions during the months immediately preceding the breakup of the Yugoslav Federation in the summer of 1991. Everywhere, one heard of mutual recriminations being uttered by members of the different ethnic groups, particularly the Serbs and the Croats, against one another. What had been taking place was the formation of numerous political parties, with programs that were radically incompatible with one another, and the development of a free press, much of it sensational and venomous in character, in all regions of the country. One evening, which happened to be the evening of Orthodox Easter Day of that year, I was the guest of my old friend and colleague Svetozar Stojanović at his apartment in Belgrade. He explained to me that the Tito regime, through its control of textbooks and the media, had worked to reduce and, ideally, to expunge the painful memories of terrible human rights violations that had occurred during World War II, when the country had been divided by the German (and, on the Dalmatian Coast, Italian) Occupation forces and bitter hostilities had internally split the individual ethnic communities themselves. This policy of suppression of certain memories had been, in fact, remarkably successful in achieving its aims, at least for several decades. Stojanović had been a child during the War, too young to remember much, but he mentioned an aunt of his who had recently begun, as a result of sensationalist stories in the news media, vividly to recall old events about which she had not thought for all that intervening time. Hers was apparently not an uncommon experience. Stojanović himself had recently visited Jasenovac, the site of an enormous massacre, genocidal in intent, of Serbs during the World War – the emotional and symbolic equivalent, for Serbs, of what Auschwitz is for Jews. It had been a very emotional experience for him. Nevertheless he, along with two other philosophy colleagues from the old *Praxis* Group who came by to visit that evening, Mihailo Marković and Dragoljub Mićunović, still harbored some hope that the total break-up of the country and ensuing violent war that many were already predicting could somehow be averted. Let me now cite a few sentences from Stojanović's book, *The Fall of Yugoslavia: Why Communism*

Failed, that was published just a few years later, in 1997:

> The karst pits into which Serbs were thrown alive by Ustashis in Herzegovina re-
> mained concreted over, and their relatives were not allowed to take out their bodies
> and bury them. These 'concreted pits' have become a metaphor for the communist
> illusion that enforced silence is the best way to deal with terrible crimes among
> nations. Perhaps that was why, not only due to his personal insouciance, Tito never
> visited Jasenovac!
>
> As I am criticizing others, I am obliged to admit that neither I, brought up as a child
> in the spirit of Yugoslav brotherhood, nor my wife, a Serbian from Croatia who had
> just managed to flee from there in 1941, spoke to our sons about what had happened
> to their mother and her family during the Second World War, When they saw on tel-
> evision the bones from those pits in Herzegovina being exhumed and buried on the
> eve of the Serb-Croat war in 1991-1992, they reproached us bitterly for our silence. For
> me, that scene was a turning point in the sense that I firmly decided to devote my full
> moral attention and my research to Jasenovac in the future. (p. 78)

Let me raise the following question, obviously an outsider's question, yet one
that also, I think, deserves our "moral attention": even if, as Stojanović says,
"enforced silence" was not the best possible way to deal with these crimes,
how much better, if at all, was the path taken after the silence had been broken
and the most bitter historical memories were encouraged and promoted and
indulged in? That path, of course, was the path of the brutal war that drowned
"Yugoslav brotherhood" in waves of blood and that is still recent enough for
all of us to recall, though I suspect ever more dimly in most cases. Meanwhile,
especially among members of the younger generations, the phenomenon of
Yugo-nostalgia was reappearing even as Stojanović was completing his book. In
her 1996 dissertation, *A Critique of Nationalism*, my Doctoral student, Natalija
Mićunović, Dragoljub Mićunović's daughter, wrote as follows:

> The newly developed, although in a limited way ever-present, feeling of Yugo-nos-
> talgia has as its referential nostalgic point a picture of Yugoslavia as it never existed.
> Of course, it is true of every nostalgia: we forget the intensity of painful situations,
> experience worse, get older, and altogether it is pleasant to remember the past. In
> the stories of many people from Yugoslavia, you will hear that it was a paradise.
> Everybody lived well, everybody loved each other, etc. That things were better then
> than during and just after the war is true for obvious reasons. But of course, in the
> tragedy of sacrifice lies greatness, and afterwards, the rewards of independence and
> hegemony were supposed to be sweet – such was the nationalist argument. Well, not

everybody enjoyed the greatness of tragedy, and the rewards were not delivered. So, as is always necessary for the existence of any social change, a great many people changed their minds. (78-79)

She goes on to say that she is perhaps less cynical, though more aware of the tragic, than most people in this respect, to wit, that she truly believes that many though by no means all former nationalists really did change their minds, and did not merely pretend to do so out of opportunism.

In sum, the case of former Yugoslavia shows once again how elusive is the notion of historical fact even when the history is recent enough for us, or at least for others with whom we are acquainted, to have lived through it. It also shows just how inextricably interwoven with myth are all the so-called "hard facts", such as industrial production, numbers of persons killed and buildings destroyed, etc. And it further reminds us that, if one of the chief purposes of education is to promote happiness, then the teaching of history free and uncensored is likely as often as not to run counter to that purpose. Hegel, of course, despite the ultimate optimism of his theodicy, was very well aware of this when he wrote, in his *Philosophy of History*, of the "moral embitterment – a revolt of the Good Spirit (if it have a place within us)" that is occasioned by considering the spectacle of "History as the slaughter-bench at which the happiness of peoples, the wisdom of States, and the virtue of individuals have been victimized." Should history, then, be taught indiscriminately? Again, I repeat, *quaeritur*.

My second case study, with which I will conclude this presentation, is, in my opinion, more complicated with respect to the questions both of what it means to suppress history and of the value or disvalue of doing so, but it has the advantage of being *zu Hand* – namely, the American invasion and occupation of Iraq. On the one hand, observers have claimed that those who planned and carried out the invasion had forgotten the lessons of the war against Vietnam, or the Soviet experience in Afghanistan, or the British experience in Iraq after World War I, etc. Many have gone so far as to say that the planners have disregarded and repudiated, especially through the Bush Doctrine that assumes a right to attack, at any time, any nation that is considered a potential future threat, the whole past history of American foreign policy, which supposedly always used to condemn and reject acts of aggression. But surely that is false, alas, except in some very limited senses. It is true that the Bush Doctrine, by encompassing the entire world, goes further than the Monroe Doctrine of the early nineteenth century, which was confined to the Western Hemisphere and did not envisage actually attacking those European colonies that still existed in the Americas. However, much of past United States history has been, stories told in children's history textbooks notwithstanding, one of expansion – obviously! – and aggression, from George Washington's annihilation of the mixed Indian-French inhabitants of the part of Indiana where I now live, through the revolt of the American slaveholders in Texas against the Mexican government that had sovereignty there and the invasion and annexation of nearly one-half of the rest of Mexico in the subsequent war, on and on through bellicose adventures great and small, from the Spanish-American War to the brilliant conquest of the formidable fortress island of Grenada during the First Bush Dynasty, and beyond. In short, although I have no doubt that the foreign policy stances of the Second Bush Dynasty, when taken as a whole, do in fact amount to a qualitative historical change, one of sufficient magnitude and importance to warrant the serious attention of us philosophers, it seems to me at least questionable to claim either that they are the result of total historical amnesia on the part of this leadership or that they represent a total repudiation of all past policies. Nor am I sure whether to be happy or sad about this observation.

However, there was one very small, apparently insignificant moment that was reported by the press during the period soon after the invasion, when it became clear that the invaders were not going to be greeted with many bouquets of flowers by a grateful Iraqi public, that seemed to me at the time, and still seems to me now, an excellent example of putting history to very bad use – of employing an historical reference that might better have been forgotten, never taught, and never learned. According to that report, the group of conservative ideologists centered around Paul Wolfowitz, the defense advisor who played a major part in advocating and planning the war, and who, along with some of his colleagues, is known to be an admirer of the work of the late Leo Strauss, had become fond of applying an old Latin saying to those same ungrateful Iraqis: "*Oderint, dum metuant*" – let them hate us, as long as they fear us. I must confess that at the time I first read about it I was not familiar either with the line itself or with its source. But I am now. It comes from *The Lives of the Twelve Caesars* by Suetonius, who claims that it was a favorite saying of the especially brutal Emperor Gaius Caligula. It is he who, in the same text, is said to have urged his soldiers to take their time when beating a condemned person to death, so that the latter might fully experience his dying; Caligula is also said to have expressed the wish that the whole Roman rabble had a single neck, so that he could hang them all at once. The saying, *Oderint, dum metuant* itself was originally a line in a play, *Atreus*, by Attus, and is cited in a quite different context by Cicero in *De Officiis*.

Wolfowitz is certainly not alone, in more modern times, in being attracted to this line. As I should have remembered – and I must particularly ask the forgiveness of our Danish hosts for not having remembered – it is cited at the beginning of a paragraph in Kierkegaard's *Seducer's Diary*: the Seducer is confident that he has made his conquest of Cordelia, and his point is that it is mistake, while connecting fear with hatred, not to realize that fear and love often go together as well, as is now the case for Cordelia with respect to himself. But so, of course, we should remind the Seducer, do hatred and love, as we see in Juvenal's famous line, *Odi et amo*; whereas Machiavelli, whom Wolfowitz' mentor Leo Strauss pretended exoterically to abhor while esoterically admiring him (or so it is said), equally famously answered his own question as to whether it was better for a prince to be loved or feared by opining that, in cases where it is not possible to achieve both, it is better to be feared, but that in any event a prince should avoid being hated. This was one of many lessons that Machiavelli, a great student of history, claimed to have learned from it. But as far as ancient Rome was concerned his focus, in the *Discorsi*, was on the time of the Republic, not on the later Imperial period of the Caesars. It is probably not an accident that among some American neo-Conservatives, who do not mind being hated by Others, meaning Aliens or non-Americans, it has now become very fashionable to speak in positive terms of "Empire". (This goes together, of course, with the revival of interest in Rome.) While Caligula was eventually assassinated, he did rule for 29 years, which is quite a long time. Perhaps, then, with an eye on Roman Imperial history, neo-Conservatives should consider rescinding the Twenty-second Amendment to the United State Constitution, which, in part as a reaction to the long rule of Franklin Roosevelt, restricted Presidents to two four-year terms in office, in order to try to extend the Second Bush Dynasty for another 24 years or so. They might even propose it as a companion amendment to the one now favored by their leader, which would define marriage as heterosexual and thus prohibit marriages between members of the same sex. This latter development, it seems to me, shows a clear tendency on the part of members of the American Right to extend Caligula's slogan to fellow citizens as well; Bush's initiative in this sphere has already, predictably, been denounced by some prominent individuals as hateful and divisive. Let them hate us, the Bush response seems to be, as long as they fear us and bend to our will; history, as many an earlier ruler has said, is on our side.

We are living, in fact, at a time at which hatred and fear abound. And the invocations of historical referents about which I have been speaking seem not to have contributed to ameliorating that situation; on the contrary. Should history, then, be taught?

What is Historical in the History of Philosophy? Towards an Assessment of Twentieth-Century European Philosophy[1]

Dermot Moran

'Lack of a historical sense is the hereditary defect of philosophers ... So what is needed from now on is *historical philosophising*, and with it the virtue of modesty.'

(Nietzsche 1878)

The Project:
A Critical Assessment of Twentieth-Century Philosophy

Thanks to a Senior Fellowship from the *Irish Research Council for the Humanities and Social Sciences,* I am currently collaborating with a team of international philosophers on a challenging philosophical project, namely, a critical assessment of twentieth-century philosophy, one that identifies its significant innovations and accomplishments, as well as the problems bequeathed to our current generation of philosophers. In this paper I want to reflect on some aspects of this problematic: how to approach twentieth-century philosophy; how to gain an overall perspective on its traditions, and specifically on the commonalities between these emerging traditions, commonalities that are, in many ways, more significant that their opposition and divergences. The overall aim is to identify the challenges still being generated by the legacy of the twentieth century. To paraphrase Croce's 1906 question concerning Hegel: what is living and what is dead in twentieth century philosophy?

1   Earlier versions of this paper have been presented as the Plenary Session, Society for European Philosophy Conference, *European Philosophy and the Human Condition*, University College Cork, Saturday 14th September 2002, and at the Organization of Phenomenological Organizations (OPO) Conference, Prague Academy of the Sciences, Prague, Friday 8th November 2002. I also acknowledge gratefully the support of the Irish Research Council for the Humanities and Social Sciences (IRCHSS).

There are, currently, remarkably few overall studies of twentieth-century philosophy; even the 10-volume *Routledge Encyclopedia of Philosophy* contains no entry for 'Twentieth-Century Philosophy'.[2] Yet it is clear that the very *meaning* of philosophy changed in profound ways over the last hundred years, ways that are certainly not even documented, never mind fully understood. How are we even to begin to appreciate the philosophical legacy of that turbulent, terrifying, but enormously productive twentieth century? Historians are apt to speak of 'long' centuries, and certainly the twentieth century must seem to us now to be one of the longest. Extraordinary technological advances coupled with political catastrophes are marks of the age. Moreover, philosophy bears a grave responsibility: like it or not, disastrous ideologies have been inspired in part by the appropriation or misappropriation of various philosophies – Marx-Leninism, Maoism, fascism, and so on. There is, undoubtedly, a fascinating chapter to be written in the sociology of knowledge concerning the relation of philosophy to other developments in the century, here however I shall be concerned with philosophy's self-representation, philosophical reflection on its own history. I shall largely exclude external factors, and largely concern myself with an *internalist* account of the history of philosophy, philosophy as interpreted by philosophers.

The Legacy of the Nineteenth Century
Nevertheless, some 'external' features need to be mentioned. Certain aspects of philosophical practice are in direct continuity with patterns set in the nineteenth century. For instance, the academic *professionalisation* and specialisation of philosophy that began in the early nineteenth century (usually dated to Kant) becomes pervasive in the twentieth, with the end of the 'man of letters' (Descartes, Leibniz, Hume). Scholarly interest in the history of philosophy also becomes completely professionalized (stimulated largely by Hegel's interest in the subject) and has been carried to new heights in the twentieth century.

While the critical review of the history of philosophy begins with Aristotle, and there are many ancient compendia of philosophical positions, e.g. Cicero and

2   Routledge has devoted three volumes in its *History of Philosophy* series but two volumes deal with analytic philosophy (seen as the dominant tradition – including epistemology, metaphysics, philosophy of language, ethics, philosophy of science) whereas one volume – edited by Richard Kearney dealt with Continental philosophy. The opportunity to compare and contrast was lost by this decision to go for separate studies of the traditions. A useful collection of articles on the analytic tradition is Juliet Floyd and Sanford Shieh, eds, *Future Pasts. The Analytic Tradition in Twentieth-Century Philosophy* (Oxford: OUP, 2001).

Augustine, nevertheless the history of philosophy practised entirely for its own sake seems to be a product of nineteenth century. Both the Hegelians and the Neo-Kantians (e.g. Windelband) wrote histories of philosophy, as did the Neo-Thomists (Gilson), who for instance, emphasised the dominance of classical realism in medieval philosophy to the detriment of the nominalist or even Neoplatonic influences. It is important to recognise how recent many of our historical discoveries are in philosophy, to realise, for example, that more has been learned about all aspects of medieval philosophy in the twentieth century (its figures, texts, sources and influences) than in the whole period from the 17th to the 19th centuries. Similarly, thanks to the 1844 manuscripts, a new version of Marx emerged in twentieth century. European universities especially in Germany, France and England developed critical editions of Plato, Aristotle, and so on. But compare what we know of Heidegger now, based on the *Gesamtausgabe* and, simularly, what we knew at the time of his death in 1976. The same can be said of Kant, Nietzsche and Kierkegaard who receive their critical editions in twentieth century.

An important innovation in the practice of philosophy in the twentieth century that cannot go unnoticed is the admission of women into the profession in large numbers from the mid-twentieth century onwards. The First World War played a role in ensuring that Husserl's classes consisted largely on women in the late war years. Edith Stein, for example, who wrote her doctorate under Husserl, demanded the right to be accepted for the Habilitation degree, and wrote letters to the Education ministry in an attempt to force reluctant academic professors to take on women.[3] Hannah Arendt was prevented from completing her Habilitation because she was Jewish. Simone de Beauvoir attended the Ecole Normale Supérieure in Paris in the twenties, and Elizabeth Anscombe was a student of Wittgenstein in the forties, but it was not until after the Second World War that women began to graduate in philosophy in large numbers and to enter the profession.

The Reaction to Idealism

German philosophy provided the dominant inspiration in European thought during the nineteenth century. The first half of the nineteenth century in Ger-

---

3   Gerda Walther, another student of Husserl's in Freiburg, records his reluctance to see women in the academic profession.

many was dominated by the philosophy of Hegel and his immediate students. But, contrary to the claims of the early phenomenologists and logical analysts, Hegel never really went away, although interest in his work went underground so to speak in the latter half of the nineteenth century, to resurface in different fashions in the course of the twentieth century. Russell was initially a committed Idealist, strongly influenced by the Hegelianism of Bradley and McTaggart. In fact, Russell and G.E. Moore saw their own 'analytical' philosophy as directly opposed to Hegel's 'synthetic' philosophy.[4] Refracted through the early Marx's writings, Hegel influenced the Frankfurt school, e.g. Herbert Marcuse or Theodor Adorno (especially his 'negative dialectics'). Georg Luckacs: *History and Class Consciousness* played a role also in the rehabilitation of Hegel via Marx. In the thirties, a new 'phenomenological' Hegel emerges in the writings of Alexandre Kojève, Jean Wahl, and later Jean Hyppolite. Hans-Georg Gadamer claims to have revived interest in Hegel in post-war German philosophy. In the sixties Walter Kaufmann and John Findlay helped 'translate' Hegel for English-speaking audiences and analytic interest in Hegel developed with Charles Taylor and others. Most recently, in the US, we have seen the social Hegelianism of Brandom and McDowell and Brandom has even written of seeking to introduce the 'Hegelian' phase of analytic philosophy (paraphrasing Sellars who spoke of Wittgenstein's Investigations as the Kantian phase of analytic philosophy that succeeded its earlier 'Humean' phase). Interestingly, for the twentieth century, as Terry Pinkard has observed, Hegel's most influential text, one that he himself regarded as merely introductory to his system, is *The Phenomenology of Spirit* (1807), a work largely ignored by nineteenth-century philosophers.

The latter half of the nineteenth century in German philosophy was dominated by the slogan 'back to Kant' ('*zurück zu Kant*'), and Neo-Kantianism had a strong influence both on Frege (whose teacher was the Neo-Kantian Hermann Lotze) and on Husserl (who was in close contact with Paul Natorp and Heinrich Rickert). The influence of Kant can also be traced through the twentieth century especially in debates over the nature of the a priori and the rule of reason. Rawls' political philosophy, for instance, owes a heavy debt to Kant. Indeed, it is extraordinary how influential Kant continues to be in the sphere of moral philosophy.

---

4   See David Bell, 'The Revolution of Moore and Russell: A Very British Coup,' in Anthony O'Hear, ed., *German Philosophy Since Kant* (Cambridge: CUP, 1999), pp. 193-208.

Most commentators agree that early twentieth-century philosophy was united in its rejection of German Idealism, and in its suspicion of speculative systems. In this it followed a certain empiricist and positivist streak found in late nineteenth-century philosophy – in Mill, Brentano, Mach and Comte. The broadly anti-metaphysical and empirical trends of the late nineteenth century ensured that the dominant approach at the turn of the twentieth century in Germany was epistemological. The chief problem was: how to secure objective knowledge in response to the challenges of *scepticism* and *relativism*. Dilthey's philosophy of world views, for example, appeared to Husserl as leading to relativism. Epistemology is still at the heart of Russell's *Problems of Philosophy*. But very soon, with the emergence of both phenomenology and the linguistic turn, epistemology was dethroned in favour of issues concerned with meaning.

The Effects of War

Even while attempting an internalist history of philosophy, the effects of two world wars on European philosophy simply cannot be ignored. The First World War was catastrophic in its human and political consequences, and it broke up the old order in Germany. In philosophical terms, as reported by Hans-Georg Gadamer, it loosened the grip of Neo-Kantianism and other nineteenth century traditions, and to open students up to the new movements, including Husserlian phenomenology, *Lebensphilosophie* (Simmel, Dilthey), existentialism (Kierkegaard and Nietzsche), and mysticism (Eckhart). The First World War also had important consequences for the development of analytic philosophy in the UK. It woke Bertrand Russell up from his detached mathematical and metaphysical concerns. As Ray Monk recounts in his biography of Russell, Russell was horrified by the enthusiasm for war gripping Britain in 1914, with the Cambridge University authorities, for instance, putting up a notice recommending that every able-bodied student join the Officer Training Corps. In response, Russell embarked on writing a number of philosophical articles on the ethics of war, which, though they might not measure up to the politically correct standards of our day in that they defended the war of a more advanced civilisation on a lesser, nevertheless demanded serious reasons for war and argued against the kind of irrational pride and rivalry that was driving 'civilised States' to war. These articles were considered so shocking at the time that journals such as the *New Statesman* refused to publish them.[5] Indeed, Russell's opposition to the war

---

5   Ray Monk, *Bertrand Russell. The Spirit of Solitiude* (London: Jonathan Cape, 1996), pp. 383ff.

and to conscription effectively destroyed his academic career. In 1916 he was dismissed from Trinity College for publishing a pamphlet defending a conscientious objector. He was prevented from taking up a job in Harvard because Britain would not issue him a passport. Particularly shocking for Russell was that his friend and protégé Ludwig Wittgenstein had enlisted in the Austrian army and was effectively fighting for the other side. Russell wrote to Ottiline Morrell, his first wife:

> It seems strange that of all the people in the war the one I care for much the most should be Wittgenstein, who is an 'enemy'.[6]

The First World War gave Russell a taste for activism, and led to him being jailed in 1918, but otherwise it was more or less welcomed by other academics (Broad was also against it). In Germany, Max Scheler made a living writing patriotic pamphlets while living in Berlin. Edmund Husserl too was broadly supportive of Germany's war aims, even though he lost one son in 1916 with his second son seriously injured, and his chief assistant Adolf Reinach also died on the front. Martin Heidegger was serving on the Western front with the meteorological division, and corresponding with Husserl, while Ludwig Wittgenstein was composing the *Tractatus* while a serving soldier in the Austro-Hungarian army. Meanwhile, Gadamer escaped the call up because he (as he later regarded it) rather luckily contracted polio and was exempted from military service.

The Second World War and in particular the anti-Jewish policies of the Third Reich had an even more decisive impact on the philosophical community. The rise of Nazism had a disastrous effect on the academy in Germany, giving rise to the mass migration of intellectuals, with members of the Vienna Circle and the Frankfurt School moving to the UK and US. Neo-Kantians also left Germany, including Cassirer. Nazism also cost the lives of important philosophers such as Walter Benjamin and Edith Stein. Meanwhile, the War also had a motivating effect on US philosophy. In the early thirties Martin Heidegger was becoming the most prominent philosopher in Germany but he effectively linked his academic career to the National Socialist Movement when he accepted Rectorship of Freiburg University in 1933 and as a result his teaching career lay in ruins along with the collapse of Germany in 1945. The young William Van Orman

---

6   Ray Monk, *Bertrand Russell. The Spirit of Solitiude*, op. cit., p. 374.

Quine, who himself had studied in Vienna, was so horrified by the prospect of the rise of the Nazis that he enlisted in the Navy and fought in Italy:

> I felt that Western culture was on the verge of collapse and all I was doing was philosophy of logic.[7]

According to Jean-Paul Sartre, for instance, this war divided his life in two. Philosophically, he moved from an earlier 'bourgeois' idealism to a commitment to Marxism. But after the war, as Adorno too has recognised in a different context, everything changed. Scandinavian philosophers who routinely did doctorates in Germany before the Second World War shifted to the United States and now wrote in English rather than in German. French philosophy cut itself loose from German philosophy and flourished as a vigorous and extraordinarily diverse set of interests. The second half of the century saw a steady drift towards America (including the large number of British philosophers, e.g. Colin McGinn, who left the UK for US universities during the Thatcher years) and the recognition of a distinct voice emerging in the US. The accounts of the education of American philosophers such as Quine or Richard Rorty are striking in that their orientation was entirely towards Europe. Quine studied logic at Harvard with Whitehead but was disappointed by what he found there, and so, having good German, he travelled to Europe to study in Vienna (where he spent six weeks with Carnap), Prague and Warsaw (where he met Polish logicians including Tarski, Lesniewski and Lukasiewicz). Rorty was first taught by Carnap and others at Princeton, as was Putnam. Indeed, the influence of European philosophy in the US was such that Arthur Danto claims that a distinctive American academic philosophy only emerged in the 1960s.

The Emerging Division Between Analytic and Continental Philosophy

In particular, and most relevant to the rest of this paper, the dislocation of the war brought about a separation between Anglophone philosophy and philosophy on the European Continent, helping to cement the emerging distinction between analytic and continental philosophy. One of the most notable features feature of twentieth-century philosophy is the development of two dominant

---

7   Quoted in Giovanna Borradori, *The American Philosopher. Conversations with Quine, Davidson, Putnam, Nozick, Danto, Rorty, Cavell, MacIntyre and Kuhn*, trans. Rosanna Crocitto. (Chicago: University of Chicago Pr., 1994), p. 33.

intellectual traditions, named—at least in the Anglophone world—as the 'analytic' or 'Anglo-American' and 'Continental' or 'European' philosophical traditions.[8] The labels are a stumbling block: European philosophers have never been comfortable with the label 'Continental', since they see themselves as doing philosophy in the traditional sense (and upholding the tradition of historical scholarship). They see 'Continental' as a label imposed on them from without, often from a rather narrow Euro-sceptical British or American perspective.[9] Recently philosophers in this tradition have begun to express a preference for describing their tradition as 'European philosophy', a title that recognises the long and unbroken European tradition from the Greeks through to German Idealism, hermeneutics and Neo-Kantianism. The problem is that European philosophy includes LaPlace, Comte, Frege, Carnap, Schlick, Popper and Wittgenstein alongside Nietzsche, Foucault, Deleuze, and Lacan and again seems to be mirroring the British Euro-Sceptics in excluding Hume, Mill, Russell and Ayer from the cast of acceptable Europeans. On the other hand, the term 'European' philosophy also seems to exclude all those in the USA who write about Heidegger, Derrida and others, excluding thereby Richard Rorty, John Sallis, Jack Caputo, or Charles Taylor. A recent meeting of SPEP (The Society for Phenomenology and Existential Philosophy) struggled with this difficulty and tried to propose the title 'Society for Continental Philosophy' but the move was resisted by those who felt it was vague – which continent? Martinich and Sosa are in a similar predicament with regard to the term 'analytic' philosophy, which they believe most accurately characterises the work of Moore and Russell and other British philosophers up to the mid-century. They suggest the term 'Anglo-German philosophy' to recognise the important contribution of Carnap, Feigl, Reichenbach and others. This division between 'analytic' and 'Continental', then, is most unhappy, as Simon Critchley has pointed out; however, at present we do not have a more suitable nomenclature and we shall continue to use these terms as they were used largely by followers of the traditions themselves.[10] These traditions are widely held to have developed separately, with opposing aspirations and methodologies, and, indeed, to be fundamentally hostile

---

8   For reasons of space in this essay I shall leave aside two other extremely important twentieth-century movements, namely *pragmatism* and *Marxism*, both in effect reactions against German Idealism.

9   See Tom Baldwin's comments in his review essay "Two Approaches to Sartre," *European Journal of Philosophy* Vol. 4 No. 1 (April 1996), pp. 81-2.

10 Of course, the term 'analysis' was used by Russell and others in contrast with the 'synthetic' method of the Neo-Hegelians. Continental philosophers (certainly European ones) did not use that label, which emerged seemingly in the US in the sixties.

to one another. Certainly they have evolved their own distinctive ideologies. Crudely, analytic philosophy has been seen as interested not in the history of ideas but in 'doing philosophy'. It was, initially at least, anti-metaphysical in that it thought of metaphysical speculation as the mind idling, unconstrained by logic. Certain forms of analysis had a strong sympathy for positivism.

More recently, the analytic tradition has largely embraced naturalism and what critics might call 'scientism', the view that philosophy itself is really a part of the exact sciences. Continental philosophy, on the other hand, is often seen as anti-scientific and humanistic in orientation. I believe, however, that more careful scrutiny will actually show that these traditions emerge from common sources in nineteenth-century philosophy and address many of the same problematics, albeit with differing emphases and conclusions. Both Continental and analytic philosophy, for instance, are interested in *naturalism*, diagnosed quite early in the twentieth century as a major threat to philosophy by Husserl in his essay *Philosophy as a Rigorous Science* (1910/1911) but advocated by Quine with proposed the naturalisation of epistemology, and by philosophers who have extended the naturalisation project to ethics and philosophy of mind. However, analytic philosophy cannot be seen as exclusively committed to naturalism, given the powerful anti-naturalist arguments of John McDowell and others.

Both traditions are sensitive to language and meaning, aware of the problem of multiple and competing interpretations, sensitive to the challenge of science and technology, reacting to the challenges of scepticism and relativism, and so on. Both traditions began as committed to some form of foundationalism but now are radically shifting ground and abandoning their supposed 'founding' methodologies. For instance, descriptive phenomenology soon faced the challenge of hermeneutics, which emphasised the clash of interpretations. Similarly, structuralism gave way to deconstruction with its conception of the limitless deferral and dispersal of meanings. In analytic philosophy, the Carnapian project of securing an ideal language was gradually replaced by a robust philosophical confidence in ordinary language, which itself has been gradually eroded by the problems associated with radical translation, etc.

Inaugural Moments and Grand Narratives

In trying to write the history of twentieth century philosophy, one must be careful not to impose a 'grand' narrative nor to be deceived by many of the grand narratives which contemporary philosophers themselves espouse. Analytic philosophers no less than Continental philosophers have showed a suspicion of these grand narratives. Rorty speaks of 'downbeat' stories; other analytic philosophers want to offer 'deflationary' accounts of truth, meaning, and so on. But while one must be suspicious of the veracity of grand narratives, one must also be aware of the many grand narratives that were proposed. Freud and Husserl were themselves authors of such grand narratives, self-conscious founders of new disciplines – inscribing themselves into history as the founders of psychoanalysis and phenomenology. Husserl, of course, was always an ambiguous founder; he saw himself as radicalising the project of first philosophy (*proté philosophia*), but also reading the history of modern philosophy as the progressive discovery of the reduction in his 'critical history of ideas' (*kritische Ideengeschichte*). But there were many other 'inaugural moments', from the Manifesto of the Vienna Circle to Jacques Derrida's typically ambiguous proclamation of a new science of *grammatology*, the science of writing, (a call taken up by Kristeva) while at the same time explaining how the metaphysical closure of the epoch could prevent it being established as such:

> By alluding to a science of writing reined in by metaphor, metaphysics and theology, this exergue must not only announce that the science of writing –grammatology – shows signs of liberation all over the world ... I would like to suggest above all that, however fecund and necessary the undertaking might be ... such a science of writing runs the risk of never being established as such and with that name. ... For essential reasons: the unity of all that allows itself to be attempted today through the most diverse concepts of science and writing is in principle more or less covertly yet always, determined by an historico-metaphysical epoch of which we merely glimpse closure. I do not say the end.[11]

In other words, and in rather typical manner, Derrida wants both to participate in the grand gesture of the founding of a new science and at the same time protect himself against the inevitable failure concealed in such vaulted ambition.

---

11   J. Derrida, *Of Grammatology*, trans. G. C. Spivak (Baltimore: Johns Hopkins, 1976), p. 4.

Martin Heidegger, too is a curious case, both a 'modern' and a 'postmodern' in many ways, and yet one who wants to speak of, and diagnose, 'epochs'. Heidegger not only developed a narrative that linked the practices of the ancient Greeks, an interest itself stimulated by nascent German neo-Thomism, with those of Husserl, but also married the hermeneutic tradition of Dilthey and Schleiermacher with the descriptive phenomenology of Husserl. Heidegger too has an idiosyncratic history of philosophy with its narrative of 'the history of Being', which, for instance, bizarrely characterises Nietzsche as a metaphysician, albeit one who diagnoses nihilism as the contemporary meaning of Being. Heidegger and Derrida want to see western philosophy in terms of an occlusion of the meaning of being, or the all-pervasive dominance of an understanding of being in terms of presence. In phenomenology, it is astonishing how so many French thinkers – Levinas, Sartre, Merleau-Ponty, Derrida, for instance – had the same totalised view of the history of philosophy. They were all formed in the same Ecole Normale Supérieure and accepted its view of the history of philosophy, very much a 'totalised' package.

There are many examples of the grand gesture and indeed the Geneva philosopher Kevin Mulligan has characterised continental philosophy as 'melodramatic'.[12] How many philosophers in the twentieth century issued apocalyptic pronouncements, proclaiming the 'end of philosophy' or, with Foucault, the 'end of man'? Heidegger sees the end of philosophy as coming with Nietzsche who 'completed' metaphysics and gave 'planetary thinking' the form it will have for decades to come. Philosophy is ended because a certain form of philosophy has been incorporated into this planetary thinking:

> With Nietzsche's metaphysics, philosophy is completed. That means: it has gone through the sphere of prefigured possibilities. Completed metaphysics, which is the ground for the planetary manner of thinking, gives the scaffolding for an order of the earth, which will supposedly last for a long time. The order no longer needs philosophy because philosophy is already its foundation. But with the end of philosophy, thinking is not also at its end, but in transition to another beginning.[13]

The rhetoric of end is always associated with the rhetoric of beginning.

---

12   Kevin Mulligan, 'Post-Continental Philosophy: Nosological Notes,' *Stanford French Review* Vol. 17. 2-3 (1993).

13   M. Heidegger, 'Overcoming Metaphysics,' from *Vorträge und Aufsätze* (Pfullingen: Neske, 1954), trans. in *The End of Philosophy*, ed. J. Stambaugh (NY: Harper & Row, 1973), pp. 95-96.

Analytic philosophy, too, at various times has proclaimed an end to philosophy as a discipline distinct from science. There is science and there is stamp-collecting. There is no such thing as 'philosophy'. It is at best a set of questions for which the proper scientific method for answering them has not yet been defined. Even where philosophy is still accepted as a separate discipline, there is also a more widespread rejection among analytic philosophers of philosophy as traditionally practiced through the critical study of classic texts. Just say 'no' to the history of philosophy, is a slogan in point. Philosophy as scientific analysis is supposed to be different in character to what is often disparagingly characterised as 'the history of ideas'. Yet, A. J. Ayer, for instance, in his autobiography, *A Part of My Life*, describes his Oxford training in philosophy as primarily being a kind of critical engagement with the history of philosophy, writing essays on Leibniz and others, a form of philosophy he practiced in his own books.

Carnap and Ayer proclaimed the elimination of metaphysics from philosophy. Metaphysical statements literally have no meaning, they are nonsensical, at best 'poetry', not subject to the criteria of truth or falsity. Metaphysicians have been 'duped by grammar' and philosophy must be distinguished from metaphysics, Ayer proclaims in *Language, Truth and Logic*. Ayer goes further and denies that metaphysical statements can be cherished alongside poetic statements as statements of nonsense that still have emotive value. While poetry is rarely literal nonsense, metaphysics always is and is of no scientific value. But Heidegger too has commented on the kind of 'nothingness' or lack of content of philosophical assertions. Although Carnap reacted violently against Heidegger's conception of philosophy, there are closer and more complex connections between their positions as Michael Friedman has shown.

The Origins of Analytic and Continental Philosophy

Let us consider a little more closely the origins of both analytic and continental philosophy. Both these prominent twentieth-century movements have their origins in the same set of interrelated concerns, including: the scientific status of logic (and its relation to mathematics); the nature and extent of the new science of psychology (which had been inaugurated in the final quarter of the nineteenth century by Wundt and Brentano and Titchener and others; and the challenge posed by reductive naturalism to the traditional philosophical enterprise. These problematics are interrelated: prominent philosophers in the nineteenth century (e.g. J. S. Mill) had explained logic in terms of psychology and the internal processes of the human mind (so called 'psychologism') and twentieth-century philosophy begins with Frege, Russell, Husserl and Wittgenstein, all rejecting this explanation in order to defend the ideality and independence of logical truths. A kind of Platonic realism about logical entities and a rejection of psychologism are hallmarks of the beginning of twentieth-century philosophy whether it be Moore or Russell or Frege or Husserl. Bertrand Russell once characterised the nineteenth century as the age of mathematics. It is interesting that the major developments in mathematics and logic were of central interest to philosophers – Husserl, Frege, Russell, Whitehead, Wittgenstein. Quine and Putnam were both fascinated by mathematical logic. Karl-Otto Apel has spoken of a similar fascination with formalisation in German philosophy in the sixties, a fascination still evident in the work of certain Scandinavian philosophers.

As Hilary Putnam has pointed out, in the early twentieth century philosophers read each other without any conscious sense that they belonged to alien traditions, or that one was philosophy while the other was not. Russell and Husserl were both deeply influenced by the crisis of foundations in mathematics and by Cantor's work on infinite numbers. Russell's early work was in the philosophy of mathematics and his famous paradox was not only known to Husserl but may even have been anticipated by him. Husserl carefully read works of Frege, which the author had sent to him. His copies, held in the Husserl Archives in Leuven, are heavily annotated, and, in particular, Husserl comments on Frege's context principle, which Michael Dummett sees as one of the inaugural moments of analytic philosophy.

In his book *Origins of Analytic Philosophy* Dummett locates the linguistic turn in Frege's 1884 *Die Grundlagen der Arithmetik* where he articulates the context principle that only in the context of a sentence does a word have meaning.[14] Sentences express thought but the decomposition of thought into its components is achieved through the decomposition of sentences. Dummett sees it as crucial to the rise of analytic philosophy that thoughts were stripped of their subjective mental character, thought was 'extruded from the mind' as he puts it. Yet this is precisely true also, as Dummett recognises, of Husserl. The compo-

---

14 Michael Dummett, *Origins of Analytic Philosophy* (London: Duckworth, 1993), p. 5.

nents of thoughts could be tracked through the composition of language once the 'disguised' logic of language had been unmasked.

In contrast to their views on meaning, Frege and Husserl, the founders of the analytic and continental traditions, parted company in their evaluation of the role of mathematical formalisation in logic. When Russell went to gaol in 1918, he took with him Husserl's *Logical Investigations* with the intention of reviewing it for *Mind*. Unfortunately, the review was never written, but the gulf between Husserl and the advocates of formal mathematical logic was by then fairly well established. Husserl regarded the development of symbolic logic as a calculus which did not penetrate the significant philosophical questions of meaning, whereas he himself was interested in transcendental logic, reviving the Kantian problem of how it is that logical acts achieve objectivity. This issue of the nature of transcendental logic has only recently reappeared in analytic philosophy, inspired by contemporary forms of Neo-Kantianism.

Of course, once a new tradition is inaugurated there will always be those who claim it had prior incarnations. Thus, the 'linguistic turn' in analytic philosophy (initiated by Frege but really developed by Russell and Wittgenstein) is also paralleled in Continental philosophy with the concern for language and interpretation of Heidegger, Gadamer and others. But, interestingly, efforts have been made to trace the linguistic turn in philosophy back to Herder, Hamann, and other figures in the German Enlightenment, and this is legitimate, but is possible only because of the particular shape that the linguistic turn took in analytic philosophy highlighted this kind of turn in earlier thinkers. Nevertheless, the forms of thinking involved are different. In analytic philosophy, for instance, the linguistic turn is given specifically scientific garb, whereas the turn to language in eighteenth-century thought is an attempt to achieve a universalisation of thinking, freeing thinking from the peculiarities of local inscription in language. But even among analytic philosophers, a pre-history to what Austin calls 'the way of words' is given, which recognises specifically analytic philosophy in the work of Socrates, Plato and Aristotle. Thus you get the emergence of another grand narrative – this time within analytic philosophy – according to which the best philosophy has always been analytic philosophy whether it be the practice of definition in Plato's *Theaetetus* or Aristotle's different senses of the term *ousia*.

If the nineteenth-century saw philosophy becoming thoroughly professio-nalized and academicized, it also saw, with Hegel, philosophy coming to pro-duce a philosophical reflection on its own genesis. An increasing self-aware-ness about the nature and limits of philosophical practice is evident in philoso-phy since Kant. But it was in Hegel's lectures, that for the first time the history of philosophy itself became philosophical. Hegel saw the need for that side of philosophy, which was to be 'its time comprehended in thought' (*ihre Zeit in Gedanken gefasst*). Incidentally, Rorty thinks this idea of philosophy freed it from the need to offer explanation and instead allowed philosophy to take the position of celebration. Rorty has recently written:

> ... I happily join with Charles Taylor in thinking that Hegel's importance lies chiefly in his historicism, and specifically in his redescription of philosophy as its time held in thought. One happy consequence of this redescription seems to me that it frees philosophers from the need to give explanations. It lets us relax and be frankly and openly celebratory (or in Heidegger's case, frankly and openly nostalgic).[15]

Whether philosophy is able to comprehend the times in which it emerged and of which it is supposedly the rational representation, is an open question, but it is at least true that the effort to comprehend our philosophical time is itself a philosophical (rather than sociological) challenge.

To think about the twentieth-century philosophical legacy, one has to be aware of the enormous and complicated hermeneutical tasks involved. In one sense, one must be resolutely Hegelian. We cannot take history to be either 'bunk' or 'one damn thing after another'. The historical development of philosophy through the century must itself have philosophical significance, but the recog-nition of that significance must not endanger the very understanding of radical contingency which underlies human action in history. Hegel himself recog-nised the tension between concept and contingency, between the rationality which philosophy demands and the chaos of what happens, and claimed that:

> ... the only thought which philosophy brings with it is the simple idea of reason – the idea that reason governs the world, and that world history is therefore a rational process.[16]

15 Richard Rorty, 'Comment on Robert Pippin's 'Naturalism and Mindedness: Hegel's Compatibilism',' *Europe-an Journal of Philosophy* Vol. 7 No. 2 (August 1999), p. 215.

16 G. W. F. Hegel, *Lectures on the Philosophy of World History. Introduction*, trans. H. B. Nisbet (Cambridge: CUP, 1975), p. 27.

But precisely this assumption of rationality is what is in question in contemporary philosophy. On the other hand, any scientific enterprise, any enterprise of understanding surely begins from the assumption of rationality, that there is an identifiable order even in apparent chaos. Heidegger for instance and I think Gadamer here follows him sees it as belonging to the meaning of philosophy to say something essential about the spirit of the age. Heidegger, Gadamer, Blumenberg, Cassirer and Arendt, all want to characterise the essence of *modernity* for instance. Foucault wants to diagnose contemporary civilisation using the mirror of the history of madness. His employment of the Nietzschean figures of genealogy and diagnosis confirm that he too believes that it is possible to penetrate to the essence of a time or a period. This is a kind of phenomenological essentialism, one that needs much fuller study.

In any event, to write a history of twentieth-century philosophy is not, as Hegel correctly recognises, merely to assemble a list of all the philosophical works and tendencies. It is also an attempt to seize *the rationale* at work in the processes. For example, Lyotard is doing just that in diagnosing the postmodern condition. In precisely this sense, I believe that the history of philosophy is relevant to philosophy, in contrast to the way in which the history of physics or medicine is not relevant to the current practice of these disciplines. Concepts and problems have histories, as I have argued elsewhere, and understanding those histories is important to understanding and contextualising the concepts themselves. I am glad to see that I am supported in this approach by an analytic philosopher interested in the history of analytic philosophy. Peter Hylton has written in his elegant *Russell, Idealism and the Emergence of Analytic Philosophy*:

> Philosophical problems, and the concepts in which they are formulated, and the assumptions on which they rest, have a history; and this history is surely a legitimate subject of study.[17]

Moroever, Hylton argues it is not just a subject of interest in historical terms but it is of philosophical interest too. That is, it challenges our conceptual frameworks.

The Meaning of Europe
Certainly for the first half of the century, western philosophy was quite specifically European philosophy. As in the later half of the nineteenth-century, the

---

17 Peter Hylton, *Russell, Idealism and the Emergence of Analytic Philosophy* (Oxford: Clarendon, 1990), p. 13.

intellectual centres were in Germany, Austria, France, and Britain – in Marburg, Göttingen, Vienna, Prague, Paris (with Bergson), Cambridge (with Russell and Wittgenstein), Oxford (Ryle, Grice, Austin, Dummett) and London (A. J. Ayer). But, especially since 1945, the axis moved persistently westward, specifically towards the United States, and since the 1960s Australia has emerged with a distinctive kind of analytic philosophy of a materialist and realist variety (Armstrong, Smart, etc.).

But the Europe in question for the first half of the century is a very small Europe: mostly Germany, France, Austria, Poland and Britain, with some developments in Russia. What of philosophy in Greece, for instance, or Portugal? In the late nineteenth-century, formal logic flourished in the Lvov-Warsaw schools, but after 1945 academic philosophy in general forgot Poland (Taski for example remained in the US) and indeed the whole Eastern bloc, with the possible exception of a small number of thinkers (such as Kolakowski in Poland), or in Hungary (Lukacs), Prague (Patocka) and Belgrade with the Marxist school, some now discredited due to their extreme Serbian nationalism. In 1932, as we have seen, the American philosopher W. V. O. Quine thought it worthwhile to leave Harvard, where he had studied with C. I. Lewis and Whitehead, to visit Vienna, Prague and Warsaw, in order to learn about the latest developments in logic. Gilbert Ryle similarly recommended A. J. Ayer to study with Moritz Schlick in Vienna. Tarski[18] on truth, for instance, is essential to understanding the work of Donald Davidson. But such thinkers as Tarski and Carnap became completely absorbed in the American context after the war, whereas post-1945 Poland together with its philosophers remained locked in a Soviet cul-de-sac from which it is only now beginning to emerge.

I must emphasise how small philosophical Europe is. In the first half of the twentieth century, it did not include Greece or for that matter Portugal or Scandinavia. If Wittgenstein went to Norway, it was because of his professed desire

---

18 Tarski was born in Warsaw in 1901 (The family name was changed in 1924.) Between 1918 and 1924 Tarski studied at the University of Warsaw where he received his doctorate in mathematics under the direction of S. Lesniewski. In 1926 he was appointed as a lecturer. In 1939 Tarski set out for a lecture tour of the USA and was prevented from returning to Poland by the outbreak of the Second World War. He then briefly held positions at Harvard University, the City College of New York and the Institute for Advanced Study at Princeton. In 1942 he was appointed to the mathematics department of the University of California at Berkeley, where he remained until his retirement in 1968. (*Routledge Encyclopedia of Philosophy*, Version 1.0, London: Routledge).

for darkness, not philosophical company and the same is true of his sojourns in the West of Ireland, where I doubt he ever visited University College Galway. If academic philosophy continues to flourish in Athens, for instance, it was on the basis of German-led classical scholarship and traditional philosophical practice (probably including now a large dose of anglo-american philosophy imported in). This is still the case, a glance at most European philosophical syllabi sees the enormous importance of Gadamer, for example, who probably does not appear at all on the syllabi of most English-speaking universities. So 'Europe' in philosophical terms still means, predominantly Germany, France and the UK, and if new university departments are being developed in Hungary, Slovenia, and elsewhere, it is largely due to support from British and Western European philosophers (as happened in East German universities after re-unification).

Tradition and Forgetfulness

In charting the history of twentieth-century philosophy, another hermeneutic scruple to bear in mind is the manner in which thinkers are inscribed into a tradition, either self-consciously by themselves or else by their followers. The French philosopher Maurice Merleau-Ponty, writing in 1958 to commemorate the centenary of Husserl birth, has an interesting reflection on the nature of tradition:

> Establishing a tradition means forgetting its origins the aging Husserl used to say (*La tradition est oubli des origines disait le dernier Husserl*). Precisely because we owe so much to tradition, we are in no position to see just what belongs to it. With regard to a philosopher whose venture has awakened so many echoes, and at such an apparent distance from the point where he himself stood, any commemoration is also a betrayal (*toute commémoration est aussi trahison*)...[19]

Indeed, it is a singular feature of the main traditions of twentieth-century philosophy that they saw themselves as new movements, which broke decisively with the past. Husserl, Freud and others saw themselves as founders of new disciplines. The rhetoric of the Manifesto of the Vienna Circle is similar. Nevertheless, as Merleau-Ponty points out, to establish something as new means self-consciously separating it from all that has gone before. Yet this separation can never be carried out completely. For instance, in order to succeed in France,

---

19 M. Merleau-Ponty, *Signes* (Paris: Gallimard, 1960), p. 201, trans. R. McCleary, *Signs* (Evanston: Northwestern U.P., 1964), p. 159.

Husserl's phenomenology had to be absorbed into the French tradition in a particularly distinctive way. Sartre harnessed Husserlian phenomenology to Cartesianism whereas Levinas links him with Bergson. Indeed, Husserl himself deliberately sought to inscribe himself into the French tradition in philosophy by emphasising his affinity with Descartes during the lectures given on his visit to Paris in 1929. Similarly, Hegel – whom Husserl, following his mentor Brentano, regarded as ungrounded speculative system-builder and hence the opposite of a true phenomenologist – was grafted onto the phenomenological tradition by Merleau-Ponty, largely through the mediation of the reading of Hegel to be found in the lectures of Kojève also given in Paris. Sartre self-consciously developed existentialism, but later, in his *Critique of Dialectical Reason*, he deliberately inscribed it as a moment within a larger conception of dialectical materialism.

In the analytic tradition similar insertions and re-inscriptions into traditions occur but they are usually not explicitly trumpeted. David Pears began his book on Russell by arguing that he was responding to the challenge of scepticism. Indeed, both Pears and Ayer portray Russell as an empiricist philosopher following in the footsteps of Hume. But, in fact, as Peter Hylton has shown, and as we have seen earlier, Russell was more immediately influenced by the idealism of Bradley and McTaggart. He was a practicing metaphysician, frequently introducing abstract metaphysical entities into his explanations as no empiricist would have done. Indeed, Russell, influenced by Green and Bradley, regarded empiricism as false and as having been effectively refuted by idealism.[20] Thus he could write in his *History of Western Philosophy*:

> David Hume ... developed to its logical conclusion the empirical philosophy of Locke and Berkeley, and by making it self-consistent made it incredible.[21]

Russell then was no Humean. But philosophical misreadings of this kind can have creative consequences. When Ryle advised Ayer to study with Schlick it was because he thought the Vienna Circle were pursuing Wittgenstein's programme in philosophy. Wittgenstein himself was soon to distance himself from the Circle and show that his philosophical interests were quite different. And, as we have seen, Heidegger inscribed phenomenology into the older Greek

---

20 Hylton, *Russell, Idealism and the Emergence of Analytic Philosophy*, p. 22.

21 B. Russell, *A History of Western Philosophy*, 2nd ed. (London: Allen and Unwin, 1961), p. 634.

tradition of philosophy, even claiming that the meaning of phenomenology was better understood by Aristotle than by his mentor Husserl! Derrida extracted the deconstructive moment from Husserlian *Abbau* and Heideggerian *Destruktion* and Nietzschean *Zerstörung* to make it into a kind of permanent principle of interpretative change. It is interesting to see that deconstruction will probably be reabsorbed into the longer tradition of hermeneutics.

The Beginning of the Century

Let us try to get a sense of how things were at the beginning of the century. In intellectual terms, we may consider the dawn of that century as marked by three important events: the death of the isolated figure Friedrich Nietzsche (1844-1900), who would become in his own words a 'posthumous man', and the publication of two works that would transform European thought: Sigmund Freud's *Traumdeutung* (*Interpretation of Dreams*, 1899), which inaugurated psychoanalysis, and Edmund Husserl's *Prolegomena zu reinen Logik* (*Prolegomena to Pure Logic*, 1900), which broke decisively with the prevailing *psychologism* in the understanding of logic and mathematics and led to the development of phenomenology. One may be tempted to see Friedrich Nietzsche as the philosophical voice of the century – his writings seem to touch on all the central themes – the problem of *history* and the fragmentary nature of inheritance and tradition, the need to engage with creative destruction – philosophising with a hammer – in order to free up sedimented meanings, *naturalism* and the way of integrating the human with the rest of nature, especially after Darwin, the recognition of the need to have ears behind one's ears in the interpretation of others, the ironic probing of dreams of mastery, the recognition of the hidden ties between reason and force. Yet, even a sympathetic reader of Nietzsche such as Richard Rorty himself believes that Nietzsche was really only integrated into philosophy through Heidegger, and before that was a figure of mainly literary inspiration, influencing Shaw for example. Similarly, Freud had almost no impact on philosophy – certainly in European philosophy prior to Ricœur in France and to some extent Adorno and the Frankfurt school most notably Marcuse. Sartre was seen as having dismissed Freudian analysis in *Being and Nothingness* (1943). It was not until the sixties (with Adorno and Marcuse, Wollheim, Derrida, Foucault, Deleuze and Guattari, and others) that Freud entered the philosophical scene.

So perhaps Nietzsche and Freud are not in fact the archetypal twentieth-century figures, certainly if one considers the nature of the their respective influences on philosophy. The situation is quite different with Husserl, who, as Merleau-Ponty put it, casts a long shadow over the twentieth century.[22] Almost every European philosopher in the first half of the century had some contact direct or indirect with Husserl. Of course, as we know Husserl himself was isolated and humiliated by the rising Nazi movement, a movement in which his successor Heidegger enthusiastically participated. Any history of twentieth-century philosophy must face that great betrayal by Heidegger – a betrayal which was interpreted as being a kind of Nietzchean philosophising with a hammer. Heidegger hated the ensconsed academic practice in the university and saw Nazism as a chance for university renewal and at the same time as a vehicle for cultural renewal. *Erneuerung*, the very term of course of Husserl's project in the *Kaizo* lectures of the twenties.

Husserl's *Logical Investigations* as Breakthrough Work

The *Prolegomena* was the first volume of Husserl's massive and ground-breaking *Logische Untersuchungen* (*Logical Investigations*), [23] the second volume of which, appearing from the publisher Max Niemeyer in two parts in 1901, inaugurated phenomenology as the project of descriptively clarifying the 'experiences of thinking and knowing'. With this work, Husserl believed he had made a start in clarifying problems that were at the heart of contemporary science and philosophy, problems concerning the nature of the experience and determination of meaning in the broadest sense. In this work, he used the term 'phenomenology' to mean a kind of descriptive psychology (such as practiced by Brentano and Meinong), a way of describing what shows itself as it shows itself in its essential forms, seeking to avoid speculation and remaining true to the evidential situations, what Husserl called somewhat misleadingly 'the things themselves' (*die Sachen selbst*). Husserl's primary principle – a radical variant of empiricism – is to accept as evident only what shows itself to be so in intuition. Intuition is the keystone of his philosophy. Intuition refers to the primary grasp of the presence of entities.

---

22 M. Merleau-Ponty, 'The Philosopher and his Shadow', *Signs*, op. cit., pp. 159-81.

23 Edmund Husserl, *Logische Untersuchungen*, erster Band, *Prolegomena zur reinen Logik*, text der 1. und der 2. Auflage, hrsg. E. Holenstein, Husserliana XVIII (The Hague: Nijhoff, 1975), and *Logische Untersuchungen*, zweiter Band, *Untersuchungen zur Phänomenologie und Theorie der Erkenntnis*, in zwei Bänden, hrsg. Ursula Panzer, Husserliana XIX (Dordrecht: Kluwer, 1984), p. 6, trans. J.N. Findlay, *Logical Investigations*, revised with New Introduction by Dermot Moran with a New Preface by Michael Dummett (London & New York: Routledge, 2001), 2 volumes. Hereafter 'LU' followed by Investigation number, section number, and volume and page number of English translation, followed by German pagination of Husserliana edition. Henceforth 'Husserliana' will be abbreviated to 'Hua' and volume number.

As Husserl put it in the Foreword to the Second Edition, and as he would subsequently stress, the *Investigations* was his 'breakthrough work' (*Werk des Durchbruchs*, LU I 3; Hua XVIII 8). It certainly made his reputation as a philosopher, being praised by the foremost philosophers of his day in Germany, including Paul Natorp,[24] Wilhelm Wundt, who welcomed its anti-psychologism, and Wilhelm Dilthey, who saw it as providing the method to investigate lived experiences in their concreteness. In personal terms, it also afforded Husserl the opportunity of moving from Halle to Göttingen. But, in terms of its philosophical significance the import of the *Investigations* is many faceted. On the one hand, it abjured psychologism and defended a broadly Platonist account of numbers, logical forms, and other ideal entities. They are what they are independent of their being thought or known. On the other hand, Husserl recognised that ideal entities and meanings are only reached by consciousness through a set of determinate acts whose essential natures and interconnections can be specified. There are acts of intending meanings, acts of recognising, judging, and so on. These acts can be understood as themselves making up a framework of idealities. Husserl's subsequent recognition that these idealities are themselves embedded in the transcendental ego moved his thought in a transcendental direction, renewing his links with the more dominant tradition of Neo-Kantianism.

Husserl moved to Göttingen in 1901 as the self-proclaimed founder of phenomenology, and, through the influence of the *Investigations* on a group of philosophers in Germany, a phenomenological 'movement' (*Bewegung*) began to emerge in the first decade of the century with Adolf Reinach, Alexander Pfänder, Johannes Daubert, Moritz Geiger and others. Through the fascination which the *Logical Investigations* provoked, Husserl effectively revolutionised existing philosophy in Germany, changing the very way philosophy was practiced, shifting the focus from the history of ideas and from epistemology to an attempt to describe what he called 'the things themselves' (*die Sachen selbst*). Until Husserl himself came to have a significant influence, German philosophy had been dominated by Neo-Kantianism (divided into the so-called 'South German and 'Marburg' schools) which accepted the fact of science, and whose project was to specify the preconditions of objective scientific knowledge.

24 Paul Natorp, 'Zur Frage der logischen Methode. Mit Bezug auf Edm. Husserls Prolegomena zur reinen Logik,' *Kantstudien* VI (1901), pp. 270-283.

Furthermore, united in opposition to Hegelian speculative idealism, various forms of positivism were on the rise in Germany, influenced by John Stuart Mill and the older British Empiricist tradition as well as by Comte. Husserl's teacher, Franz Brentano, for instance, was a strong advocate of this positivism and of the unity of exact philosophy and science. Husserl's phenomenology had a profound effect. Issues of knowledge had to be given a much deeper analysis. No longer could the study of the history of philosophy substitute for philosophy. So, perhaps unsurprisingly, I see the publication of the *Logical Investigations* as the most important moment, the inaugural moment for European philosophy in the first half of the twentieth century.

The Rise of Analytic Philosophy

It is only in the past decade that philosophers have begun to think of analytical philosophy as a historical movement and as a tradition, rather than as *the* method of philosophy. There is also increasing recognition that the nature of the analytic tradition has radically altered over the decades. Who are the founders of analytic philosophy? Although the older Empirical tradition of Hume and Mill is clearly in the background most commentators see Gottlob Frege (1848-1925) as inaugurating analytic philosophy with his recognition of the distinction between the *grammatical form* of a sentence expressing a categorical judgement (S is P) and the logical form which was best expressed by the notions adapted from mathematics of *function* and *argument*. Frege was able to break free of psychologism in one move by showing that logical reasoning could be more accurately expressed in mathematical terms putting all reference to the subjective nature of judging aside. He clearly distinguished between the act of judging and the judgement or proposition asserted. Similarly, Frege regarded it as the task of philosophy 'to break the power of the word over the human mind' as he puts it in his *Begriffschrift* (1879). His distinction between *Sinn* and *Bedeutung* in his 1892 article was seen as a helpful disambiguation of two different senses and hence as an example of the kind of clear and illuminating analysis favoured by philosophers.

However, the archetypal text that inaugurated anaytic philosophy is usually held to be Bertrand Russell's famous 1905 article, 'On Denoting', published in *Mind*,[25] which also enshrined the difference between logical and grammatical form, became a model of its kind and the paradigm of analytic philosophy. Russell's target is Meinong's object theory which allowed any grammatically acceptable subject of a sentence to stand for or name an object. Russell, in contrast, shows the difference between a referring or denoting expression and one which has a different logical form and serves as a description. Russell sets out his method in a manner that makes clear that logic must solve paradoxes:

> A logical theory may be tested by its capacity for dealing with puzzles, and it is a
> wholesome plan, in thinking about logic, to stock the mind with as many puzzles as
> possible, since these serve much the same purpose as is served by experiments in
> physical science. I shall therefore state three puzzles which a theory as to denoting
> ought to be able to solve; and I shall show later that my theory solves them.

Following on from the paradigm of Russell's analysis, the task of analytic philosophy was seen, in Fregean terms, as freeing logic from the enslavement of language. In part this would lead to the pressure to develop ideal languages, it also led to the recognition that many traditional philosophical problems were actually insoluble because their linguistic form was 'systematically misleading' as Ryle would put it. Analytic philosophy now came to recognise the need to distinguish between genuine and 'pseudo-problems' (Scheinprobleme) in philosophy.

Besides his actual logical analysis, Russell must be given enormous credit for establishing the style and manner of analytic writing in philosophy. The form of philosophical writing became the lucid essay, as exemplified in the writings of G. E. Moore, preferably published in one of the newly founded journals such as Mind (e.g. his 'The Nature of Judgement,' Mind 1899). Whole systems of thought were condensed in a series of propositions. In Russell's view, for instance, idealism could be reduced to a single issue: the nature and possibility of internal relations. Similarly, Leibniz's philosophy could be reduced to a set of axioms and the question was whether they were consistent with one another. But, of course, as in many other areas of twentieth-century thought, this reduction of the complex to the simple can also be found prefigured in Kant. It was Kant for instance who made the whole extraordinarily complex issue of the meaning and scientific status of metaphysics depend on the single question of whether a priori synthetic propositions were possible. Nevertheless, the Russellian style of analytic philosophy was not universally admired. In his correspondence with Russell in early 1914, Wittgenstein states that he hopes that, in his

---

25   B. Russell, 'On Denoting,' Mind (October 1905), pp 479-93.

forthcoming lectures in Harvard, Russell will reveal something of his thinking and not just present 'cut and dried results'.[26] Certainly, Wittgenstein had put his finger on something in the manner of Russell's way of writing: Russell favoured the scientific manner of reporting results. Wittgenstein, on the other hand, recognised that the *process* of philosophising is the important thing, the *showing*, the revealing that is done in the very acts of questioning and probing. Here in fact, Wittgenstein is probably closer to Heidegger than to Russell.

The will-to-system is also evident early on in analytic philosophy. Russell was by nature a system builder trying in his books to give clarification to the central scientific and metaphysical concepts of space, time, matter, causation, the nature of relations, classes and so on. The most notable case of systematisation in point here is Wittgenstein's *Tractatus* (1921).[27] According to this book, the object of philosophy is the 'logical clarification of thoughts' and the *Tractatus* is surely an extraordinary edifice, a purely modernist construction. Wittgenstein announces that he believes he has found 'on all essential points, the final solution of the problems'.[28] But it also has unmistakeable Kantian echoes, e.g. 'the aim of the book is to set a limit to thought'.[29]

The *Tractatus* encouraged the early Vienna Circle members who were intent on promoting a 'scientific conception of the world' (their phrase). Moritz Schlick, for example, had studied physics and was struggling to find an appropriate philosophical vehicle to accommodate the insights of Einstein's Theory of Relativity and the new physics in general. Certainly the Vienna Circle gave predominance to science and dismissed the pseudo-propositions of 'metaphysics'. In the English-speaking world, A. J. Ayer's *Language, Truth and Logic* (1936),[30] had extraordinary influence, especially on those who wanted to argue that moral and religious statements were in fact literally meaningless. Side by side with the hard, formalistic, systematic side of analytic philosophy was a softer style of analysis, first typified by G. E. Moore and soon afterwards by Whitehead. For instance, Moore's 'In Defence of Common Sense' lists propositions which he claims he knows, but many of these knowledge claims embody

---

26 Ray Monk, *Bertrand Russell. The Spirit of Solitude*, op. cit., p. 340.

27 L. Wittgenstein, *Tractatus Logico-Philosophicus*, trans. D. F. Pears and B. F. McGuinness (London: Routledge & Kegan Paul, 1961)

28 Wittgenstein, 'Author's Preface,' *Tractatus Logico-Philosophicus*, op. cit., p. 5.

29 *Tractatus Logico-Philosophicus*, op. cit., p. 3.

30 A. J. Ayer, *Language, Truth and Logic* (London: Victor Gollancz, 1936)

assumptions that belong to the background of what Husserl would call the life world.[31]

Morris Weitz[32] lists a number of characteristics of analytic philosophy, including the refutation of idealism, the defence of realism and common sense (Moore), logical analysis (Russell, Ryle), logical positivism, and conceptual elucidation. Examples of logical analysis are Russell's theory of descriptions, and, building on that, Ryle's discussion of systematically misleading expressions. But the central notion of analytic philosophy appears to be elucidation or the clarification of concepts through the clarification of the linguistic forms in which those concepts appear. As Michael Dummett has written:

> What distinguishes analytical philosophy, in its diverse manifestations, from other schools is the belief, first, that a philosophical account of thought can be attained through a philosophical account of language, and secondly, that a comprehensive account can only be so attained.[33]

Central then to Dummett's characterisation of analytical philosophy is the linguistic turn.

What is difficult to understand is how logical analysis and specifically the disambiguation of logical from the grammatical form of sentences should end up being coupled with a strong defence of ordinary language. This is precisely what happened with the emergence of Oxford ordinary language philosophy in the fifties, inspired by the approach to language found in Wittgenstein's *Investigations*. Austin and Ryle were the main exponents of this approach in Britain but their approach was continued subsequently in America by Searle (a student of Austin) and Dennett (a student of Ryle). Ryle's analysis of systematically misleading expressions is employed by Dennett in his first book *Content and Consciousness* to deny that there exist 'sakes' (as in 'I did it for John's sake') and to determine which if any of our nouns denoting mental items are in fact referential.[34]

31   See Stanley Rosen, 'Moore on Common Sense,' in *The Elusiveness of the Ordinary. Studies in the Possibility of Philosophy* (New Haven: Yale U. P., 2002), p. 174.

32   M. Weitz, ed., *Twentieth-Century Philosophy: The Analytic Tradition* (London: Collier-Macmillan, 1966).

33   M. Dummett, *Origins of Analytic Philosophy* (London: Duckworth, 1993), p. 4.

34   D. Dennett, *Content and Consciousness* (London: RKP, 1969; reprinted Routledge, 1993), pp. 6-18.

It would be wrong to think that analytic philosophers are wedded to a fixed set of presuppositions, which they do not critically analyse. In fact, analytic philosophy shows a tradition of critique that gradually pared away what were thought to be foundational concepts of analysis. After Russell's analysis of descriptions, perhaps the next most paradigmatic article for analytic philosophy is Quine's 1951 paper 'Two Dogmas of Empiricism'[35] which attacked the very basis of the analytic/synthetic distinction so beloved of Neo-Kantians and Carnapians alike. This was a challenge to the very meaning of analysis, and an undermining of the theoretical assumptions that had given rise to analytic philosophy in the first place. As Grice and Strawson point out, Quine is not saying that the distinction between analytic and synthetic truths is badly drawn or vague or useless, rather that it is illusory. It is for Quine 'an unempirical dogma of empiricists, a metaphysical article of faith'.

Quine's article also included an explicit attack on the verificationist principle of meaning, which had become, as he calls it, a 'catchword' of twentieth-century empiricism. Against the 'reductionist' claim that meaningful statements can be traced back to a statement about immediate experience, Quine wants to propose that our 'statements about the external world face the tribunal of sense experience not individually but only as a corporate body.'[36] What he wants to propose in that paper is an 'empiricism without dogmas' and one that is holistic in that it sees the web of knowledge as a "man-made fabric which impinges on experience only at the edges".[37] Every statement is revisable, whether it be a statement about experience or the formulation of a logical law. Moreover, the positing of abstract entities such as classes is on a par with the positing of Homeric gods or physical objects. This positing is a matter of convenience, or as Quine puts it, 'swelling ontology to simplify theory'.[38]

The next step in this overhaul of the very meaning of classical empiricism and indeed classical analytic philosophy (as represented by Carnap or Ayer) is the attack on the scheme/content distinction in Davidson's famous 'On the Very

35 *Philosophical Review 60* (1951), reprinted in A. P. Martinich, and David Sosa, eds, *Analytic Philosophy. An Anthology* (Oxford: Blackwell, 2001), pp. 450-462.

36 *Analytic Philosophy. An Anthology*, op. cit., p. 459.

37 Ibid., p. 460.

38 Ibid., p. 461.

Idea of a Conceptual Scheme' (1974).[39] Indeed, this step is already prefigured in Quine's 'Two Dogmas' article. In that article, Quine already recognises that some sentences look more like statements about our conceptual schemes (whether we admit classes or not) while others look more like statements about brute fact ('there are brick houses on Elm St). Quine wants to deny that there is a difference in kind between these two types of statement. They are on a continuum and the decisions which to accept is 'pragmatic' according to Quine. Davidson begins his article by recognising many philosophers speak of conceptual schemes and contrast them with experience and specifically 'the data of sensation'. Even those who think there is only one conceptual scheme still cling to the idea of there being such a 'scheme'. But in particular Davidson is interested in the idea (current in modern anthropology and elsewhere – he cites Benjamin Whorf's work on the Hopi languages and their untranslatability, as well as Thomas Kuhn's *Structure of Scientific Revolutions* on revolutions in science leading to different paradigms or 'mindsets') that what makes one conceptual scheme different from another is that it is not translatable into it. Davidson is explicit that he is seeking to build on Quine's exposure of two dogmas by himself exposing the third dogma of empiricism – that between scheme and content. As Davidson recognises to give up the third dogma is to abandon anything there is to empiricism:

> I want to urge that this second dualism of scheme and content, of organizing system and something waiting to be organized, cannot be made intelligible and defensible. It is itself a dogma of empiricism, the third dogma. The third, and perhaps the last, for if we give it up it is not clear that there is anything distinctive left to call empiricism.[40]

These are paradigmatic moments in analytic philosophy, and there is evidence of a clear sense of tradition. Quine is utilising but criticising the approach of Carnap and Davidson is moving to reject a new dualism that emerges after the analytic/synthetic dualism has been jettisoned. Davidson quotes closely from Quine's article, deliberately invoking phrases like 'the tribunal of experience' and it is clear that the conception of a 'conceptual scheme' that he has in mind comes directly from Quine.

---

39 Reprinted in D. Davidson, *Inquiries into Truth and Interpretation* (Oxford: OUP, 1984), pp. 184-198.

40 'On the Very Idea of a Conceptual Scheme,' *Inquiries into Truth and Interpretation*, op. cit., p. 189.

It is interesting that there is a progressive move away from empiricism. However, as we have seen, the early Russell and Moore began from the point of view (inherited from German idealism and its British counterpart) that empiricism had been refuted. The essays of Quine and Davidson then may be seen as a corrective of the distorting empiricist interpretations of the Vienna school of the central tradition of analytic philosophy.

The changes in Wittgenstein's thought are suggestive of the kind of radical swings in the nature of philosophy that occur through the century. Wittgenstein is not alone in this progression. Heidegger too is famous for *die Kehre*, and it is evident that he moved from a commitment to pursuing fundamental ontology through the phenomenological method (in *Being and Time*) to a kind of 'other thinking' (*Anderes Denken*) in his later works. Evident in both Wittgenstein and Heidegger is a certain frustration with the manner in which philosophy has been practiced and an attempt to begin anew. Heidegger is explicit about conducting an *Abbau* or *Destruktion*, which argues that even the history of philosophy, the way the tradition of philosophy itself appears to us needs to be broken down, unpackaged and thought again. There is a strong sense in Heidegger of the kind of dilemma that Samuel Beckett's characters find themselves in: 'I can't go on; I must go on'. Indeed, as Rorty has recognised, it is important to understand that *Being and Time* and the *Tractatus* are modernist works in a very specific sense, there is an attempt to break new ground, to use an innovative style, to present *a form* of thinking.

In this essay, I have tried to explore some of the complexities involved in attempting to gain a historical perspective on western philosophy in the twentieth century, focusing in particular on the legacy of European philosophy and on the two major traditions it generated, namely analytic and Continental philosophy. In particular, I have tried to identify some of the hermeneutic scruples that must be brought to bear in order to gain a sense of the nature of the competing traditions at work. I shall end by quoting Merleau-Ponty's conception of the philosopher as a hint towards understanding the common threads that run through both traditions. He emphasises the philosopher's desire for truth, but goes on to say:

> The philosopher is marked by the distinguishing trait that he possesses *inseparably* the taste for evidence and the feeling for ambiguity.

Certainly, a philosopher such as Wittgenstein too, despite his fearsome logical intellect, also had a 'feeling for ambiguity'. In attempting to write the history of twentieth-century philosophy, one needs not just – to employ Nietzsche's phrase – 'ears behind one's ears', but also an acute sense of ambiguity as well as a talent for disambiguation.

Transformation of the Concept of People

Ove Korsgaard

Introduction

When I went to school many years ago I learned in history that the transformation from absolute monarchy to democracy in Denmark was a very successful process. Only one peaceful demonstration in Copenhagen 21st of March 1848 - and we got democracy. While it was peaceful in Denmark it was quite the opposite in other European countries. Down south it was massacre. Of course, I also learned about a war which started in 1848 in the southern part of Denmark, but I got the impression that it was a war between the ‚good‘ Danes and the ‚bad‘ Germans. It was not only me but generation after generation who was told that story in school. And it continues. In the 1990‘es my children learned more or less the same story about the successful implementation of Democracy in Denmark. However, some years ago I realized as a big surprise that what I have learned in school is only a limit part of the whole story. What we did not learn was that the concepts of *people* and *nation* changed, which on the one hand gave the possibility for democracy and on the other threatened the old state-form. We did not learn about the dilemma between political system and state-form.

The History of Concepts and Ideas

A comparison between the dictionary for the older Danish language and Modern Danish dictionary shows that the notion *folk* [people] has undergone a radical shift in meaning from *household* to *nation*. The old definition was expressed in words like war-folk, court-folk, boat-folk, country-folk harvest-folk and people’s hold, people’s payment, people’s room, people’s kitchen and people’s table.

In the pre-democratic social order the notion *people* was simply a category for the subjects. The people were always subjugated under a guardian, as for instance a master of the house, a lord of the manor, father of the country or the lord God. Although with the call for democracy the people became sovereign and thus could no longer be categorized as mere subjects. The origin of this change and transformation in the history of ideas can be traced back to Rousseau and Herder who in the 1760s and 1770s wrote key texts on pedagogic and political philosophy. Rousseau was the first to formulate the ground-breaking idea that the people hold the political power. Thus from Rousseau came the impulse to regard the people as the ultimate sovereign within a new kind of political and governmental structure. Herder also formulated a ground-breaking principle, that is, the principle of the people holding cultural power. With Herder the notion *people* also came to denote specific peoples independent of political systems. At the core of this "cultural" conception of the notion *people* is an understanding of the collective identity as a deep-set reality shaped by language and culture. This understanding of people as ethnic groups tied together by language came from Herder. Rousseau and Herder both broke with the old notion of the people as subjects. However, they put forth two distinct senses of people as the sovereign. While Rousseau tied his conceptions of sovereignty to establishing a social contract, Herder linked his to the recognition of a language pact.

At the same time two new types of folk-words appear, referring to the people in a political and a cultural sense. The political sense appears in words like people's sovereignty, the will of the people, the people's parliament, and a people's poll. The cultural sense comes out in words like folksong, folklore, folkcostume (national costume) and folkdance.

Folk as ‚class'	**Folk as ‚host'**
folkehold (people's hold)	hoffolk (court-folk)
folkeløn (people's payment)	krigsfolk (war-folk)
folkestue (people's room)	bådsfolk (boat-folk)
folkekøkken (people's kitchen)	høstfolk (harvest-folk)
folkebord (people's table)	brandfolk (fire-folk)
Folk as ethnos	**Folk as demos**
Folkeviser (folksong)	Folkevilje (the will of the people)
Folkeeventyr (folklore)	Folkesuverænitet (people's sovereignty)
Folkedragt (folk-costume)	Folkeafstemning (people's poll)
Folkedans (folkdance)	Folketing (people's parliament)

The Danish History

Now I will turn from the history of idea to the history of Denmark to see in what way this new interpretation of the concept of people effected the Danish way to democracy.

When the democratization of the Danish state occurred nationalism gradually replaced religion as the kernel of European collective identity. The process of democratization did not, however, bring about a gradual progression towards modernity. Rather, this process led to a radical destabilization, in fact, a complete breakdown of the existing multi-national and multilingual state. Only after this breakdown became the nation-state the exemplary form for the modern Danish state.

The process of democratization in Denmark is an exceptional illustration of the tension between collective identities, political systems and state-form. When democracy began to be implemented as a new political system in Europe there was as yet no fully realized nation-state. The state, the so-called United Monarchy, was still a multi-national and multilingual state consisting of the Kingdom of Denmark and the duchies Schleswig, Holstein and Lauenburg; the north Atlantic isles: Iceland, Greenland and the Faroe Islands and a few small colonies throughout the world. The majority of the population in the Danish Kingdom spoke Danish, though in Holstein they spoke German and in Schleswig half of the population spoke Danish while the other half spoke German. From the 1830'es the big question was: Could one, in a single process, implement democracy while keeping the United Monarchy together?

Democracy's problem is, of course, that it requires a demos, that is to say a people. But who were the people of the United Monarchy? Did people correspond to population? Or, were there several peoples within the state? The answer to this question depended upon the understanding of the notions people and nation. Should the notion people be understood as a political or cultural category?

The relationship between state-form and political system was, as mentioned, not clarified when democracy knocked on the United Monarchy's door, which in actuality happened in the spring of 1848. There was a great difference of opinion amongst the advocates of democracy as to the future of the state-form. Therefore, a number of royalists were against the implementation of democracy as it would threaten the existing state-form. The fundamental issue was whether democracy required a new state-form or, whether the new political system could be incorporated in the old state-form. In other words, does the demos require a state with only one d1ominating ethnos or could there be one demos in a state consisting of competing ethnos'?

The advocates of democracy proposed three different state-forms.

A Federation

Cosmopolitan democrats proposed a free constitution within a federative configuration of the state and suggested Switzerland and North America as models. According to the journalist and author Meir Goldschmidt, Denmark should – as Switzerland did in 1847 – create a "federation of states wherein the different nationalities are thriving and are ensured by the means of freedom."[1] This vision was a "rainbow-state" wherein the different nations – Holstein, Schleswig and the Kingdom – could live in the same state under a common constitution.

The Ejder-State

The national liberals in Copenhagen – who had a kind of ‚think-tank' at the University of Copenhagen – fought for a free constitution within an Ejder-state, which meant that Schleswig should be included in the Kingdom and Holstein

---

1   Goldschmidt, Meir: *Nord og Syd*, vol. 9 and 10, 1849:344

should be excluded. A big German-speaking minority within the Danish state was regarded as a threat to the future existence of the Danish nation. It was feared that a fiercely expanding Germany would use this minority as an excuse to turn against Denmark.[2] Later, history proved that this fear was not unfounded.

Two States: Schleswigholstein and the Kingdom

The national liberals in Kiel – who had another ‚think-tank‘ at the University of Kiel – fought for a free constitution within an autonomous state, which was to include Schleswig-Holstein. Essentially, they demanded that Schleswig-Holstein seceded from Denmark in order to be included as an autonomous state in the German confederation.

When the demand for democracy resulted in the fall of absolute monarchy on March 21, 1848 the differences over the state-forms broke out. The proponents of democracy in the United Monarchy could not come together on one demos. A civil war broke out. It was not a war played out between the proponents of the old and the new political systems, but a war amongst the proponents of democracy. The first battle in this civil war took place near Bov April 9, 1848. The war ended in 1850 without a solution to the fundamental problems in part because the major powers in Europe would not allow changes to the borders that had been agreed upon in the Congress of Vienna 1814-15.

From 1850 to 1864 the main question was still if it was possible and desirable to implement democracy as political system in a federation, in the Ejder-state or in two states – the Kingdom and Schleswig-holstein. Not until the defeat in 1864 to Prussia and Austria and the loss of the three duchies Holstein, Schleswig and Lauenburg did the solution appear. With the loss of the duchies, Denmark was close to fulfilling the ideal requirements of a nation-state (i.e. the co-extension of state, nation, language, culture and territory). There were, however, two elements that disrupted the idyllic image. One of these elements was that the North Atlantic isles could not, without any further ado, be regarded as a part of the Danish nation-state. The other – and a far more crucial problem – was that 200.000 Danes fell under German rule. The last matter did not get straightened out until the reorganization of Europe after the WWI,

---

2   N.F.S. Grundtvig and J.N. Madvig, for example, were afraid of a big German-speaking population within a Danish -nation-state. It could be a threat to the Danish nation's future existence.

which led to a plebiscite in Schleswig and therefore the division of the old duchy. The northern half was incorporated into Denmark; the southern part remained German.

The Ethnos-Strategy

Today, we have to ask: Why was it possible to establish a democratic federation in Switzerland and Belgium but not in Denmark? What went wrong? As

Brendan O'Leary has pointed out, there are few good examples of the establishment of democratic federations that have been able to concurrently regulate the conflict between different ethnic communities successfully. In successful cases, the communities have lived relatively segregated. "In Belgium, Canada and Switzerland the success of federalism in conflict-regulation, such as it is, had been based upon the historic accident that the relevant ethnic communities are quite sharply geographically segregated."[3] In the United Monarchy of Denmark, there was actually a relatively clear-cut division between the German and the Danish language communities that went right through the middle of the duchy Schleswig – approximately where the current border was drawn in 1920. This indicates that it was possible for the United Monarchy to become a democratic federation like Switzerland and Belgium.

However, in part because the ethnically based nationalism played a major role in the creation of the Danish nation it became impossible to found a federation like in Switzerland and Belgium. The predominant view turned out to be that the borders of the demos and the ethnos should coincide.

This emphasis on language as the "natural" foundation of socio-political unions had enormous political consequences for Europe. The politicization of language, which Herder founded but did not unfold, shaped the political basis of the growing national groups in Europe by conferring major importance to all language communities. Poets, philologists, literates and historians became the main champions in those "language-battles" that broke out in Europe during the 19th century. In the United Monarchy the two universities, in Copenhagen and Kiel, became centers for the transformation of the concept of people. The university in Copenhagen became a kind of 'think-tank' for the national liberals in the Kingdom and the university in Kiel for the national liberals in Schleswig-Holstein.

---

3   Brendan O'Leary: "Right-Sizing and Right-Peopling", *Right-Sizing the State: The Politics of Moving Borders* 2001:50.

It is ironic, or tragic, that the concepts with which the linguistic or cultural nationalism took part in the construction of a Danish national sentiment were developed by the "enemy" – the Germans. And the more the multinational United Monarchy became depended on the German conceptualization of "nation" and "national sentiment", the weaker it became. The multilingual United Monarchy was weakened as a political entity with the politicization of the language and the nationalization of the culture. There were in Denmark – as in the multinational states of Switzerland and Austria – people who warned strongly against instating an ethnic principle of nationality as a state ideology. There was a successful balancing of the ethnic tensions in Switzerland and they maintained a multinational state by clearly distinguishing "ethnos" and "demos". There was not, on the other hand, a successful creation of a multinational state in Denmark or Austria. Though the Danish multinational state ultimately collapsed in 1864, the Republic of Austria did not break down until after WWI.

Today, it is easy enough to scorn the nationalists of those days. The crucial question is, however, whether the Danish state could have survived as an independent state in Europe had it not been for the Danish nationalists' demand for the state to be transformed into a modern nation-state. For not only was nationalism in fashion during the 19th century, but the nation-states' creation of an international state-system was under way as well. And given that Ernest Gellner is right, nationalism and the establishment of nation-states must be regarded as a necessary and integrated part in the development of the modern industrialized state.[4]

What we obviously cannot know is what would have happened in Denmark if Rousseau's social contract – political nationalism – had been ascribed more importance and Herder's language contract – cultural nationalism – less importance. We can never know if this would have led to the conservation of the multinational and multilingual state-form, or, the obliteration of the entire state; Jutland swallowed up by Germany and the isles united with Sweden.

Remember to Forget

Because the ethnically homogenous nation-state was regarded as the obvious framework of democracy since 1864, the question of whether or not a functional democracy within the framework of the United Monarchy could have been

---

4   Jf. Ernest Gellner: *Nation and Nationalism*, Blackwell, 1994 (1983).

established has hardly been raised. The reason why this question has not been posed is connected to the fact that nationalism, as a homogenizing factor, not only relies on the ability to remember but also the ability to forget. After the war and in the wake of nationalism's advance, new stories and tales of what it had been like to be Danish in times gone were developed and Denmark's past as a multinational state was soon forgotten.

Nationalism stages certain historical myths and allows others to slip out of our field of vision. Such a maneuver requires an active and conscious effort in a politics of remembrance. The national history writings began to tell the tale of the Danish state as a historical power existing since the dawn of time. But in order to establish and maintain such a way of recollecting history it was necessary that historians partook in "forgetting" and "suppressing" certain events and processes related to the creation of the nation-state. To the Danes it was about "forgetting" how bloody the transition to democracy as political system and to the nation-state as state-form had been in Denmark.

It is why I did not learn about the transformation and different notions of the concept of people in school. I learned to forget the dark side and only remember the bright side of this story. However, today it seems important to remember the story we have learned to forget. Because the horizon and the context have changed, we have to look at our past and rediscover our own history in a new way.

Enlightenment Top Down Leibniz' ,Lettre sur l'éducation d'un prince'

Hans Poser

1. Leibniz on Education

History in Education should include *Education in History* or *History of Education* – at least as long as philosophers dealt with the problem of how to bring about an educated human being. Since Plato, we know that this presupposes anthropology on the one side and ideals, norms and values on the other side; and we know from him about the epistemological problem of having to explain that a human being is able to learn and to understand something which he or she encounters for the first time. The history of education mirrors the attempts to solve these difficulties – and since we did not get rid of them, we have to be aware of these attempts: this is at least the answer to the question why education in history has to be a part of history in education. But why on earth just Leibniz? Wait and see.

Leibniz is well known as a logician, as the inventor of the term *Théodicée*, as the author of the so called *Monadology*, as a specialist for formal as well as natural languages, and as a historian who emphasizes the importance of history:

- We know from his *Monadology* that the *identity of an individual* depends on its history.
- We know from his research on natural languages that the *identity of a tribe or even a nation*, defined by its language, depends on its history.
- We know from his plans for a Scientia generalis that we need a *history of knowledge as the treasure house of wisdom*.
- We know from his extended collection of juridical documents from the past, that *law has to be conservative and therefore has to know its history* in order to institutionalise and to keep justice.

Notwithstanding, we normally do not think of Leibniz as someone who dealt with problems of education. In fact, there is much more to be found than the small remarks in textbooks on the history of education, which normally mention only the Leibnizian conception of reason.[1] Leibniz himself had been responsible for the education of the son of Baron von Boineburg whom he accompanied to Paris;[2] and he wrote several essays dealing with problems of education, for example the first one *Nova methodus discendae docendaeque jurisprudentiae* written in 1667 and containing some remarks on education,[3] further on two unfinished drafts *G.G. Leibnitii Cogitata de insigni bonitate et multa sapientia Principi Juveni inspiranda* and *G.G. Leibnitii Cogitata de perfectionibus Principis potentia externa, sapientia in intellectu et bonitate in voluntate interna nec non de perfectione corporis* (which came via Berlin, Dresden and St. Petersburg to Warszawa),[4] remarks on education in connection with the plans for academies, and finally the so called "Lettre sur l'éducation d'un prince".[5]

How to educate a prince had been the theme of books since the Renaissance; Machiavelli's *Il Principe* is one of the best known, but untypical examples. In 1685 Leibniz got a manuscript of an author unknown to us dealing with the subject, and Leibniz was asked to give his comments. He made some excerpts

---

1   An overview concerning Leibniz' writings on education and their reception is given by Werner Wiater: G.W. Leibniz und seine Bedeutung in der Pädagogik. Ein Beitrag zur pädagogischen Rezeptionsgeschichte (= Beitr. z. hist. Bildungsforschung Bd. 1) Hildesheim: Lax 1985. – My own approach has been stimulated by up to now unpublished papers of Nelly Robinet-Bruyère, – "Une lecture de la Lettre sur l'Éducation d'un Prince au regard des sciences de la éducation contemporaines" and Patrick Riley, "Leibniz on Paideia", both presented on the XIIth World Congress of Philosophy, Boston 1998, and Nelly Robinet-Bruyère, "La Lettre sur l'Éducation d'un Prince et l'Europe" (they all will be published as well as an extended German version of my paper in: C. Roldan (ed.), Leibniz und die Idee Europas).

Leibniz' writings are quoted from:

A = Sämtliche Schriften und Briefe. Hg. von der Akademie der Wissenschaften (Akademieausgabe). Reihe I-VII. Darmstadt, later Leipzig, now Berlin, 1923 ff.

GP = Die philosophischen Schriften. Hg. Carl Immanuel Gerhardt. 7 vols., Berlin 1875-1890 (reprinted Hildesheim / New York 1978).

Klopp = Die Werke von Leibniz. Hg. Onno Klopp. Reihe I, 11 vols., Hannover 1864-1884.

Finster = Der Briefwechsel mit Antoine Arnauld, hg. v. R. Finster, Hamburg: Meiner 1997.

2   Klopp, I.3 / A I.1, p. 265 - 401 (Boineburg, seine Familie und sein Kreis).

3   A VI.1.261 - 364, especially Pars I, p. 266 - 292.

4   Both published by J. Kvacala, Neue Leibnizsche Fragmente über die Erziehung eines Prinzen, in: Zeitschrift für Geschichte der Erziehung und des Unterrichts IV (1914), p. 79ff. – For a short sketch of the way of the manuscripts and its (lacking) influence see Paul Wiedeburg: Der junge Leibniz, das Reich und Europa, T. I: Mainz, Anmerkungsband, Wiesbaden: Steiner 1962, fn. 92, p. 41ff. respectively fn. 39, p. 13 – 15.

5   A IV.3.542 - 557. French edition: Leibniz, Lettre sur l'éducation d'un prince. Edition, introduction et notes par Nelly Robinet-Bruyère, Paris, Vrin (in print).

and several short notes, whereas his answer consisted in the *Lettre* in question.[6] This small writing is important, for between 1690 and 1714, Leibniz made copies with small alterations, reflecting the special conditions in Berlin, in Hanover as well as in Dresden, so that he himself took the opportunity to influence the education of princes for nearly three full decades at the courts in question.[7] Moreover, what he developed in the *Lettre* corresponds to his projects of academies and their importance for education. This holds especially for the plans for an academy in St. Petersburg.

In fact, even if the King of Saxony had been impressed by the *Lettre* and even if Queen Sophie-Charlotte in Berlin installed Leibniz as one of those responsible for the education of her son who later on became the so called *Soldatenkönig*, Leibniz's ideas never have been realized: all the courts followed their traditional instructions.

2. The Necessary Perfections of a Prince

Notwithstanding these circumstances, Leibniz's ideas of education in early Enlightenment are a very typical expression of his ideas of an enlightenment top down. What is it which makes the Leibnizian ideas remarkable? Without saying it, he rejects the line of instructions for princes at that time, which aim at a knowledge of military and the rules how to behave at the court. And even if he doesn't exclude these elements totally, his main intention is to form the character and the spirit of the prince as a future emperor, who has to function as a positive example for his country. Therefore, the education of his spirit and his character are the most important points. In a way typical for him, Leibniz distinguishes between three different degrees of perfection, namely that

- which is *necessary*;
- which is *useful*; and that
- which is *embellishing*.[8]

As we will see, what is *necessary* aims at the education of a human being as such. The *utilities* concern the elements belonging to the traditional instruction of a prince already mentioned, whereas the *embellishing*, characterized as

---

6 Concerning the history of the manuscript see A IV.3.542ff. The reactions are described by Rudolf Grieser: Leibniz und das Problem der Prinzenerziehung, in: Wilhelm Totok, Carl Haase (Hg.): Leibniz. Hannover: Verlag für Literatur und Zeitgeschehen 1966, p. 511 - 533.

7 Data etc. are taken from Grieser, p. 518-521, and fn. 13, p. 530.

8 " Je conçois *trois degrés de perfection*, qu'on peut envisager dans l'Education d'un Prince, dont le premier est de *necessité*, le seconde est pour *l'usage*, le troisième est pour *l'ornement*." A IV.3.546.

highly desirable, includes the sciences on the one side, the beaux arts on the other side.

These small remarks show already, that the necessary perfections are the most important ones. They consist in four main abilities or elements of the character, which are indispensable for the prince. The prince has to be

- a morally good person (un *homme de bien*),
- a stout-hearted person (un *homme de cœur*),
- a judicious person (un *homme de jugement*), and
- an honest person (un *honnête homme*).

3. The *homme de bien*

Un *homme de bien* is a person of "piety, justice, charity, and of fully fulfilling his duties".[9] This is exactly that what Leibniz has called a *vir bonus* – a concept which can be found throughout his whole writings: "the *vir bonus* is someone who eagerly strives for justice", and "justice is well ordered charity", as Leibniz writes 1679 in his *Modalia Iuris*.[10] According to Leibniz, justice and charity are clearly properties of an *homme de bien*. To follow one's obligations is included as well, for Leibniz immediately uses an expression, which can be found throughout all his thinking and which Patrick Riley has analysed: "justice is the charity of the wise, or that which the good and wise man wants due to his nature".[11] Therefore Leibniz can explain in his *Iuris Naturalis Principia*, the vir bonus necessarily aims at the felicity of everyone.[12] All this belongs to the centre of the Leibnizian philosophy. In a letter to Arnaud, he writes: "*Justice* is the charity of the wise. *Charity* is a universal benevolence, which the wise man carries into execution in conformity with the measures of reason in order to obtain the greatest good. *Wisdom* is the science of felicity or of the means to reach a stable state of contentment, which consists in a continuous approxima-

---

9   "*l'homme de bien* a des grands sentiments de pieté, de justice et de charité, et il s'applique fortement à faire son devoir." L.c.

10   "Vir bonus est qui justitia praeditus est", and: " Justitia est caritas recte ordinata", A VI.4.2758.

11   "*Justitia* est caritas sapientis, seu quae boni prudentisque viri arbitrio congruit", A VI.4.2777; see also 2837. – P. Riley has shown that Leibniz in his terminology combines Greco-roman thinking (benevolentia) with the Christian tradition (caritas) in his iustitia universalis, namely as a universal concept of justice. See Patrick Riley: Leibniz' Universal Jurisprudence. Justice as the Charity of the Wise. Cambridge/Mass. – London: Harvard UP 1996, particularly p. 156ff.

12   "Viri boni est ad communem felicitatem procurandum niti" , A VI.4.2810, footnote 16f. (4).

tion to the highest perfection or at least in a variety within the same degree of perfection."[13]

All these remarks lead us into the very heart of Leibniz's theory of justice which he himself develops under three principles: *honeste vivere, neminem laedere* and *suum cuique tribuere*[14] – principles going back to Plato and used in the stoic tradition as well as in Roman law. The most important point, here: they hold not only for a prince but for each reasonable being! They are immediately interwoven with Leibniz's idea of a universal harmony which to enlarge is the most important obligation of human beings. This background immediately shows the fundamental difference between the Leibnizian approach and the traditional conceptions of rules how to educate a prince. It is the same idea which can be found near the end of Enlightenment in Mozart's *Magic Flute*, where Sarastro says of Prince Tamino: "- a prince. Moreover – a human being." This means that for Leibniz education, based on natural law, has to aim at the formation of a cognitive, namely wise and charitable human being.[15]

4. The *homme de cœur*

The same holds for the other necessary perfections at which education has to aim. The *homme de cœur* is someone "who cannot be easily shocked, and who maintains his freedom of the mind in each situation".[16] This is directly connected with the Leibnizian definition of vir bonus, for a good person is not only a clever, rational or wise one, but someone whose affections (which are the driving power of an action) are aiming at charity. We saw: "Justice is the charity of the wise." In his small note *De Iustitia ac amore voluntateque Dei*, Leibniz explains: "Charity is the attitude to love everyone."[17] Even if this is said with respect to God and his will, this holds for human actions as well, for the central

---

13 "Que la justice n'est autre chose que la charité du sage. Que la charité est une bienveillance universelle, dont le sage dispense l'exécution, conformément aux mesures de la raison, à fin d'obtenir le plus grand bien. Et que la sagesse est la science de la felicité ou des moyens de parvenir au contentement durable, qui consiste dans un acheminement continuel à une plus grande perfection, ou au moins dans la variation d'un même degré de perfection." To Arnauld, 23 March 1690, GP II.136 / Finster, p. 362.

14 A VI.4.2851-2853.

15 In this context, N. Robinet-Bruyière emphasizes the European and non-national character of Leibniz' concept of education, including tolerance among the religious confessions and the exchange of national specialties, aiming at a "Prince éclairé par la Raison naturelle", as she writes, "qui agisse conformément aux principes du droit naturel".

16: "L'homme de cœur n'est pas aisé à ebransler, et garde la liberté d'esprit en toute sorte d'occurrences." A IV.3.546.

17 "Caritas est habitus amandi omnes", De Justitia ac amore volutateque Dei, A VI.4.2890 and 2891.

point here is, that the will is free if and only if it follows reason. Therefore, justice is the charity, which leads the wise.

5. The *homme de jugement*

To be an *homme de jugement* is the third kind of necessary perfections. It holds for a person whose "judgements are just in each case without being lead astray by mere apperception."[18] This, too, holds for each reasonable being as such, including God and his choice of the plan of creation, namely the best of all possible worlds – whereas a human being might be mistaken and might aim at something which is only seemingly worth striving after. Therefore, the difference between *iudicium humanum* and *iudicium divinum* is discussed in these writings, which culminate in the three principles of justice already mentioned.[19] This perfection has to be supplemented by an extended knowledge on "toute sorte de matiere", for it would be impossible to judge adequately without knowledge; but here, Leibniz is thinking of the moral quality not to be disturbed by emotions and circumstances in judging.

6. The *honnête homme*

The fourth and final one of the necessary perfections demands the education of an *honnête homme*, that is, of a person "which avoids everything which is shocking".[20] Now, the characterization of someone as an honnête homme has been in many cases used for the kind of gallant behaviour without any profoundness, attributed especially at Frenchmen in the 17th and 18th century – but Leibniz says at least in two other writings that he thinks of an honourable, namely virtuous person[21] in the sense of the Latin term *vir honestus*.[22]

Altogether Leibniz's short introduction of his *Lettre* shows that the unalterable and necessary aims of education include a highly condensed conception of

---

18   *"L'homme de jugement* raisonne juste sur toute sorte de matières, sans se laisser eblouir par les apparences." A IV.3.546.

19   See A VI.4.2858

20   *"l'honnête homme* sçait garder la bienseance, et eviter tout ce qui est choquant", A IV.3.546.

21   Concerning the history of this concept see Maurice Magendie: La politesse mondaine et les théories de l'honnêteté en France au XVIIe sciècle, de 1600 à 1660, 2 vols, Paris 1925; the following period is documented by Henning Scheffers: Höfische Konvention und die Aufklärung. Wandlungen des *honnête-homme*-Ideals im 17. und 18. Jahrhundert (= Studien zur Germanistik, Anglistik und Komparatistik 93), Bonn: Bouvier 1980.

22   In 1684, Leibniz took some notes from de Sablé and d'Ailly: Maximes et Pensées diverses, where these both express just this more fundamental meaning of the term (Pens. XII, XIII; A VI.4.2734); and somewhere he explains that "honneste homme" means "vir probus et virtutibus deditus" (quoted from Wiater, p. 189).

the essence of each human being and not only of a prince: In its first instance the prince has to be *human* in the full sense of this word, including cognitive, emotional as well as moral perfections.

7. Useful Perfections

Let us for a moment have a small look at those perfection,s which are the *useful* ones. For Leibniz, these are the abilities of a prince as a statesman and a commander in chief. They are not absolutely necessary, but "very suitable"; in fact, Leibniz gives only some examples, introduced by the remark that the prince as someone who is an *homme de jugement* has the capacity to appoint capable ministers and good commanders, so that there is no need for him to have himself the qualifications to be e.g. a commander.[23] This again shows, that Leibniz is not really interested in all those topics, which in his time had been the central ones in the traditional curricula of a prince.

8. The *homme éclairé* and the *homme agréable*

As a final perfection Leibniz deals with the *embellishing* as the delighting. Even if these perfections are neither necessary nor useful, they are discussed at length, for, if someone reaches them, "it leaves nothing to be desired".[24] They consist in *knowledge* concerning sciences on the one side and *capacities* concerning the fine arts on the other side.

Let us turn to the second element of the embellishing perfections, first. These are the capacities in fine arts. They have to make sure that the prince is an *homme agréable*. But it is not only the ability to dance, to play chess or an instrument and to be able to compose which is meant, here, for some paragraphs later Leibniz makes clear: Beneath the elements which constitute an homme agréable, the fine arts encourage our imagination, and by this, they give thousands of fruitful ideas.[25] This indicates that for Leibniz the emotional side is always interwoven with the cognitive one, with which we have do deal now.

---

23 "Quand au *second degré* il est tres *utile*, qu'un Prince sçache la Politique et l'art militaire. Ce sont les deux mestiers, qu'un Prince devoit sçavoir faire. J'avoue, qu'il s'en peut passer, absolument parler", A IV.3.546.

24 "Mais quand outre ces qualités le Prince est encor éclairé en toute sorte de matieres, et agreable à tout le monde, c'est le *troisième degré* de perfection, qui sert à *l'ornement* et au plaisir, et ne laisse plus rien à desirer", A IV.3.547.

25 A IV.3.551.

The scientific knowledge (Leibniz mentions the disciplines of a whole academy) shall make sure that the prince "is enlightened (éclairé) in each matter" so that he is an *homme éclairé*. Knowledge is, as mentioned, a precondition of true judgements. When Leibniz throughout his lifetime argued for academies, following the conjunction *theoria cum praxi*, he had in mind that sciences would warrant better life conditions. But moreover, he was convinced that sciences have a moral value in two aspects: First – and that has been the Socratic standard argumentation of enlightenment – better knowledge leads immediately to morally better actions, for if we know from better knowledge that the result of an action will not increase the perfection of our life, we would abstain from it! This should become the cornerstone of Christian Wolff's ethics. Secondly – and one of Leibniz's convictions, which he shares with the Jesuit's idea of a *propagatio fidei per scientias* – sciences demonstrate the regularity, order and harmony of the world, and by this they lead us to the insight that there must be a necessary being, the wise creator of the world. Therefore, this part of the third degree of perfection which has to be introduced in the education of a prince, is in fact far away from mere embellishment.

In using these terms *éclairé* and *agréable* in his *Lettre*, Leibniz picks up a terminology which can be found in others of his writings; therefore they are the adequate terms to emphasize what Leibniz intends: the prince has to be the *representative of an enlightened mankind*, and obliged to make sure that the whole society takes part in the process of enlightenment. The metaphor of light, used in the expression "*éclairé*" has to be taken as the leitmotif within the plan for educating a prince as a human being. This holds for Leibniz's project of a Scientia generalis as well as for the plans for academies; and it is explicitly laid down in 1692 in his *Memoire pour des Personnes Eclairées et de bonne intention*.[26] There he criticizes the "corruption générale" (§2) of society and argues that "people could be much happier" (§5), if reason would be taught, spread out and used – which needs nothing but will to do so (§6).[27] Some pages later Leibniz explains: "In order to really contribute to the happiness of men, their understanding has to be enlightened, their will has to be strengthened by

---

26   Klopp I.10, p. 7-21 / A IV.4.612-621.

27   "Il ne faut que vouloir" (l.c.).

exercising virtue, namely by accustoming to follow reasons in acting. In order to enlighten the understanding one has to train the art of reasoning."[28]

In this context, André Robinet quotes from a Leibnizian letter to Chauvin: "Those who are really enlightened and full of good intentions work with all their power ... to enlarge the good for others, and if they possess the means do so, they intensely enlarge the enlightenment of men, Christian virtue, and the public felicity. This is the touchstone of the true piety."[29] Therefore, Robinet adds, Leibniz's prince has to be seen as the *Émile* of the Prussian Court.[30]

9. Conclusion

Education in history – but why on earth just Leibniz? At least in Germany we have no prince (or only some private person bearing this title); a Danish prince will be educated due to the regulations of the Danish court and not by methods of the 17th century. And enlightenment top down in a democracy? This is just the problem, whether we should deal with and teach history of philosophy.

Thinking of Leibniz, I do not want to deal with the question, *why* we are able to learn and to understand – the Leibnizian answer is the Monadology; but his *Lettre* does not touch this metaphysical question. Much more important is the question, *what* to teach, namely which the aims of education are, i.e. which norms and values we should teach today. And here, Leibniz' approach is really helpful. As in 17th century, we need today to look for
- a morally good person (un *homme de bien*),
- a stout-hearted person (un *homme de cœur*),
- a judicious person (un *homme de jugement*), and
- an honest person (un *honnête homme*).

Even if a foundation on natural law is impossible, the Leibnizian principles behind it – *honeste vivere, neminem laedere* and *suum cuique tribuere* – are absolutely fundamental ones, for they guide us to tolerance and to the obligation to enlarge harmony in our world. Instead of speaking only of human *rights*,

---

28 "Pour contribuer veritablement au bonheur des hommes, il faut leur eclairer l'entendement; il faut fortifier leur volonté dans l'exercice des vertus, c'est à dire dans l'habitude d'agir suivant la raison; et il faut tacher enfin d'oster les obstacles, qui les empêchent de trouver la verité et de suivre les veritables biens. Pour eclairer l'entendement, il faut perfectionner l'art de raisonner", Memoire, § 12f., Klopp I.10, p. 11 / A IV.4.615.

29 "ceux qui sont veritablement eclairés et bien intentionnés travaillent de toutes leur force, à leur propre instruction et au bien d'autruy, et s'ils en ont les moyens, ils s'efforcent de procurer l'accroissement des lumieres des hommes, de la vertu chrestienne, et de la félicité publique. C'est la pierre de touche de la veritable pieté." Letter to Etienne Chauvin, 4 Sept. 1696, A I.13.232.

30 André Robinet: G.W. Leibniz. Le meilleur des mondes par la balance de l'Europe, Paris: PUF 1994, p. 282.

they allow us to articulate human *obligations* among each other. As we saw, this includes *knowledge* as a presupposition – which guides us to the ideal of an enlightened person. This still holds today, only the Leibnizian terminology is somewhat old-fashioned. We cannot be sure that knowledge as such leads a human being to morality, responsibility and fulfilling obligations; but together with the Leibnizian principles we gain a starting point for such important topics of today as bioethics, ethics of technology and medical ethics.

Taking the *Lettre* as a piece of history of philosophy – why should we use it in education, be it at school or in university seminars? It is a mirror which shows *our* problems of toleration, of human rights and human obligations. The *Lettre* has to be taken not as the expression of naïve optimism, which in many cases is attributed to Leibniz, but

– against the background of a disastrous period of the 30 years war as a religious war, which enforced toleration among Christian confessions for the first time,
– against the problems caused by Louis XIV. and his politics depending on political power and rejecting tolerance,
– against the dangerous situation caused by the Turkish army which had occupied the whole Balkans and which stood before Vienna.

Leibniz argues for a balance of reason, emotion and morality. Therefore, this piece of history allows us to show timeless arguments as well as time-dependent and contingent presuppositions – and by this it makes clear that we need enlightenment in the multi cultural as well as multi religious world of today.

But what about the prince in a democracy? Some interpretations of the 19th century believe Leibniz to have understood the prince to be a kind of central monad – but there is no textual support for this interpretation, and it does not fit into the Leibnizian idea of an individual. We saw in that opera of enlightenment, the *Magic Flute*, "more than a prince: a human being" – namely an outstanding enlightened one, an homme éclairé following the charity of the wise.[31] All this shows that Kant's quotation from Horaz – "sapere aude", dare to think – is for Leibniz (and one century earlier than Kant) not only the essence of enlightenment, but also the criterion which has to be fulfilled (even today) in educating all people, for without it, Enlightenment is not possible.

---

31 Joseph Vernay pointed out that this prince is the model of an enlightened person as an ideal for the inhabitants of his empire. Joseph Vernay: Essai sur la Pédagogie de Leibniz, Heidelberg: Winter 1914, p. 59.

Le rôle de l'histoire dans l'enseignement

Jean Ferrari

Comme l'indique le titre de ma communication qui figure sur le programme, mon intention première avait été de vous parler ce matin de l'histoire et de l'histoire de la philosophie dans la formation de l'étudiant en philosophie. Mais il m'est apparu qu'en une demi-heure la tâche était impossible et comme il fut question à plusieurs reprises hier de l'histoire de la philosophie, je m'en tiendrai à la seule histoire générale. Mais avant de définir le rôle de cette histoire dans l'enseignement et d'envisager les méthodes pédagogiques dont elle fait l'objet et qui varient selon les lieux et les moments, il faut d'abord s'interroger sur la nature de cette discipline, elle aussi, diversement conçue selon les pays et les périodes de l'histoire. Mon propos s'appuiera naturellement sur l'expérience de la France et des nations francophones, non pas donnée en exemple, mais comme élément de comparaison avec ce qui se fait en d'autres aires culturelles. Nous devons tous, à cet égard, remercier l'Université danoise de l'Education, l'Institut de philosophie de l'Education et son directeur, le professeur Peter Kemp d'avoir pris l'initiative d'organiser ces deux journées, car elles obligent les philosophes que nous sommes à nous interroger sur notre rapport, non seulement à l'histoire de la philosophie, mais aussi à l'histoire en tant que discipline autonome.

Car entre la philosophie et l'histoire ont longtemps persisté de nombreux malentendus. Qu'est-ce que la philosophie, qui se situait dans l'intemporel, avait à faire avec le factuel d'événements contingents? Descartes, on le sait, méprisait l'histoire et il avait ses raisons car elle n'était pas encore constituée en discipline de connaissance. Elle s'intéressait surtout aux anecdotes et aux généalogies. Il n'est pas étonnant que Descartes, et Malebranche à sa suite, n'aient vu là qu'érudition et pédantisme. Penser, philosopher, n'est-ce pas, comme le disait Spinoza, se placer *sub specie aeternitatis*? Mais ce qui était vrai au début du XVIIème siècle ne l'est déjà plus à sa fin. Leibniz est l'un des fondateurs de l'historiographie moderne et, avec le XVIIIème siècle, apparaît l'idée que l'homme est un sujet historique, qu'il connaît un développement avec le temps. S'impose alors irrésistiblement, si l'on veut comprendre la nature humaine, l'idée d'une évolution de l'homme. Pour Rousseau, dont il fut beaucoup question hier, l'homme possède une nature et il a une histoire dont il est possible, hypothétiquement de restituer les étapes, de l'état de nature à l'état civil. Certains iront jusqu'à dire que sa nature est d'avoir une histoire. Dès lors la connaissance du passé humain prend une importance capitale. Elle paraît indispensable pour comprendre l'homme présent et l'histoire comme discipline, avec ses exigences propres, se constitue en première science de l'homme. Au même titre que la psychologie dont David Hume − qui fut aussi un grand historien − donne un échantillon avec son *Traité de la nature humaine* avec comme sous-titre *Essai pour introduire la méthode expérimentale dans les sujets moraux*, avec Voltaire, l'histoire en langue française se veut scientifique. Voltaire apparaît comme un écrivain qui non seulement écrit des livres d'histoire, ainsi l'*Histoire de Charles, roi de Suède* ou *Le siècle de Louis XIV*, mais qui réfléchit à la méthode qui doit être mise en œuvre par l'historien:

> On n'a fait que l'histoire des rois, mais on n'a point fait celle de la nation. Il semble que, pendant quatorze cents ans, il n'y ait eu dans les Gaules que des rois, des ministres, des généraux, mais nos mœurs, nos lois, nos coutumes, notre esprit ne sont-ils donc rien?
> écrit-il à D'Argenson en 1740.

Les innovations de Voltaire, par l'intérêt qu'il porte à la justice, aux finances, à l'armée, aux sciences et aux arts, en font un véritable précurseur de l'histoire contemporaine. Toutefois, lorsqu'il embrasse une vaste période de l'histoire comme dans l'*Essai sur les mœurs et l'esprit des nations depuis Charlemagne jusqu'à Louis XIII*, dédié à la marquise du Châtelet, son propos n'est pas de rapporter des faits, mais d'éclairer un sens de l'histoire, où s'affirme, par le progrès de l'esprit humain, peu à peu libéré de ses entraves, préjugés, superstitions, le règne de la raison et de la civilisation. Si c'est le hasard qui domine l'histoire, il fait assez bien les choses et Voltaire se réjouit de vivre en son siècle, se moquant de Rousseau, voulant, selon lui, retourner vivre dans les forêts.

Aujourd'hui l'importance de l'histoire est partout reconnue, de nombreuses études sont consacrées à sa méthodologie et à son enseignement. Il me semble donc que les philosophes et les pédagogues que nous sommes ne peuvent pas ne pas s'intéresser à ce qu'est l'histoire elle-même et, ensuite, à la manière dont elle est enseignée, c'est-à-dire à la fois selon quelles méthodes elle se constitue en tant que savoir et selon quelles méthodes elle est présentée aux élèves.

Mais d'abord qu'est-ce que l'histoire ?

L'histoire peut s'entendre en deux acceptions. L'histoire, c'est d'abord le devenir humain, pendant la longue suite des siècles, dans son ensemble comme dans ses plus infimes détails, c'est l'irréversible mouvement de l'espèce vers ce que certains appellent son achèvement, c'est la succession des crises, des échecs et des victoires des hommes qu'avec Pascal on peut considérer comme un seul homme qui subsiste toujours et apprend continuellement. Cette première conception de l'histoire comme totalité, que personne ne pourra jamais saisir puisqu'idéalement elle rassemblerait la vie de chaque individu, de chaque tribu, de chaque nation et les innombrables événements et interactions qui en ont marqué le cours depuis qu'il y a des hommes sur la terre, constitue une sorte d'en soi qui échappe à toute connaissance, c'est l'histoire avec un grand H. Mais l'histoire définit aussi un savoir. Elle est la connaissance que prennent les historiens de l'histoire-réalité. Elle est, comme la définissait Lucien Febvre, la science des hommes dans le passé et, comme telle, elle implique la définition claire de son objet, une certaine méthode, des procédés particuliers d'investigation. La raison qui s'y applique est celle qui construit la science, qui rend compte d'un réel donné, qui édifie, dans le cas de l'histoire, à partir de "traces", suivant l'heureuse expression de Simiand, une certaine vision de la vie des hommes dans le passé qui prétend à l'objectivité.

Aussi la raison qui s'applique à l'histoire-réalité pour forger l'histoire connaissance doit-elle opérer un travail considérable. L'objet historique apparaît comme un objet constitué et non pas donné, constitué à partir d'une double abstraction exigée par la méthode historique: l'objet historique est toujours une rectification par rapport à une première mise en œuvre de documents ; le sujet par ailleurs doit s'abstraire de l'action historique: faire de l'histoire, c'est toujours au moins idéalement faire abstraction de son engagement historique.. L'historien, ainsi que le notait Tacite, ne doit agir *nec ira, nec studio*. L'effort de compréhension qu'il doit poursuivre ne doit pas l'amener à prendre parti. Mais cette double abstraction de l'objet historique et de l'historien qui introduit un morcellement dans une totalité continue et suppose qu'on privilégie seule une dimension du temps, n'est point suffisante pour rendre l'histoire perméable à la raison. C'est pourquoi, ainsi que le disait déjà Thucydide, l'historien s'efforce de travailler avec l'idée de causalité qui fait partie de l'essence même de son exercice. La raison introduit dans l'histoire l'idée que ce qui arrive succède à un autre événement suivant une règle. Dans l'histoire réalité qui ne se donne point d'emblée comme un enchaînement cohérent, la raison recherche les suites de faits, les enchaînements qui apparaissent nécessaires. C'est l'idée de déterminisme qui rend possible les déterminations. C'est pourquoi l'historien est amené à opérer un tri. Tout, dans l'histoire réalité, n'est pas également significatif à cet égard. Il s'agit de dégager l'essentiel en mettant en lumière comme des chaînes de montage en créant une continuité signifiante par-dessus le remplissage de la vie qui se caractérise si souvent par son "décousu". L'historien au contraire est celui qui découvre des séquences, qui décrit des raccourcis cohérents.

Dès lors on voit combien il serait inexact dans cette conception de l'histoire connaissance de vouloir considérer l'histoire comme une manière de revivre le passé. C'est avant tout la raison qui est en œuvre chez l'historien pour réduire l'histoire à ses schèmes raisonnables. Car, après la découverte des causalités dispensées, il y a comme un regroupement autour d'une causalité unique qui paraît privilégiée, mais qui ne peut-être considérée ici que comme une hypothèse de travail: forces collectives, réalité des institutions, infrastructures économiques etc... L'idée d'un passé intégral n'est plus qu'une idée limite et comme la chose en soi de l'historien qui lui permet de multiplier les perspectives et les hypothèses, mais demeure comme un résidu que la raison dans son travail d'élucidation et de rationalisation de la réalité historique ne parvient pas á réduire. Les Français prêtent, peut-être à tort, à la langue allemande deux termes pour distinguer l'histoire réalité et la science historique: *Geschichte* et *Historie*. L'historien André Irénée Marrou, empruntant ici une distinction kantienne, dit qu'on pourrait parler d'une histoire noumène, impossible à connaître et une histoire phénomène, celle de la science historique.

La diversité des domaines qui relèvent de l'histoire ou plutôt la diversification de ceux-ci, liée à la *spécialisation* croissante de la discipline comme c'est le cas pour toutes les matières scientifiques au XXème siècle, s'accompagne de l'apparition de conceptions différentes de ce qu'est l'histoire et des méthodes à lui appliquer. Ainsi, la tradition historique a connu en France au XXème siècle de profondes mutations. A l'histoire purement chronologique, privilégiant les grands hommes, rois, empereurs, généraux, les événements comme les guerres et leurs batailles, les conquêtes et leurs revers, histoire justement appelée événementielle, s'est ajoutée avec l'Ecole dite des Annales (annales d'histoire économique et sociale) du nom de la Revue où s'exprimaient ces nouveaux historiens, une nouvelle conception de l'histoire. Les principaux représentants en ont été Marc Bloch (1886-1944), historien médiéviste, auteur de *Les rois thaumaturges* (1924), *Les caractères originaux de l'histoire rurale française* (1931), *La société féodale* (1939-40), *Apologie pour l'histoire,* ouvrage posthume (1951). Il fut fusillé par les Allemands en 1944. Lucien Febvre (1878-1956), influencé par le géographe Vidal de la Blache, montra les liens existant entre l'histoire et la géographie dans son livre *La terre et l'évolution humaine* (1922) (autres publications, *Un destin, Martin Luther* (1928), *Le problème de l'incroyance au XVIème siècle, La religion de Rabelais* (1942)). Sa conception de l'histoire, qui se voulait une synthèse des éléments politiques, économiques, sociaux, religieux, culturels, mentaux, est défendue avec force dans *Combat pour l'histoire* (1953). Illustrant encore superbement l'Ecole des Annales, je citerai, un peu plus près de nous, Fernand Braudel (1902-1985). Dans *La Méditerranée et le monde méditerranéen à l'époque de Philippe II* (1949), il a tenté de concilier les recherches historiques avec les sciences voisines, notamment la géographie, mais aussi la sociologie, l'économie. Il s'attache à ce qu'il appelle l'histoire longue, en particulier de l'Europe et plus particulièrement de la Méditerranée. Il décrit l'évolution profonde des infrastructures économiques qui sont une des conditions majeures de l'évolution des sociétés. Autres ouvrages du même auteur qui sont devenus des classiques de l'historiographie française: *La Méditerranée, l'espace et l'histoire* (1985), (Champs Flammarion) et *Ecrits sur l'histoire* (même éditeur, 1969) qui est une réflexion sur l'épistémologie et les méthodes mises en œuvre dans la recherche historique.

Ces profondes transformations de la recherche historique qui s'attache désormais à ces ensembles cohérents en mouvement que sont les civilisations ne pouvaient pas ne pas avoir d'effet sur l'enseignement de l'histoire dans les lycées et à l'Université, des modifications de programmes qui ont commencé à apparaître dans les années 60 avec le bouleversement et le presqu'abandon de la chronologie des grands événements au profit de synthèses plus ambitieuses rassemblant histoire, géographie, économie, démographie etc...

Si je prends la situation actuelle de l'élève, puis de l'étudiant en philosophie, je puis dire, que, en France, et cela vaut dans la plupart des pays francophones comme la Suisse, la Belgique et le Québec sans parler de certains pays d'Afrique qui se sont inspirés du modèle français, l'histoire est une matière obligatoire depuis les petites classes jusqu'à la classe de Terminale à l'issue de laquelle l'élève affronte les épreuves du Baccalauréat, elle y figure soit à l'écrit soit à l'oral. Au terme de ses études secondaires l'élève est supposé avoir parcouru toute l"histoire des origines à la période contemporaine, de son propre pays d'abord, mais aussi des principales puissances mondiales, des grandes civilisations et avoir, en définitive, une culture historique suffisante pour commencer, en quelque discipline que ce soit, ses études supérieures.

L'ordre d'apprentissage de cet ensemble peut varier selon les programmes en constante évolution et modification qui font le bonheur des éditeurs de manuels scolaires. Le manuel d'histoire joue un rôle essentiel et sa présentation est le reflet de la manière dont on conçoit, à un moment donné, l'enseignement de l'histoire. Il est clair qu'entre le manuel du début du XXème siècle, celui des années 50 et ceux de ce début du XXIème siècle, les différences sont tout à fait considérables. Ainsi pendant des décennies de l'enseignement de l'histoire au XXème siècle en France, le manuel utilisé dans les établissement publics était le "Malet et Isaac" et, par exemple, les programmes en 1957 étaient les suivants: L'Orient et la Grèce (classe de sixième), Rome et les débuts du Moyen Age (classe de cinquième) Le Moyen Age (classe de quatrième), Les Temps modernes (classe de troisième), XVIIème et XVIIIème siècles (classe de seconde), L'époque révolutionnaire, 1789-1851 (classe de première), Histoire contemporaine, 1852 -1939 (classes de philosophie, mathématiques et sciences expérimentales). L'ordre chronologique des époques était clairement respecté et c'est seulement en terminale que l'élève parvenait à l'histoire contemporaine. Les manuels de géographie faisaient l'objet de volumes séparés. Un peu plus de vingt ans plus tard, dans les années quatre-vingt, les programmes étaient totalement modifiés, avec l'abandon de l'enseignement relativement élitaire qui avait prévalu jusque là. J'ai retrouvé un manuel de mon fils qui devait être en troisième en 1985. Un unique manuel intitulé *Espaces et civilisations* couvrait l'histoire, la géographie, l'économie et l'éducation civique et avait exigé la collaboration d'une douzaine d'auteurs. Le programme ne concerne plus les temps modernes, mais le XXème siècle sous tous ses aspects. Surtout, et depuis ce trait n'a fait que s'accentuer, la place de l'information historique, à vrai dire du savoir historique présenté par l'auteur du manuel, est devenue très réduite par rapport à ce qui est appelé "documents", photos, articles de journaux ou de revues commentés ou non par l'auteur du manuel. Cela donne un ensemble assez chatoyant, mais relativement confus, où seul celui qui dispose déjà d'une bonne culture historique, d'une échelle chronologique sûre, est susceptible de s'y retrouver. Or, d'après les professeurs d'histoire que j'ai interrogés, ce n'est pas le cas de la majorité des élèves qui manquent de points de repère et sont pour ainsi dire perdus dans le flot d'information disparates.

On peut donc dire, mais nous pourrons si vous voulez en discuter, qu'il y a une véritable crise, comme dans d'autres disciplines, de l'enseignement de l'histoire dans l'enseignement secondaire dont pâtit, comme les autres élèves, le futur philosophe, malgré l'intérêt qui, en général, est porté à la matière.

Il paraît clair que, sur le plan pédagogique, il eût été préférable, aux dires même des professeurs, d'enrichir les anciens schémas plutôt que de les bouleverser. L'ancienne méthode faisait appel à l'imagination, voire à l'émotion. Que l'on songe par exemple à telle page de Jules Michelet (1798-1874) sur la Révolution française où le lyrisme du style l'emporte sur toute autre considération, où le récit de la bataille de Valmy qui prend des allures d'épopée. L'évocation est si vive qu'on a le sentiment d'y être. Le patriotisme se nourrit de ces héros et ces grandeurs passées. Michelet mêle à la description proprement historique vie et enthousiasme qui le conduisent souvent à la partialité. C'est un historien engagé qui juge, qui condamne, souvent à tort ; se comparant aux autres historiens, ses contemporains, Michelet écrivait, à propos du but de l'histoire: "Thierry (A) y voyait une narration, Guizot une analyse, je l'ai nommée résurrection et ce nom lui restera". Il a conçu l'histoire comme une résurrection intégrale du passé qui fait appel à l'imagination du cœur et est portée par une philosophie de l'histoire où l'homme est le Prométhée de lui-même, se libérant peu à peu de toutes ses entraves. On conçoit la part d'illusion d'une telle ambition mais on imagine aisément quelle sorte de professeur devait être Michelet et, comme il est plus difficile aujourd'hui de passionner les élèves avec des statistiques comparant les économies de l'Europe et des Etats-Unis.

Dans l'enseignement de l'histoire aujourd'hui, tout n'est pas cependant négatif et je voudrais seulement faire ici deux remarques, l'une qui concerne l'esprit même dans lequel est enseigné l'histoire et qui permet d'échapper à l'exigence nationaliste d'autrefois qui voyait dans l'histoire un puissant moyen, au risque de quelques trahisons de l'objectivité, d'attacher l'élève à son pays et de développer son patriotisme ; ainsi Michelet au XIXème siècle: la grandeur de la France, ses héros, ses grands hommes, ses victoires, son empire. C'est à cette forme de l'histoire que songe Valéry, lorsqu'il écrit dans ses *Regards sur le monde actuel*:

> *L'Histoire est le produit le plus dangereux que la chimie de l'intellect ait élaboré. Ses propriétés sont bien connues. Il fait rêver, il enivre les peuples, leur engendre de faux souvenirs, exagère leurs réflexes, entretient leurs vieilles plaies, les tourmente dans leur repos, les conduit au délire des grandeurs ou à celui de la persécution, et rend les nations amères, superbes, insupportables et vaines.*

L'Histoire justifie ce que l'on veut. Elle n'enseigne rigoureusement rien, car elle contient tout, et donne des exemples de tout.

Texte qui prenait un sens particulier si l'on songe à l'époque où il fut écrit, où le nazisme triomphant faisait appel à l'histoire pour justifier les conquêtes qu'il se proposait de faire. Après la deuxième guerre mondiale, on a assisté à un examen de conscience des historiens de tous les pays européens et aussi des auteurs de manuel pour corriger cette image trop complaisante à l'égard de soi-même, pour ne rien dire qui puisse exciter la haine et l'esprit de nostalgie ou de revanche. C'est ainsi que va être publié en 2006 un manuel d'histoire franco-allemand, destiné dans les deux pays aux trois dernières années de lycée. Le caractère scientifique revendiqué par l'historien d'aujourd'hui impose cette utilisation de l'histoire.

Ma deuxième remarque concerne l'histoire immédiate et la nécessité dans laquelle se trouvent les professeurs de présenter à leurs élèves des événements contemporains dont la matérialité entraîne souvent des jugements contradictoires. Déjà, il y a une trentaine d'années, le stalinisme pouvait susciter des réactions vives de certains élèves dont les parents admiraient encore Staline considéré comme le petit père des peuples, et le vainqueur du fascisme qui méritait considération et respect: alors que pour d'autres, les camps de concentration, le goulag, condamnaient son régime au tribunal de l'histoire.

Aujourd'hui en France, lors même qu'on envisage – et cela me paraît une utile réforme – de faire entrer dans l'enseignement de l'histoire des domaines qui en étaient jusque là exclus comme l'histoire des religions, il faut s'attendre à des débats, voire à des violences dans certains cas. La laïcité à la française est souvent mal comprise et difficile à tenir. L'objectivité la plus fortement affirmée peut toujours être soupçonnée de partialité dans la mesure où ce dont il est question dans l'histoire, c'est toujours de l'homme. Dans une conférence qu'il fit autrefois et qu'il a repris dans son livre: *Histoire et vérité* (1955) sur l'objectivité et la subjectivité en histoire, Ricœur disait:

Nous attendons de l'histoire qu'elle soit une histoire des hommes et que cette histoire des hommes aide le lecteur instruit par l'histoire des historiens, à édifier une subjectivité de haut rang, la subjectivité non seulement de moi-même, mais de l'homme. Mais cet intérêt, cette attente d'un passage, par l'histoire, de moi à l'homme n'est plus exactement épistémologique, mais proprement philosophique car c'est bien une subjectivité ou réflexion que nous attendons de la lecture, de la méditation des œuvres d'historiens: cet intérêt ne concerne déjà plus l'historien qui écrit l'histoire mais le lecteur, singulièrement le lecteur philosophe...

Henri-Irénée Marrou dans son livre *De la conscience historique*, publié comme celui de Ricœur aux éditions du Seuil en 1954, ne dit pas autre chose:

A l'histoire, écrit-il, il ne faut pas demander plus, ni autre chose, que ce quelle peut fournir. Pas plus qu'elle ne décharge le philosophe de la responsabilité de formuler le jugement de vérité, elle ne prétendra par exemple dicter à l'homme d'action, en vertu des précédents ou des analogies qu'elle lui fait connaître, une décision d'ordre politique. L'histoire ne peut assumer dans la culture humaine, dans la vie le rôle d'un principe animateur ; son vrai rôle, infiniment plus humble, mais à son niveau réel et bien précieux, est de fournir à la conscience de l'homme qui sent, qui pense, qui agit une abondance de matériaux sur lesquels exercer son jugement et sa volonté ; sa fécondité réside dans cette extension pratiquement indéfinie qu'elle réalise de notre expérience, de notre connaissance de l'homme. C'est là sa grandeur, son "utilité".

C'est cette idée de l'histoire, maîtresse de vie, chère aux Anciens, qu'il faudrait restaurer dans l'enseignement de l'histoire.

Il me paraît donc très important que le professeur d'histoire présente toujours l'histoire qu'il enseigne comme une reconstruction faite par les historiens, selon des perspectives et des méthodes qui peuvent différer mais qui visent à une certaine objectivité. Il doit rappeler qu'entre ce qui s'est vraiment passé et qui ne peut jamais être saisi dans sa totalité par l'historien et le récit qu'il en fait ou l'analyse qu'il en propose, il y a une distance à laquelle il faut rendre l'élève sensible, non pas pour cultiver en lui le scepticisme, mais pour l'aider à développer son propre jugement, sa propre réflexion.

En histoire, comme d'ailleurs en philosophie, le danger est celui du dogmatisme alors qu'il faut au contraire développer l'esprit critique, la mise en question de la première hypothèse qui peut paraître plausible. Si l'on évoque par exemple l'attentat meurtrier de Madrid du jeudi 11 mars, on peut considérer, dans un premier temps, qu'un passé récent semblait donner des indices probants selon lesquels l'ETA pouvait en être l'auteur, mais, très vite, d'autres indices ont paru désigner la piste islamiste. Toutefois, ancré dans sa première interprétation qui paraissait lui être la plus favorable, le gouvernement, bien à tort, a continué, de bonne ou de mauvaise foi, à privilégier la piste de l'ETA, ce qui a en partie expliqué qu'il ait perdu les élections, accusé qu'il fut de flagrant délit de désinformation. Un exemple comme celui-là, correctement interprété, permet au professeur de montrer aux élèves comment l'objectivité en histoire a un caractère spécifique. Elle se construit peu à peu à partir de traces ou d'indices de clarté. Mais le doute et le soupçon sont des attitudes qui aident l'historien à établir une vérité historique, à l'opposé de la présomption et de la précipitation dénoncées par Descartes.

Sans être professeur d'histoire, mais passionné d'histoire et attentif aux problèmes actuels de son enseignement, il me paraît qu'il devrait être possible de combiner trois choses sans en sacrifier aucune: 1 – un cadre chronologique solide pour permettre aux élèves de situer les événements dans leur époque et ici le recours à l'histoire événementielle paraît incontournable. 2 – des synthèses périodiques dans l'esprit des Annales et de l'histoire longue en faisant comprendre le lien avec le présent. 3 – l'histoire vivante, récits, documents à interpréter qui donnent le goût de l'histoire, le goût de l'interrogation, le goût de la recherche, à partir d'un doute premier qui appelle examen et vérification des preuves avant d'avancer des hypothèses provisoires. Sous ces conditions, l'enseignement de l'histoire demeure d'une très grande utilité, parce qu'elle réunit analyses abstraites et situations existentielles, parce qu'elle oblige à prendre en considération le temps, non pas le temps des astres, mais le temps des hommes avec ses lenteurs et ses accélérations, parce qu'elle donne un nombre infini d'exemples qui ne se répètent jamais, même si certaines analogies paraissent s'imposer d'une époque à l'autre; l'histoire, me semble-t-il, est un merveilleux outil de formation du futur philosophe et il est intéressant de remarquer qu'en Italie, par exemple, son enseignement est lié à celui de la philosophie. Ce qui nous conduirait à nous interroger sur l'histoire de la philosophie et son lien avec l'histoire générale, mais ce serait un autre sujet.

What Kind of History Shall We Teach?

Evandro Agazzi

The matter we usually teach and learn under the general label "history" in schools and universities consists almost entirely of more or less detailed presentations of political, diplomatic and military events, of chronologically ordered lists of kings, emperors, dynasties, wars, battles, treatises, revolutions and the like. As a consequence the "makers" of history are considered to be sovereigns, generals, great prime ministers, exceptionally gifted diplomats, political leaders. Much more seldom are presented religious movements or leaders, and only to the extent that they have produced military or politically relevant consequences (more or less in the same "deterministic" way as certain economic phenomena). Mention of literature, arts, philosophy, and even of science and technology is only occasional, marginal and this because it is tacitly understood that such domains are also treated from an historical point of view, but in their *specialized* histories (history of literature, of music, of philosophy, of science, and so on). The obvious presupposition of this attitude is that *general history* is essentially the political-military one, but this presupposition is patently unaware that this alleged "general" history is indeed *partial*.

The thesis I want to advocate in this paper is that *general history* must be broader in scope, not so much in the *professional* work of the (general) historians who can continue to cultivate it according to the standards of a long tradition that has implicitly circumscribed its principal sectors, but as far as its *teaching* is concerned, and shall try to justify my claim by pointing out that the issue is not that of "adding new contents" to the matter of the textbooks of history, but to consider the teaching of history under a *different perspective*,

History as Memory

Such a perspective results from a consideration of the most significant *aim and sense* of knowing history. These cannot be equated with the most general *motivation* that can induce people to be "interested" in history, a motivation that we could perhaps indicate as the "curiosity" about the past and that is perfectly legitimate but, as such, cannot reveal the real aim and sense of historical investigation and teaching.

A first indication of this aim and sense is contained in the classical definition of history as *memoria rerum*, that is, as an effort of preservation of the "memory" of things and facts produced by humans. Already at the very beginning of his *History*, Herodotus (the "father of history") explicitly declares that his aim is to avoid that "the beautiful and admirable deeds accomplished by the Greeks and the aliens" should become obscure and forgotten because of time. In this declaration we find that history is conceived as a kind of homage that humankind pays to herself, through the preservation and appreciation of the noble and remarkable achievements that humans (independently of their belonging to any particular country) have attained and keep a supra-temporal value and significance that can be granted by the only means we have at our disposal with respect to what has gone away in time, that is, *memory*. But memory is much more than a simple catalogue of facts. According to a sense that had already been introduced by Saint Agustin, memory has a genuine ontological status, being in a way the *presence* of the past. In this sense we can say that any human being is memory, meaning by this that anyone is what he/she is as the holistic result of all his/her past existential situations and experiences, from the fact of being born in a given place, within a given culture and family, to the fact of having received a given education, of having adhered to a certain religion, of having shared certain moral values and rules, of having met certain persons, taken certain decisions, cultivated certain professional or non professional interests, and so on. This view expresses a correct understanding of the *genetic* constitution of any individual personality, that is, an understanding that takes into account not only its *internal development* (as does, for instance, the "genetic psychology"), but also the contribution of the external circumstances to the concrete constitution of this personality. This view is by no means *deterministic*, but simply expresses the awareness that human freedom of action always manifests itself in the framework of certain *conditions* (and this is different from saying that what we are is the result of the "environment" in which we have existed). We could summarize the content of these remarks by saying that human beings, though sharing a common *nature*, differ from one another because of their respective *histories* (considering these as the conjunction of their individual constitution and their existential vicissitudes). As a consequence, knowledge of her particular history is an indispensable condition for the *understanding* of an individual person.

The above can be repeated in a strict analogical sense about human communities of different size and kind, as well as about the contents and aspects of human civilization. For example, there is a sense according to which a family *is* the present of its past, such that its "individual" characteristics preserve something like an "imprinting" of its history that is often only implicit and not conscious, but whose knowledge can strongly contribute to the "sense of identity" of the family itself. This is why the cult of the ancestors is present in all cultures. This is why those families that wanted to be considered *distinguished* in comparison with the rest of their community normally attributed great importance to the explicit reconstruction of their past history, of their genealogical tree, and also to the material preservation of objects and souvenirs of their past members. A similar discourse can be easily extended to small political communities, such as the ancient Greek *poleis* or the "free" cities of the European Middle ages and Renaissance, but also (under more elaborated conditions) to the "nations" of modern history. Indeed a "community of history and destiny" is the characteristic usually considered as the basis for the constitution of a *national identity* (that has been often compatible with differences of religion, language and race within the same nation).

The Present of the Past

As we have said, not only human communities, but also fundamental domains of human culture present the feature of being in some way the present of their past. Let us consider, for example, religions. It would certainly be inadequate to consider *present* Christianity simply as the religion that considers Jesus Christ as the Son of God and accepts his teaching. This can be considered at best the "core" of Christianity, but many factors of cultural, philosophical, social, political nature have accompanied and shaped the *history* of Christianity, also in its very theological and institutional aspects, such that only a consideration of this history can allow one to understand *the reasons* of the present state of this religion, its differentiated forms of institutional organization, its doctrinal controversies, its way of interacting with the rest of human institutions, that amounts to a better understanding of this religion as it actually is at present.

Examples of a different kind are those of special sectors of human culture, such as philosophy, music, literature, science, whose historical nature appears not only from their being embedded in particular socio-cultural environments (as is underscored with special emphasis nowadays), but also from the fact that their present state is to a considerable extent the "result" of their *internal history*. This can be particularly evident in the case of literature, where internal subdivisions, articulations and differences are not simply due to the different languages in which the literary works are written, but much more to the special historical tradition that characterizes the works belonging to a given linguistic area, whose authors have been and still are inspired by their direct acquaintance with certain masterpieces, models, styles, topics of their tradition. The same can be repeated for philosophy, in which it is true that – in a given epoch – thinkers have treated problems that were particularly debated at that time but, nevertheless, they have usually formed their thinking by reading and meditating the works of other philosophers (and, quite often, with special profit from the reading of philosophers belonging to a remote past).

What we have said indicates that only superficially can we believe that, in order to do a "good work" in a given field, what we really need is simply a good command of the *present* state of this field (i.e. practice of its current methods, knowledge of its up-to-date results, familiarity with the most recent specialized literature, etc.). Indeed, an historical knowledge of its past development can often be of real use, especially in the humanities. But, even in the case of the sciences, the simple fact of necessarily needing to acquire an adequate specific *preparation*, for instance in the form of the acquisition of a body of background knowledge contained in textbooks, already means that, in order to do our "present" work, we rely on the historical heritage of the work done by past scientists and preserved in a seemingly a-historical way in our textbooks or journal articles. The fact that most scientists are unaware of this historical dependence of their investigation and can produce, nevertheless, a "technically" unobjectionable work does not imply that a "qualitatively" better work would not be that in which also a deeper *understanding* were produced by an historical consciousness of the state of the discipline.

The Historical Determinateness of Cultural Domains

The moral of the above remarks is that an historical reflection and presentation is highly recommendable in all domains of human culture, and this not only stresses the value of the "specialized histories" that exist concerning every such domain, but indicates at the same time that such histories cannot be reduced simply to an "internal" chronological reconstruction of the deeds, facts, results, works of a given field, since consideration of the "external" cultural environment can be equally significant.

This conclusion, however, entails in turn another one. The historical determinateness of any cultural domain does not consist only in the fact that this domain has *received* influences and various *inputs* from its cultural environment, it also consists in the fact that several *outputs* have been sent from this domain into its environment. In other words, the historical relation we must consider is that of a *feedback-loop* according to which all domains of human culture interact with their environment and, via this interaction, interact more or less directly and significantly, with all the other domains. Recognizing this is tantamount to admit that every cultural domain is at the same time *history-made* and *history-maker*, that it is to a certain extent a *product* of history and a *producer* of history. This awareness, that concerns, so to speak, the ontology of history (that is, history as the set of *res gestae*, of human deeds and actions) must have its counterpart in the epistemology of history, that is, in *historiography* or the description and interpretation of human actions and deeds. This reconstruction cannot obviously take into account the almost infinite totality of human events. A selection of the most *significant* is indispensable, and the real problem consists in the determination of the criteria of significance we must adopt when our purpose is that of reconstructing the *global* features of human history in the course of time.

The Contribution of History for Understanding the Present

A suggestion regarding this problem comes from the idea presented above, according to which we are our history, in the sense that we are the present of our past. This implies that, in order to adequately understand "what we are" now, we have to know our past, we have to know how we have come to be what we are now. In the notion of "what we are now" (understood in a collective and not in an individual sense) we include, for instance, the present political organization of our country, the forms of its economy, its legal regulations, its most accepted customs, its religious beliefs, its ideological trends, its artistic expressions, its "way of life". It should be obvious that, in order to understand these dimensions of our present, a consideration limited to the great political and military events of the twentieth century (such as the two world wars, the Russian revolution, the rise and fall of fascism, nazism and communism) would not be sufficient. Quite the contrary, it is more than probable that a better understanding of such "great" historical events would be attained through the consideration of certain "ideas", expectations, worldviews, value-choices, prejudices that formed the "mentality" of people and were at the root of certain individual and collective decisions whose palpable effects were those great events. Therefore, a serious historiography that would help us understand our recent history should contain much more information and reconstruction regarding these neglected aspects of our real cultural life.

The same, however, is true (and even more) regarding past history, and for two different reasons. First of all, it is clear that, if we can believe that the historical reality of ancient Greece (for example) has still a significance for us, for understanding "what we are", this is not because the Greeks were able to defeat the Persians at Marathon, or because Pericles ruled Athens in the most glorious period of its history, but rather because the poetry of Homer, the tragedies of Eskilos, Sophocles and Euripides, the masterpieces of Greek sculpture and architecture, the doctrines of Plato and Aristotle, and so on, have remained as an heritage of what we still consider as *our* civilization, such that we still approach and admire them as if they were part and parcel of our culture. The second reason is that, even if we are only interested in knowing and understanding what ancient Greece "really was", it is much more informative to know what the great achievements of the Greeks in the field of art, science, literature, philosophy have been, what was their political organization, what their form of democracy, what their daily way of life, rather than knowing a list of battles, treatises, and the names of a few political leaders. Unfortunately the textbooks we use at schools for teaching history are still far from being redacted according to this spirit. They perpetuate a tradition of historiography that limits the attention to the military and political events. What we need are textbooks in which history be much more presented as a complex network of cultural dimensions, in which literature, philosophy, science, arts, religion find a proper place, along with a reconstruction of the concrete forms of social life and customs. The presence of these contents would amply compensate the reduction of the space devoted to the boring lists of battles, wars, treatises, kings and diplomats that often make of the study of history an exercise of memory and a show of erudition.

History and Intercultural Understanding

There is a last and perhaps more important reason for promoting this kind of *culturally oriented* teaching of history. One of the most urgent problems of our time, a problem that will become even more urgent in the near future, is that of the *mutual understanding of different cultures*. It is not enough, in order to attain this understanding, to promote the spirit of *tolerance*. This is very important, but is limited to an intellectual-moral attitude, whereas what we need is that tolerance be a consequence of the understanding of the *reasons* of the difference between ourselves and the alien. Most of these reasons cannot be captured by a logical or sociological analysis, but are simply given by the fact that the alien is "what he is" because has a *different history*. Knowledge of this history is therefore one of the best means for promoting mutual understanding, for seeing why certain attitudes or customs are not expression of bad will, hostility, arrogance, intolerance, but only of what is "normal" within another cultural heritage. Understanding does not necessarily entail adhesion or acceptance, but certainly produces a more friendly attitude, to the extent that it is the opposite of *violence*, and this should already stress its absolute primacy. The major need of the present world is certainly *peace*, and this cannot be imposed through force. Peace can only be the result of tolerance and understanding, and since understanding is greatly helped by an appropriate knowledge of history, we must promote a teaching of such a kind of history if we want to serve the ideal of peace through education.

Aesthetic Immersion and Education

Basilio Rojo Ruiz

Introduction

There is no doubt that art testifies to each historic period; history, then, is linked to art. Through art we penetrate what Miguel de Unamuno calls *Intrahistory*: what moves concrete actions in space and time, which we classify in terms of geography and dates. Art shows us the political, psychological, economic and sociological ... sides of the thinking of an era, but even more so, when it reaches deep levels, it reveals basic structures of human nature and the universe. This is where the aesthetic approach becomes linked with history and philosophy, revealing knowledge that, in a certain way, points out paths of order and growth and the importance of history-art in education.

Facing our current world problems and the absence of a guiding light, knowledge appears again as a possible means of improvement: "What happens is that we do not have enough certain knowledge to attempt the construction of a *good world*. We do not possess the knowledge to be able to teach *individuals* to love each other, at least not with much confidence".[1] The way of reason plays, no doubt, an important role, but the side of sentiment in a historical-artistic-philosophical-pedagogic approach may also give us some valuable ingredients.

In the next section a line of thought will be pursued from an artistic-historical perspective, which will lead to structural orders in a process of aesthetic immersion.

Immersion

In our initial process of sensitive perception we are in the categories of present time and space, paying attention to the peculiarity that is in front of us. In this

---

1 Maslow, Abraham; *El hombre autorrealizado*, Kairos, Barcelona, 1968, p. 14.

initial phase we need to pay careful attention to the details with a work of *fruition and atemperancy* (Zubiri), which considers the particular way of being as a concession to their own letting be (Zubiri). The constellation aspect of the different elements thus plays its role and begins to emerge from a supraphysical level of time expansion. Gadamer points this out with the following comments: "What emerges is something that we have not seen before. Even when it is a portrait, when you know the person that is portrayed and you think that the picture resembles him, it is like you have never seen him before. Up to that point it *is* him. One has been introduced by the seeing, so to speak, and the more one does that, the more there is that emerges".[2]

We are then introduced to elements of mental affection that carry the personal and communitary history of a group of humans and put us into the emotions and vital experiences that we share. Thus, the mere objective side is overcome in a "between" reality (Buber) and at the same time the artistic work *educates* us to see it and to be conscious of its suprasensitive reality. There is no doubt that this process begins to awaken stirrings in the heart (Pascal) and the linking relation.

The opinion of Maslow is worth noting. In an explanation of what he calls *knowledge of the being* vs. *ordinary knowledge* he writes, "The knowledge of the being seems to enrich perception. The repeated fascinating experience of the face that we love or the picture that we admire, makes us enjoy it more and allows us to see more and more aspects of it in different ways. We can call it intra-objective richness".[3]

I mentioned before that the constriction of space and present time is overcome by what is termed in modern psychology transpersonal experiences; "Transpersonal experiences ... involve primarily transcendence of the usual spatial and temporal barriers".[4]

Here, an idea of the human being and reality that exceeds mere materialism must be introduced. According to old and modern schools of psychology, the human being is *soma, psique and pneuma*. At the level of emotive affections and history, psychology is considered social science and we would be at the level of the psyche. Obviously, an analysis of art carried out strictly on the level of quantity would be short. According to Gadamer, "The work of art is not a

---

2   Gadamer, Hans-Georg; *Estética y hermenéutica*, Tecnos, Madrid, 2001, p. 299.

3   Maslow, o.c. p. 116.

4   Grof, Stanislav; *The Psychology of the Future.* 2000, p. 57.

product that is ready once we have done the job. It is not an object that you measure with some established pattern. A real and effective work of art does not lend itself to measurement, not even for the number of bits. It is not just a bunch of information, like a newspaper, a travel chronicle or a novel. Nothing that you can manipulate in that way in a picture is what distinguishes it as art".[5]

This immersion process that starts at the sensitive body level moves on to a psychological level and finally reaches a spiritual level in a series of continuous connections, in which the levels are only a methodological distinction to facilitate comprehension and analysis. "But, as it has always been sustained by those who espouse the perennial philosophy that humans are comprised of not only body and psyche but also spirit ... body is always temporary, spirit is always eternal, and psyche is an amphibious creature, fated by the laws of human existence to join up to certain point with his body, but capable, if he wants, to experience his spirit and to identify with him ... the spirit will always continue as it is eternal, but the human being is constituted in such a way that his psyche cannot always be identified with the spirit. In the statement "Now I am eternal, now I am temporal" the subject is psyche, who moves from time to eternity when it identifies with the spirit and returns from eternity to time, by will or unwilled necessity, when it wants to identify with the body and is obligated to do so," states Aldous Huxley in an attempt to explain this network of our being.[6]

When this process of aesthetic-historical immersion goes on in an expanded temporality we end up at the level of the spirit and temporality reaches infinitum. Here we have the concept of what is "classic", in other words, what touches deep structures or knowledge of being.

It seems that at the level mentioned above, one accedes not with reason alone, but also with sentiment as a superior faculty at a spiritual level and its affiliation with being; such affiliation will be called value - value developed as a question that acts in a historical and aesthetic approach.

The development of being in terms of sentiment results in the peak experiences (Maslow) that convalidate existence.

About the Peak

Beginning with the sensitive approach, the sensitive intelligence (Zubiri) or the intelligent sense follows a path in a parallel way: reason and sentiment. The

---

5   Gadamer, o.c. p. 298.

6   Huxley, Adolf; *La filosofía perenne*, 1944, p. 232.

aesthetic analysis goes beyond the peculiarities of the work and interrelates the elements in a constellated potentiation driving language concepts and a temperance to details. Strictly speaking, we cannot say that they are parallel approaches, but they are paths in close communication like capillaceous vases with a constant interrelationship.

Next, we come to the field of emotions and mental affections. The mere objective character of a work of art being thrown in front of me also starts to have a *subjectal* character (involving the subject) that refers to my point of living and, certainly, to my transpersonal happening: "This term means literally < reaching beyond the personal> or <transcending the personal>. The experiences that originate at this level involve transcendence of our usual boundaries (our body and ego)".[7] The work of art then starts *to happen*. "... in a work of art it happens that it only has its being when it is executed"[8] and, one may add (I think without betraying Gadamer), in reviving the creative process of the dynamic spectator. Then it happens that a work of art gradually exceeds its mere vicarious character of representation or historical testimony to reach by degrees ontological levels: "What illustrates this model is the ontological impossibility of separating the picture from what *is represented*".[9]

Our will to follow intellectual analysis or rational plans makes place at the work of sentiment, and thus "intelligence and will create distance and drive, generally, their activity aside. They have always in front of them an object. Sentiment, on the other hand, is the perfect way of being, that is, spirit and subjectivity. The target that it points at is the being, if it slows in its moving surface or descends to the immutable depths: the being and the <finding> of the being in itself"[10]

In the moments described above, the limit of the rational process and the cause-effect relation in time are found: "When a work of art plays its fascination, all opinions and everything opinionated disappear".[11] "Incommunicability is the note that shares physical and spiritual sentiments. The difference that separates them, anyway, is enormous. The first ones, as they are more pure physically, suffer from forgetfulness, and soon fraternize with nothingness.

7   Grof, o.c. p. 56.

8   Gadamer, o.c. p. 302.

9   Gadamer, Hans-Georg; *Verdad y Método I*, Sígueme, Salamanca, 1999, p. 188.

10   Haecker, Theodor; *Metafísica del sentimiento*, Rialp, Madrid, 1959, p. 72.

11   Gadamer, Hans-Georg; *Estética y hermenéutica* , Tecnos, Barcelona, 2001, p. 298.

The second ones, on the contrary, being more spiritual, resist the injury of forgetfulness, because they are protected with a shell of eternity".[12] That is what Maslow calls *peak experiences* (mentioned above), in which intentionality is no longer sustains itself and convalidates existence: "Peak experience is felt as a self-validating and self-justified moment that has in itself its own intrinsic value".[13] In other words, to try in time to grasp eternity. It does not mean that it is easy or that it exempts us from the passivity of the analytical cruise and the sentiment keel: "What a strange thing! Of the different ways of being human, what has more difficult access is sentiment ", exclaims Haecker.[14] Nevertheless, nothing is denied: "Everything may be a term of an aesthetic sentiment. It is enough that instead of considering the qualities that it really has, I handle the fruition and complacence in it as being reality. It is, from my own point of view, the essence of the aesthetic phenomena" says the master Zubiri.[15]

---

12 Haecker, o.c. p. 89

13 Maslow, o.c. p. 119.

14 Haecker, o.c. p. 72.

15 Zubiri, X.; *Sobre el sentimiento y la volición*, Alianza, Madrid, 1992, p. 346.

The Use of History[1]

William Sweet

Critical discussion in and about history is lively today, but – at least at first look – there seems to be little agreement. Not only is there no consensus in this discussion, but it is far from settled what questions may be asked.

Those who are interested in what history is, what its purpose (if any) might be, what historians (claim they) do, and what it is to *write* history, find themselves confronted with cultural and literary analyses of history (for example, of history as literature or as a quasi-literary product); with debates of whether histories are simply chronicles or whether they are narratives with underlying principles and with goals; and with 'internal' discussions among historiographers about what is involved – and whether anything *need* be involved – in the practice of writing history.

For many, of course, history is not *just* such an interest; it is important to life – and it is particularly significant at a time when the conventions and norms of religion and science no longer hold firm. People want to know who they are and where they come from, and so they turn to history – to family or local history, to genealogies and chronicles, but also to stories and accounts of historical figures, of nations and civilisations, and even histories of the world. But here, too, little appears settled, for we have institutional histories, 'people's histories,' academic histories – and we are told that all histories are ideological, each promising to tell things 'as they were' and yet frequently leaving out more than they include. So the underlying assumptions involved in the writing of history concern not only scholars, but anyone struck by the uncertainty that exists at the beginning of the 21st century.

---

1   An earlier version of this essay was presented at the Institut for Pædagogisk Filosofi - Danmarks Pædagogiske Universitet, København, Denmark, on March 25, 2004. As well, I draw on material that will appear in the Introduction to my book *The Philosophy of History: a re-examination* (Aldershot: Ashgate Publishers, 2004).

I.

If we look at history – academic history – as it is engaged in today, we see that many historians find themselves confronted with challenges concerning the presuppositions of history. So, while some may go no further than to admit that there is a distinction between history as 'event' or a series of events, and history as a discipline, historians and historiographers (and philosophers as well) raise the issue of what history is – whether it is a science, a social science, an art, a "corpus of ascertained facts",[2] a social practice (that inevitably reflects ideologies and models of gender), or a 'conceptual structure' that makes no claim to be 'about' people or events. Some historians and philosophers go further, raising such questions as whether there are any *facts* or only *judgements* – whether one can ever *know* the past and, if so, how one could attain it. Others raise the points that, even if the past can be known, one cannot conclude anything from this knowledge – and that historical understanding or explanation is not even possible.

As historians (and philosophers) today consider and reconsider questions central to what history is and what it is about, the answers they give certainly divide them. But it seems that the source of this division does not lie in the interpretation of data, but in how one answers the more basic questions of the possibility and status of historical knowledge. In current debates, then, what one takes history to be, what it is to do history, and so on, are influenced by what is generally called 'historicism.'

'Historicism' is an ambiguous – or at least vague – term. It appears in the movement called the 'New Historicism' that has been influential in literary and cultural studies.[3] The term has also been used in (what is for an Anglo-American audience) a somewhat idiosyncratic sense by Karl Popper, where it is equated with a kind of grand narrative determinism – that, "through studying the history of society, we can detect patterns and recurrences which will enable us to predict the future"[4] – which, to Popper, not only denies human freedom but suggests that there may be some way in which to engage in 'social engineering' to create the perfect society. And the term refers as well to a movement rooted in 19th- century German scholarship in religion, philosophy, and history, concerned with the basic questions of how knowledge – and particularly judgements

---

2   Carr, 1961, p. 6 (see the bibliography at the end of the paper).

3   Cf. Michaels, 1987; Greenblatt, 1988; Veeser, 1989.

4   Popper, 1957.

of value about what is 'known' – are possible when we recognise that the conditions under which we know are in flux, that human knowledge is limited, and that what we know has an essentially subjective character which seems to preclude absolute objectivity and the possibility of making definitive judgements.[5]

Historicism in its most widespread and popular sense today is close to this third description. It holds that "human phenomena cannot be understood in isolation from their historical development and from their significance to the particular historical period in which they existed"[6] – that "the nature of any phenomenon can only be adequately comprehended by considering its place within a process of historical development"[7] – and it emphasises the particularity (and possibly incommensurability) of past events compared with present events. Because of this, it is often equated with a kind of historical relativism. Historicists reject the claim that there can be "a purely ahistorical perspective on human affairs"[8] and hold that there can be no understanding events or the actions of agents as events or actions of a certain type; events have meaning and significance only within a particular context. *Everything* is subject to "interpretation." Historicists also suggest that, at best, the only legitimate judgements (e.g., value judgements) we can make about these events are those we could have made *at the time* (– so that, by extension, we have relativism).

Historicism, then, challenges not only the possibility of historical understanding, but the giving of 'historical explanations,' and it would also appear to challenge the possibility of history itself as being anything other than "something spun out of the human brain".[9]

Historicism has become entrenched within our intellectual culture; at least, one finds a widespread acceptance of many of its underlying principles. Some scholars have become so convinced of the relativity of claims of knowledge and meaning, that they are reluctant to claim that we can say anything true about the past. Indeed, they question whether 'truth' is a proper historical concern. This has contributed to the development of a post-modern approach to history and to a philosophy of history which rejects any attempt to present the past "as

---

5   Cf. Iggers, 1995; Megill, 1997; Hoover, 1992.
6   Martin, 1991, p. 103.
7   Gardiner, 1995.
8   Kemerling, 2003.
9   Carr, 1961, p. 30.

it really was",[10] any claim that there are any principles or rules or models of history, and any attempt to see history as a science – particularly an explanatory science. This approach is also resolutely anti-foundationalist.

The postmodern 'solution' or response, then, has been to focus on issues other than knowledge, objectivity, and meaning, and to see history as a construct – as a narrative that does not have a particular logic or character to it[11] – and not to be concerned with seeking to explain events.[12] Some have chosen to discuss the character of historical writing as literature, or in relation to gender or politics or ideology.[13] Others, having similar views, have become more open to seeing even historical 'fiction' as a source of knowledge and understanding.

There are, of course, those who resist this. There seems to be something wrong in just giving up on history, or saying that it has no use. Some scholars have suggested that the post-modern turn, exemplified by its fundamental historicism, "is self destructive and can lead to solipsism".[14] Others have tried to argue that reality exercises a constraint on theory, and that the objections of the post-modern sceptic just are not borne out.[15] Some argue that, no matter how persuasive – or how difficult to refute – it is, this post-modern approach to history is "methodologically irrelevant" to historians, so that "hardly anyone... *acts as if* he or she" believes it in practice.[16] Still others acknowledge the legitimacy of the issues raised by historicism about the "historical sensitivity" of knowledge claims or the relativity of knowledge, but seek to avoid post-modern or relativistic conclusions (whatever this might mean); this is a strategy suggested by Hilary Putnam's 1981 *Reason, Truth, and History* and also acknowledged, at least in part, by E. H. Carr.[17] There are those who return to such philosophers as R.G. Collingwood, whose recognition of the contextual character of knowledge nevertheless claims to allow room for genuine historical understanding. And there are other responses besides.

Nevertheless, historicism presents us with a number of challenges. Is history *passé* – a 'thing of the past'? Why should anyone seek to understand history?

---

10 Ranke in Carr, 1961, p. 5.

11 Ricœur, 1983-85.

12 Cf. the essays in *A New Philosophy of History*, Ankersmit and Kelner, eds., 1995.

13 Smith, 1998.

14 Hoover, 1992, p. 355.

15 Cf. Appleby, Hunt, and Jacob, 1994.

16 Martin, 1995, p. 327.

17 Carr, 1961.

Can we ever speak of objectivity in history? To see better the present debates in history, and to help in answering or responding to these three challenges, it may be useful to review briefly how matters got to where they are today. After all, the present debates about history and historicism, like all events, are 'historical'; they are products of what has come before.

II.

History – by which I mean the activity or discipline of history – is old. The "Father of History" in the west is commonly held to be Herodotus (c 490-425 BCE), and it is perhaps no surprise that he is also sometimes referred to as the "Father of Lies." It was his *History*, written at the time of the Peloponnesian War that sought to do more than chronicle or relate a series of events; its aim was to interpret events, explain them, and draw a lesson from them.

But a key moment in the discussion of history occurred more than 2,000 years later, in the late 19th- and early 20th- centuries. Following on 18th- century models of history reflected in the work of scholars like Edward Gibbon and William Robertson, the 19th- and early 20th- centuries were still a period of detailed, comprehensive historical accounts, and included attempts to describe the course of events, not just in a nation or an empire, but in the world as a whole. In the Anglo-American world, for example, Robert Labberton (1812-1898), Edward Augustus Freeman (1823-1892), Thomas Keightley (1789-1872), and H. G. Wells (1866-1946)[18] continued to provide grand historical accounts. (On the continent, Oswald Spengler (1880-1936) may be included as well.[19]) Here we see instances of historians writing works that were not mere chronicles, and which explicitly sought to interpret events, to put them into a 'meaningful' order, and to suggest some kind of direction in them. A model of such endeavours – and perhaps the greatest project in history in the 20th century – was that of Arnold Toynbee (1889-1975). In his magisterial twelve volume *A Study of History* (1934-61), Toynbee produced a comparative study of 26 civilizations, analyzing their development, and discerning not only a pattern, but a "lesson." Focussing on civilisations rather than nations or empires, Toynbee allowed that there can be a development in history – that history is not cyclical – but neither is it necessarily a straight line of progress from the past to the future.

---

18 See Wells, 1920.

19 See Spengler, 1939

Yet the 19th- and early 20th- centuries were, in many respects, also a watershed in the writing of history. From the mid-19th century, an increasing number of scholars – particularly philosophers – argued that undertaking large, narrative histories was highly problematic. The stirrings of this concern, first found in the historical and literary criticism of Biblical texts in the early to mid-19th century (e.g., in Friedrich Schleiermacher [1768-1834]), and inspired by the work of J.G. Herder and G.W.F. Hegel, came to have an influence in dealing not just with texts, but with any talk about events in a historical past.

These 'stirrings' did not influence just 19th-century German thought; it had an impact far beyond its borders. Critical reflection on history was undertaken by many of the leading Anglo-American philosophers and, while this interest may not have been pervasive, it was acute. F. H. Bradley (1846-1924) raised a number of fundamental questions in his *Presuppositions of Critical History* (1874). Influenced by the German Biblical scholarship and criticism, Bradley argued that (historical) testimony does not stand as a fact on its own, but must be evaluated from the perspective of the historian. History, then, must be "critical" – it cannot pretend just to be a "copy" of what happened in the past. The historian must select, and must also be aware of the presuppositions of the approach she or he brings to historical enquiry. For Bradley, the historian's judgement is the basis of history; "The historian ... is the real criterion".[20] Bradley does not deny that there are facts; he simply rejects the view that these facts exist independently of the historian and are there for scholars just to collect. While Bradley's position is not (narrowly) historicist, it recognises the inseparability of (value) judgement from event and the importance of understanding historical events within their contexts. Bradley's view, R.G. Collingwood later wrote, was a "Copernican revolution in the theory of historical knowledge".[21]

Bradley's colleague, Bernard Bosanquet (1848-1923) has seemed to many to take an even more cautious and sceptical view of history. When confronted with "mechanistic" accounts of history or accounts that emphasized the fundamental role of "great individuals," Bosanquet was struck by their "fragmentary" and dead quality. He was suspicious of any history *qua* narrative or *qua* chronicle of the contingent events of the past which proposed to give a "total explanation" – and of the historian who sought to provide an explanation of "the

---

20   Bradley, 1968, p. 78.
21   Collingwood, 1946, p. 240.

minds and natures of great men as if he was God's spy".[22] Such history was a "fragmentary diorama of finite life processes unrolling themselves in time," consisting of "mere conjectures," and "incapable of any considerable degree of being or trueness".[23] And thus Bosanquet wrote what some take to be a remark dismissive of the whole practice of history – that history was "the doubtful story of successive events".[24]

Bosanquet did not, however, mean to reject the value of history, or imply that history could not be done, or say that there is no point in studying history, or hold that history is merely "one damn thing after another."[25] (He was, for example, the author of *A History of Aesthetic* (1892) and, like many 'speculative philosophers' of the period, had been schooled in the Greek and Roman classics and had a deep appreciation of history and tradition.) Bosanquet's objection was, however, that history – when it is understood simply as a series of contingent events in a narrative – ignores the general; it is not a concrete universal. And so Bosanquet proposes that, rather than concern ourselves with this kind of history, we should turn to art and religion, both of which bring together the particular and the general. Thus, Bosanquet could write a history of aesthetic – of the development of aesthetic consciousness in and through particular works of art – but not be interested in a history of art.

We see this "critical" approach to history in R.G. Collingwood (1889–1943) as well. Influenced by Benedetto Croce (1866-1953) and by the idealism of his teachers in Oxford, Collingwood is best known for his *The Idea of History* (posthumously published in 1946). Here, Collingwood develops some of the insights of the idealist tradition by arguing that "All history is the history of thought ... and therefore all history, is the re-enactment of past thought in the historian's own mind".[26] An experienced archaeologist and a distinguished historian of Roman Britain, but a philosopher by inclination, training, and profession, Collingwood had the experience to reflect seriously on history.[27] He argued for a closer relation between history and philosophy than was generally held, and insisted that philosophy must understand itself as a historical discipline – that

22 Bosanquet, 1912, p. 79.

23 Bosanquet, 1912, pp. 78-79.

24 Bosanquet, 1912, p. 79.

25 Despite Bosanquet's view of history, he is not an ally of the post moderns, and would not hold that since we can't know the past itself, there is nothing to know and, in consequence, history is simply explained away.

26 Collingwood, 1946, p. 215.

27 See Collingwood, 1923, 1926, 1930, 1936.

philosophy's task was to articulate the "absolute presuppositions" characteristic of an age or way of thinking, and that the truth and falsity of philosophical claims must be understood in their context. Yet Collingwood believed in the possibility of historical knowledge and historical explanation through the method of re-enactment. (i.e., a "re-thinking" of the historical actor's thoughts). Collingwood focused on the historical figure as an agent – on what he or she thinks – rather than on just what the person does. Explanation, then, requires understanding – and hence the appropriateness of re-enactment.

Collingwood has been called a historicist.[28] Perhaps rightly so – though if it is, it must be in a sense that is consistent with Collingwood's rejection of relativism and subjectivism. Indeed, whether Bradley, Bosanquet, or Collingwood actually held strongly historicist views, in the sense in which the term is used today, is doubtful. For while they raise some problems in giving historical explanations, they do not deny that this is possible, nor do they claim that there can be no history or historical truth.

One of the key features of these three thinkers, then, was that they identified some central problems in the practice of history. And so, by the mid-20th century, the study of history was much more critical, and there were serious questions about the nature of that activity itself – and indeed, of what it was to do history.

III.

This 'moment' in the philosophical reflection on history described above – though I am speaking here of a 'moment' that lasted some 50 years – was a 'watershed'. And it evoked two radically different responses in the understanding of history in the Anglo-American world.

The first was a move to formal or critical philosophy of history; this can be said to begin in the middle of the 20th century, about the time of the death of Collingwood in 1943. In a 1952 essay, "Some Neglected Philosophic Problems Regarding History," Maurice Mandelbaum presented what was becoming clear to many who engaged in, or thought about, history, and that was that how one 'did' history was rooted in an issue in the philosophy of history – that there was a distinction between "formal" and "material" approaches to the field.

---

28 Strauss, 1952; Mink, 1987. See, especially, the essays "Collingwood's Historicism: A Dialectic of Process," and "Collingwood's Dialectic of History," pp. 223-45 and 246-85.

"Formal" philosophy of history dealt with "a philosophical concern with the problem of historical knowledge" and attempted "to interpret the historical process itself";[29] "material" philosophy of history sought to provide "some 'meaning' within the whole of man's historical experience".[30] Much the same distinction was made, at the same time, by W.H. Walsh – between critical and speculative philosophies of history – the former dealing with such questions as "the nature and validity of historical knowledge" and the latter being "attempts to give an over-all, 'metaphysical,' interpretation of the course of events".[31]

Speculative philosophy of history, then, was that which hailed back to Augustine, and through Bossuet to Vico, to Hegel and Marx, on to Spengler and Toynbee and up to Karl Löwith and Niebuhr.[32] Here, one found accounts that professed to discern a pattern within history, to find a principle that serves as an axiom of interpretation and explanation, and therefore to give a meaning to the historical process.

Formal or critical philosophy of history, however, did not have such ambitions. It focused on the assumptions underlying history – for example, about the nature and objectivity of historical knowledge. Other questions included whether we can establish causal relations among events and, if so, whether they have a general character. Broadly, formal philosophy of history was concerned with epistemological and logical problems. Because of this focus on the analysis of the fundamental concepts of historical practice, most philosophers of history in the 20th-century Anglo-American tradition can be seen as formal philosophers of history. It is an approach that one sees reflected early, in Herbert Butterfield[33], in E.H. Carr[34], and in other historians. And there were attempts by philosophers to ensure that history could be a truth-bearing discipline: by Karl Popper and C.G. Hempel – who insisted that unless history provided causal explanations involving "covering laws," it had no title to call itself a science[35] – and by those like William Dray who insisted that explanations with 'law governing' rules or general statements were possible in history, even if

---

29 Mandelbaum 1952, p. 317.
30 Mandelbaum 1952, p. 318.
31 See Oakeshott, 1952.
32 Löwith, 1949; see also Jaspers, 1953.
33 Butterfield, 1931
34 Carr, 1961.
35 Hempel 1966, 1963, and 1942; Popper, 1949.

these rules did not have a necessary character.[36] Formal philosophy of history was widely accepted, no doubt, because of the awareness of problems with the selection process used by historians in gathering data and the adequacy of any resulting knowledge – but also because of suspicion of speculative philosophies together with (or perhaps because of) the anti-metaphysical and anti-systematic tendencies of mid-20th century philosophy.[37]

Whether one can make a rigid distinction between speculative and formal philosophy – whether each does not implicitly lead the philosopher to questions characteristic of the other – is a fair concern. Nevertheless, by the mid-1960s, Anglo-American historiography and philosophy of history was almost exclusively formal, and the dominant questions were the formal (epistemological) questions of explanation, of objectivity, and of whether history can be a science.

But there was a second response to the late 19th- and early 20th- century discussion of history that went beyond many of the mid-twentieth century "epistemological" questions of explanation and objectivity. Some found many of the concerns of philosophers and historians simply question begging – for they presumed that there *can* be explanation and objectivity when such things are simply not possible. Such challenges were – and are – pressed by those who, explicitly or implicitly, adopt the 'principles' of postmodernism.

The term 'postmodern' is, like many terms to describe intellectual movements, vague[38] – but in general one can say that it is rooted in the conviction of the legitimacy of historicism and, by extension, of the inappropriateness or impossibility of claims of objectivity and truth.[39] Drawing on Hegel, Martin Heidegger, Michel Foucault, Jean Baudrillard, Roland Barthes, and Jean-

---

36 Dray, 1957

37 Outside of the Anglo-American world are figures like Wilhelm Dilthey (1833-1911) and Raymond Aron (1905-1983). Despite dealing in his later works (e.g., *Introduction to the Human Sciences*, 1883) with the question of whether there can be a "foundation of the human sciences" – a question which bears indirectly on the possibility of a philosophy of history – Dilthey also addressed the issue of historical understanding, and thus can properly be regarded as a critical philosopher (see Dilthey, 1962). Similarly, Aron (1961) provides a powerful critique of positivism, but also proposes the use, in history, of an imaginative reconstruction that is more than empathy.

38 Sweet, 1997.

39 Historicism was not, at first, particularly influential on historians or historiographers; neither was it immediately adopted in philosophical circles. Thus, Karl Marx provided a purely objectivist and materialist philosophy of history which was - notwithstanding later works by Benedetto Croce (*Storia come pensiero e come azione*, 1938; Engl. Tr. 1941), Reinhold Niebuhr (*The Nature and Destiny of Man*, 1939), and Oswald Spengler (*Der Untergang des Abendlandes*, 1918; Engl. Tr. 1939) - the last profoundly influential philosophy of history.

François Lyotard, postmodern historians insist that both "upper case" history and "lower case" history have collapsed. (The former is "a way of looking at the past in terms which assigned to contingent events and situations an objective significance by identifying their place and function within a general progressive schema of historical development usually construed as appropriately progressive",[40] the latter is "the study of the past 'for its own sake'"[41]). Thus, speculative and formal philosophy of history are both rejected.[42]

Many see the postmoderns as taking the late 19th-century theory of 'critical history' to its logical conclusion – that, by recognizing the role of the historian in history, we must also challenge many of the pretensions to truth and objectivity of history itself. And so, inspired explicitly or implicitly by the historicism of the 19th- and early 20th- century German and Anglo-American philosophers, postmoderns asked: Is there room for the concept of truth in history? Is it proper to attempt to judge (morally) the motives and actions of agents in the distant past? Or is all this ruled out of court, given the questionable status of historical knowledge? Today, then, while some scholars may still hope that there is a 'meaning' to history, few would claim that reason, observation, or experience *shows* that there is and, like pluralistic postmodern philosophers, many have come to accept the possibility that there is no such meaning at all. Some have gone so far as to suggest that, because historical objectivity is impossible – there always being bias in the posing of questions and in the selection of data – history should become more focussed on advocacy.

Of course, while postmodernism is influential – largely because of the persuasiveness of some features of historicism – it is not without its critics.[43] And so it would be presumptuous to hold that postmodernism expresses the consensus of historians or philosophers of history, and a mistake to think that contemporary philosophy of history has entirely left behind the debates and controversies of the preceding generation. Nevertheless, in the scholarly literature today, a large – perhaps an inordinately large – amount of time is spent discussing the various post-modern criticisms (and there are many) of history, historiography, and the philosophy of history. And thus the three challenges of historicism raised earlier need to be addressed. But I would suggest that the preceding

---

40 Jenkins, 1997, p. 5.

41 Jenkins, 1997, p. 6.

42 Keith Jenkins and Hayden White (1973) have had a significant influence here.

43 E.g., Brunzl, 1997; Evans, 1997; cf. Fox-Genovese, 1999.

'history' of how we arrived at where we are may provide us with some responses to these challenges.

IV.

As we have seen, postmodern historicists press the points made by those like Bradley, Bosanquet, and Collingwood concerning the place of the historian in history, the pretensions of a value-free historical science, and the alleged independence of historical knowledge. But do these points in fact lead us to, or oblige us to hold, the conclusions of the postmodern historicist? Consider the first question raised earlier, in section I: Is history a thing of the past? When we ask such questions as 'What is it to have knowledge of the past?' or 'What are the conditions for the possession of historical knowledge?' it may seem that we cannot avoid ending up in some kind of subjectivity – for how (as Bradley noted) can history be done without reference to the standpoint or the context of the historian?

But does this – as some postmodern critics maintain – eliminate the possibility of the study of history as a study of what has happened in the past? As students of R.G. Collingwood remind us, "the possession of a point of view by the historian should not be confused with bias"[44], and we can acknowledge the inevitability of having a perspective without being committed to arbitrariness or relativism. After all, it is obvious that any historical account is given from a point of view, and that this point of view may not have been available to the historical agents. But this does not entail that there is incommensurability in the accounts or bias. Historians can or do know what their presuppositions are, are normally open to debating and criticizing them, and seek to avoid unreflective bias. Historians recognize that their histories are always written from a perspective representative of their time, and yet seek to organise or present them in a way that allows them to engage the past in a 'critical' and self-critical way. In other words, a "critical history" (to use Bradley's term) recognises the inseparability of context from historical knowledge while, at the same time, avoids the potentially relativistic consequences of postmodern historicism.

Yet – a postmodern might claim – even if we can have historical knowledge, history is nevertheless *just* a "thing of the past", that neither bears on contemporary discussion, nor can be subject to any kind of (contemporary) normative

---

44 See James Connelly, 'Is History a Thing of the Past?', in Sweet (2004), pp. 27-42, at p. 39.

assessment. Substantive critical commentary on the actions or the motives of past historical agents is not possible; (as Quentin Skinner[45] seems to hold) we are prohibited from making such (putatively anachronistic) attributions and limited to merely formal commentary.[46] Collingwood, however, would allow we *can* reasonably know what past historical agents held "on their own terms"; this is, in part, what is undertaken when we engage in re-enactment. And because we focus here on historical agents as agents – decision makers – we can hold them responsible for their views (as Collingwood does in *The New Leviathan*). Thus, we can appropriately make substantive critical comments (as distinct from simply formal remarks) about a past historical agent's blindness or lack of blindness on an issue – at the very least, provided that there are reasons to believe that that person could have had his or her position challenged by others who lived at that time.[47]

This is not to ignore that Collingwood's re-enactment theory is not without its difficulties, and later scholars, such as William Dray, have tried to develop Collingwood's insights in a way that avoids these problems. Nevertheless, it is clear that Collingwood did not see the role of the historian in doing history as providing any reason to doubt that there is something called the past, or that we can have access to the past – and there is certainly no logical connexion between Collingwood's claims and the postmodern 'conclusions' putatively drawn from them.

But even if history is not just a thing of the past, what – if anything – are we to do with history? Why seek to understand history? Even if we grant that we can know the past, are not past events also unique – the results of events that, strictly, can never take place again? And doesn't it follow that history is, therefore, of little help to us?

I think that there are two responses to this, implicit in the accounts of Bradley, Bosanquet, and Collingwood. The first is that we seek to understand history because it is required in order to make sense of the present. The postmodern challenge to historical knowledge and understanding – based on the concern that our location in the present and in a 'different' place always impedes any genuine knowledge – is misplaced, for neither the present nor one's aims for the

---

45   See Skinner, 1969.

46   See Catherine Wilson, "Postformalist Criticism in the History of Philosophy", in Sweet, 2004 pp. 43-62.

47   Ibid.

future can be known unless they are already understood in the context of the past. Indeed, ignorance of the past severely inhibits action in the present.[48] For Collingwood, for example, we must know the past in our own lives in order to know our own 'presuppositions', and these serve as guides for action and our own personal development.[49] Again, it is by a study of the past that we can have a "trained eye for the situation in which one acts"[50] – and thereby can bring about progress.

Second, not only do we need to have some understanding of the past to make *sense* of our own present (i.e., to 'make ourselves'), but we need to know the past so that we can be aware of the present in a broader sense. Collingwood would point out that a re-enactment by the historian of the thinking of the historical actors allows us to understand it as a process that is historical and relative, and yet does not require explanation of the past in terms of principles or laws. Thus we do not need a casual theory to explain why an agent acted or chose as he or she did, or a law-like account of history. And so, even if we accept the putative uniqueness of historical events, there can still be an understanding of the past.

Still, some postmodern critics argue that such 'knowledge' of the past can never be genuine because it can never succeed in being objective; it is 'just' a perspective. (It is ironic that a principal argument for this, presupposes the correspondence theory of truth, which postmoderns generally reject.) These postmodern critics would add that historical explanation involves historical understanding – and understanding is a process that is historically relative and value laden. But there can be no objectivity – not in history or in any social science or even science. And it is precisely its claim to objectivity that makes conventional or traditional history suspect. Many postmodern historians would consider that a "narrative" is sufficient to provide all we need (and all we can have) *qua* explanation.

Nevertheless, Bradley and Collingwood (who saw himself as completing Bradley's 'Copernican Revolution'[51]) – both figures whose work lies at the origin of this historicist critique – would insist that objectivity can still be achieved.

---

48 See Franz Schreiner and Mostafa Faghfoury, "Temporal Priority and a Better World", in Sweet, 2004, pp. 119-127. Here, they argue for a similar point, drawing on the work of Wilhelm Dilthey.

49 Lionel Rubinoff, "History, Philosophy and Historiography: Philosophy and the Critique of Historical Thinking", in Sweet, 2004 pp. 163 – 196, at p. 191; cf. Collingwood 1946, pp. 226; 230.

50 Ibid., p. 175.

51 Ibid, p. 174.

Indeed, they would argue that objectivity can be achieved not in spite of, but because of, the fact that historians write from a point of view. By re-enacting the thought of agents, Collingwood says, one is attempting an objective picture – by taking into account all the relevant details that one can, being ready to adjust or to correct error, and so on.[52] It is true, of course, with the writings of different historians we have before us a multiplicity of perspectives. But, first, historians would standardly allow that these perspectives and presuppositions are open to discussion and critique – and that, to do so, they admit that there is enough that is shared to allow for the possibility of the engagement of, and a reconciliation between, differing views. And, second, to the extent that this diversity remains, there is no sufficient reason to believe that that the result is less, rather than more knowledge. Consider a Marxist and a feminist account of a historical event. Each would draw attention to details the other might not. But by having both to hand, we may have a better understanding than only one – even a 'best' one on its own – might provide. While the multiplicity of different accounts does not cumulatively provide a general principle or law, i) what counts as good research is the same, ii) one recognises and overcomes certain problems in the selection of data and in the selection process, and the result is that iii) one may have a better *understanding* of the event even if not a better *explanation* of the event. If none of this were the case, why take feminist or Marxist criticism seriously? In short, there is no good reason to assume that objectivity entails that exactly or only one correct perspective does or can describe best how events took place. Such an "interperspectivism" among historians, taking its inspiration from Collingwood, would thereby allow one to claim that one's knowledge is objective. This does not mean that historical truth is absolute and unchanging, but that it meets a standard, appropriate to the object of study, where 'the past' and the historian's self awareness of doing history and his or her judgement lead to understanding the event.

As a result, if we adopt a broadly Collingwoodian conception of re-enactment – which contains elements of narrative – we may have both a better understanding of the agency of historical actors, and a basis for objective knowledge of the past.[53]

---

52   Ibid, p. 179.

53   See for example, Karsten Steuber, "Agency and the Objectivity of Historical Narratives", in Sweet, 2004, pp. 197-222.

In short, we can take some of the basic claims of postmodern historicism, and see that, if we look at their roots, this origin not only does not entail post-modernism, but may provide for a more robust account of history as objective. While taking seriously the three challenges of historicism enumerated at the beginning of this paper, we can allow that historical explanations are not value free, and yet objective; we can still claim that we can have knowledge and understanding of the past; and we can hold that understanding the past is an activity that is done not just for its own sake, but because it bears on our capa-cities to understand ourselves and the world around us, and to respond thoughtfully to what may happen in the future.

V.

The preceding remarks present some reasons for holding that there is a use for history today.

'Doing' history today cannot ignore the arguments of postmodern critics and of all those who would argue that the 'subjectivity' of the discipline of history makes it impossible to carry out. It requires reassessing or rethinking what it means to have historical understanding, and what it is that historians do.

Nevertheless, in this paper I have suggested that, if we return to the work of some of the key figures in Anglo-American philosophy of history, we can see that a postmodern, historicist critique of the 'use' of history need not succeed. I have argued, first, that history is not just a thing of the past. This does not mean that history is just a series of events that the historian merely identifies and puts into some externally determined right order. It requires a critical effort on the part of the historian as well as an act of interpretation. But neither does this mean that there is nothing in 'the past' that we must respond to.

Second, I have argued that the issues of historicism and historical under-standing have to be carefully and fully assessed. As paradoxical as the notion of knowledge of what does not exist – i.e., the past – may be, it is obviously neces-sary both for our social practices and for our ability to understand the present; this suggests that the subjectivist or post-modern may simply be posing a set of pseudo problems. This is not to deny that the questions have force, but perhaps the issue of the nature of the past is just like the issue of the nature of time – a puzzle about which Augustine remarked, "If no one asks me, I know what it is. If I wish to explain it to him who asks me, I do not know".[54]

---

54 Augustine, 1993, Bk. 11, ch. 14, sect. 17.

Third, I have argued that there is no sufficient reason to abandon the search for objectivity.

Rather than rule out objectivity *tout court*, it seems plausible to hold that there are different ways in which we might understand objectivity – with some ways more likely to be fruitful than others. Here, we need to explore the notion of standpoint or perspective, what it entails, and whether (and how) it is consistent with objectivity and the possibility of making judgements about the past.

And finally, I have suggested that, in returning to, and reassessing, the work of figures such as Bradley, Bosanquet, and Collingwood - who were central in the critical understanding of history - we may be able to resist the temptations of historicism. Despite the many difficulties that critics note, we may still have confidence that history is possible, that there can be some kind of historical understanding, and that we can learn lessons from – and make criticisms of – history.

There is a use for history.

Bibliography

Ankersmit, F.R. and Kelner, Hans, ed. (1995), *A New Philosophy of History*, Chicago: University of Chicago Press.

Appleby, Joyce; Lynn Hunt; Margaret Jacob (1994), *Telling the Truth about History*, New York: Norton.

Aron, Raymond (1961), *Introduction to the Philosophy of History: An Essay on the Limits of Historical Objectivity* [*Introduction à la philosophie de l'histoire: essai sur les limites de l'objectivité historique*, 1938], trans. George J. Irwin, London: Weidenfeld and Nicholson.

Augustine (1998), *The City of God against the Pagans* [*De Civitate Dei*], ed. trans. R.W. Dyson, Cambridge: Cambridge University Press.

Bosanquet, Bernard (1912), *The Principle of Individuality and Value*, London: Macmillan.

Bosanquet, Bernard (1892), *A History of Aesthetic*, London: Swan Sonnenschein, 1892. 2d ed., 1904; reprinted in *The Collected Works of Bernard Bosanquet*, 20 volumes, ed. with Introductions, notes, and annotations by William Sweet, Bristol, UK: Thoemmes Press, 1999. Vol 4.

Bossuet, Jacques-Bénigne (1976), *Discourse on Universal History* [*Discours sur l'histoire universelle à monseigneur le Dauphin. Pour expliquer la suite de la religion, & les changements des empires*], ed. Orest Ranum, trans. Elborg Forster, Chicago: University of Chicago Press.

Bradley, F. H. (1968), *Presuppositions of Critical History* (1874), ed. introd. and commentary Lionel Rubinoff, Chicago: Quadrangle Books.

Brunzl, Martin (1997), *Real History: Reflections on Historical Practice*, London; Routledge.

Butterfield, Herbert (1931), *The Whig Interpretation of History*, London: G. Bell and Sons.

Carr, E.H. (1961), *What is History?* New York: Random House.

Collingwood, R.G. (1926), *Roman Inscriptions and Sculptures belonging to the Society of Antiquaries of Newcastle upon Tyne*, Newcastle-Upon-Tyne: Northumberland Press Limited.

Collingwood, R.G. (1923), *Roman Britain*, London: Oxford University Press, H. Milford.

Collingwood, R.G. (1930), *The Archaeology of Roman Britain*, London: Methuen & Co.

Collingwood, R.G. (1936), *Roman Britain and the English Settlements*, with J. N. L. Myres, Oxford: The Clarendon Press.

Collingwood, R.G. (1946), *The Idea of History*, ed. T.M. Knox, Oxford: Clarendon Press.

Collingwood, R.G. (1924), *Speculum Mentis*, Oxford: Clarendon Press.

Collingwood, R.G. (1942) *The New Leviathan, or, Man, Society, Civilization and Barbarism*, Oxford: Clarendon Press.

Condorcet, Jean-Antoine-Nicolas, Marquis de (1979), *Sketch for a historical picture of the progress of the human mind* [*Esquisse d'un tableau historique des progrès de l'esprit humain*], trans. June Barraclough; introd. Stuart Hampshire, Westport, Conn: Hyperion Press.

Croce, Benedetto (1941), *History as the Story of Liberty* [*Storia come pensiero e come azione*], trans. Sylvia Sprigge, London, G. Allen and Unwin Ltd.

Croce, Benedetto (1921), *Theory and History of Historiography* [*Teoria e stòria della storiografia*], trans. Douglas Ainslie, London: George G. Harrap & Co.

Dilthey, Wilhelm (1962), *Pattern and Meaning in History: Thoughts on History and Society*, New York: Harper.

Dray, William (1995), *History as Re-Enactment: R..G. Collingwood's Idea of History*, Oxford: Clarendon Press.

Dray, William (1957), *Laws and Explanations in History*, Oxford: Oxford University Press.

Evans, Richard J. (1997), *In Defence of History*, London: Granta Books.

Fox-Genovese, Elizabeth, ed. (1999), *Reconstructing History: The Emergence of a new Historical Society*, London: Routledge.

Gardiner, Patrick (1995), "Historicism," *The Oxford Companion to Philosophy*, 1995.

Greenblatt, Stephen J. (1988), *Shakespearean Negotiations: The Circulation of Social Energy in Renaissance England*, Oxford:†Clarendon Press.

Hegel, Georg Wilhelm Friedrich (1944), *The Philosophy of History* [*Vorlesungen über die Philosophie der Geschichte*], trans. J. Sibree, New York: Willey Book Co\.

Hempel, C. (1966), "Explanation in science and in history" (1962) in Dray, W. (ed). *Philosophical Analysis and History*, New York: Harper & Row, pp. 95-126.

Hempel, C. (1963), "Reason and Covering Laws in Historical Explanation," in Hook, Sidney (ed.), *Philosophy and History*, New York: New York University Press.

Hempel, C. (1942), "The Function of General Laws in History," *The Journal of Philosophy*, 39, 35-48.

Herder, Johann Gottfried von (1968), *Reflections on the philosophy of the history of mankind* [*Ideen zur Philosophie der Geschichte der Menschheit*], abridged, with introd. Frank E. Manuel, Chicago: University of Chicago Press.

Hoover, Dwight W. (1992), "The New Historicism (in Historiography)," *The History Teacher*, 25 (3), 355-366.

Iggers, Georg G. (1995), "Historicism: The History and Meaning of the Term," *Journal of the History of Ideas*, 56 (1), 129-152.

Iroegbu, Pantaleon (2002), "Hegel's Africa," in Sweet, William (ed.), *Philosophy, Culture, and Pluralism*, Aylmer, QC: Editions du scribe, pp. 79-98.

Jaspers, Karl (1953), *The Origin and Goal of History*, New Haven: Yale University Press.

Jenkins, Keith, ed. (1997), *The Postmodern History Reader*, London: Routledge.

Kemerling, Garth (2003), "Historicism," in Kemerling, Garth (ed.), *A Dictionary of Philosophical Terms and Names*, http://www.philosophypages.com/dy/h5.htm#hism

Löwith, Karl (1949), *Meaning in History*, Chicago: University of Chicago Press.

Mandelbaum, Maurice (1952), "Some Neglected Philosophic Problems Regarding History," *The Journal of Philosophy*, 49 (10), 317-329.

Maritain, Jacques (1957), *On the Philosophy of History*, ed. Joseph W. Evans, New York: Charles Scribner's Sons.

Martin, Raymond (1995), "Forum on *Telling the Truth about History*", *History and Theory*, 34(4), 320-339.

Martin, Rex (1977), *Historical Explanation: Re-enactment and Practical Inference*, Ithaca: Cornell University Press.

Martin, Robert (1991), *The Philosopher's Dictionary*, Peterborough, ON: Broadview Press.

Marx, Karl, and Engels, F. (1947), *The German Ideology*, New York: International Publishers.

Megill, Allan (1997), "Why was There a Crisis of Historicism?" (Review Essay of *Heidegger, Dilthey, and the Crisis of Historicism*, by Charles R. Bambach), *History and Theory*, 36, 416-429.

Michaels, Walter Benn (1987), *The Gold Standard and the Logic of Naturalism: American Literature at the Turn of the Century*, Berkeley: University of California Press.

Mink, Louis O. (1987), *Historical Understanding*, ed. Brian Fay, Eugene O. Golob, and Richard T. Vann, Ithaca: Cornell University Press.

Niebuhr, Reinhold (1941-43), *The Nature and Destiny of Man; a Christian interpretation* (Gifford lectures, 1939), 2 vols. London: Nisbet & co. ltd., Vol. I, 1941; Vol. II, 1943.

Niebuhr, Reinhold (1949), *Faith and History. A Comparison of Christian and Modern Views of History*, New York: Scribners.

Oakeshott, Michael (1952), "Review of *An Introduction to Philosophy of History*. By W. H. Walsh," *Philosophical Quarterly*, **2** (8), 276-277.

Popper, Karl (1957), *The Poverty of Historicism*, London: Routledge & Kegan Paul.

Popper, Karl (1949), "Prediction and Prophecy and their Significance of Social Theory," in Beth, E. W., Pos, H. J., and Hollak, J. H. (eds.), *Proceedings of the Xth International Congress of Philosophy*, Amsterdam, Aug. 11-18, 1948, Amsterdam: North Holland, Vol. 1, 82-91.

Putnam, Hilary (1981), *Reason, Truth, and History*, Cambridge: Cambridge University Press

Ricœur, Paul (1983-85), *Temps et récit*, 3 vols. Paris: Seuil [*Time and Narrative*, trans. Kathleen McLaughlin and David Pellauer, Chicago: University of Chicago Press, 1984].

Rubinoff,Lionel. "History, Philosophy and Historiography: Philosophy and the Critique of Historical Thinkhing", in Sweet (2004): 163-196

Skinner, Quentin (1969), "Meaning and Understanding in the History of Ideas," *History and Theory*, 8, 3-53.

Smith, Bonnie G. (1998), *The Gender of History: Men, Women, and Historical Practice*, Cambridge, MA: Harvard University Press.

Spengler, Oswald (1939), *The Decline of the West* [*Der Untergang des Abendlandes*, Vol. I, 1918, Vol. II, 1922], trans. Charles Francis Atkinson, New York: A. A. Knopf.

Strauss, Leo (1952), "On Collingwood's Philosophy of History," *Review of Metaphysics*, 5, June, 559-586.

Sweet, William (1997), "Modernity, Postmodernity and Religion," *Journal of Dharma*, 22 (3), fall, 199-207.

Sweet, William (2004), *The Philosophy of History: a Re-examination*, Aldershot: Ashgate Publishers.

Toynbee, Arnold (1934-61), London: Oxford University Press.

Veeser, H. Aram, ed. (1989), *The New Historicism*, London: Routledge.

Vico, Giambattista (1948), *The New Science of Giambattista Vico*, trans. Thomas Goddard Bergin and Max Harold Fisch, Ithaca, NY: Cornell University Press.

Voltaire, François Marie Arouet de (1965), *The Philosophy of History* [*La Philosophie de l'histoire*], pref. Thomas Kiernan, London: Vision.

Walsh, W. H. (1966), "The Limits of Scientific History" (1961), in Dray, W. (ed.), *Philosophical Analysis and History*, New York: Harper & Row, pp. 54-74.

Wells, H. G. (1920), *The Outline of History: being a plain history of life and mankind*, by H. G. Wells; written with the advice and editorial help of Mr. Ernest Barker, Sir H. H. Johnston, Sir E. Ray Lankester, and Professor Gilbert Murray, and illustrated by J. F. Horrabin, New York: The Macmillan Company.

White, Hayden (1973), *Metahistory: The Historical Imagination in Nineteenth Century Europe*, Baltimore: The John Hopkins University Press.

Zinn, Howard (1970), *The Politics of History*, Boston; Beacon Press.

The Complexity of Education in the Current World

Thalía Fung Riverón

Education is a process of fixating and creating knowledge, habits, feeling, traditions, religious attitudes, and values of every kind that is inherent to man. In the contradictory educational process of a society, generations are trained and reformed, identity values are carried out, and at the same time, openings which go beyond concrete communities and societies are originated.

To pretend that philosophy is reduced only to the academy, is to reduce its spectrum which covers the knowledge given in science; but also those which are a product of common experience, originating in artistic expressions, standardized behaviors, and those which are developed as their opposition. However, instruction is an indispensable foundation to establish communication. To the extent that new communication media enhance inter-subjective relations, writing and computer communication have become landmarks due to their far-reaching effects, each with different degrees of exclusion. They are also more indispensable to developing life on a human basis, with education stressing the external aspect.

Every society uses reproductive means which are imposed, as well as ideology, for its reproduction (simple and enlarged). Education is presently encountered in one or the other, although the field of ideas is a priority.

A complete vision, which is a truly world vision of education, shows us that in different regions of the planet, the organizing categories of the reproductive educational thinking of society are diverse. Although since ancient times, writing has developed a determinative role of exceptional importance due to its ability to collect and transmit oral tradition, to inform about new and previous knowledge, to transfer feelings, traditions, stages of development of awareness, identities and universal things throughout all times. In a word, it constitutes the cultural inheritance by which a philosophical perspective allows the analysis of language from its external and internal visions to the world.

It seems that everybody agrees that philosophy is not enclosed within systems. On the contrary, its knowledge is in its greatest understanding of the condition comprising the general relation of man to man and man to world. José Martí gave an extraordinary value to education in its broad sense, saying that "to educate is to place the current man in conjunction with his history in order to explain the present and to foresee the future, is to prepare man for life". For Martí, culture is the only way to reach liberty. This was condensed in the well-known phrase "TO BE LEARNED IN ORDER TO BE FREE", by which he identifies himself with modern ideas, but contextualized by educational and political ideas and relations of the America he calls "ours".

Throughout the XXth century, with the advance of technological revolutions, the distance between the accesses to knowledge between majorities and minorities has become greater as science reaches unsuspected levels. Even at the beginning of the XXIst century, a greater number of persons are unable to read and to adapt to new situations.

Anyway, I consider that throughout the XXth century, the tendency for the unification of science and consciousness began to develop separately in the context of modernity, in which scientific coherence does not require a consideration of value for its ideological content. Although this has not advanced, in my personal opinion, in a complete way, it marks a tendency within the particular sciences and even in the methodology of scientific knowledge. And this is not circumscribed to the use of the results of science, but affects the process of production of scientific knowledge itself.

Now then, if writing stressed a difference in knowledge, today's science makes the relationship among men more asymmetrical to the extent of creating highly privileged cognitive elites. The understanding for this framework requires a reflection which goes beyond the disciplines and corresponds to philosophy in its several aspects.

Every philosophy develops from the field that has been chosen as its action environment. It is a role of critical awareness in the epistemological, axiological, cognitive, aesthetic, linguistic, ethical and moral relations, and in general social ones, inter-subjective as well as intra-subjective. But the established science have been put into question by turbulences caused by man-nature relationships with thus far unknown consequences. And in this order of relations, the education of men has a sine qua non role.

One of the conditions for such a connection to be evaluated is found in the tendency recorded by scientists in their multi-disciplinary teams of the unity of scientific knowledge, which is a result of a cognitive and evaluative need.

Education in the current world has to respond to the urgent needs of mankind and at the same time, its method can not only deal with it on a world level, but also on a local one.

It takes global and local thinking and at the same time, something more than a minimum of instruction and education in the role of men, not only as citizens, but also in their relationships with others that go beyond their community. Although their community relationship is decisive, it requires the knowledge of urgencies and emergencies faced by the community because it will affect in a direct and even immediate way each individual.

Philosophy in the educational field can constitute an essential guide in social education, academic education, and in scientific research. In a word, it consists of evaluating the socialization of knowledge at the global level and its possibility of understanding the problems of the concrete man. This will allow man's self-perceptions to clarify his situation in the world. In my own criterion, from all philosophies generated in every time and place, we can draw general things to think about the current world.

In fact, until now, our outline for a greater systematization and diffusion has been western philosophical thinking. This has deprived us of understanding the diversity of nature and the social diversity of men and has given us a paradigm assessed as untouchable.

Technological and scientific transformations force us to consider a new and alternative approach.

Today, in science, an approximation is produced between those classified by Dilthey as natural sciences and human sciences. This classification, which has its basis in the universities and research centers, shows that it contradicts results reached by cognitive and evaluative means, and states the possibility of overcoming the difference between fact and value judgments.

Philosophy of science and philosophy of education cannot stop investigating this problem. The work done by natural scientists, including the applied mathematicians, must evoke an orienting response by philosophers.

Philosophy is just in time to join the critical analysis of relations between the sciences and their mediations, to appraise the relevancy of its ways, and to rank the problems that affect the world in an endless list, from philosophers' diverse positions with regard to the world and man.

The questions that developed disciplines such as environmentalism and bioethics have asked are questions which philosophy did not ask before. It seems that philosophy has been left out of the discussion, with the exception of questioning, at a given moment, whether the new bioethical knowledge would be the philosophy of the XXIst century.

Of course, philosophy has answers for that reductionist position. It can recover its critical role and also establish the socio-cultural limits for those new knowledges.

Philosophy, regardless of its last names, which are valid beyond any doubt, has to develop itself out of its respective environments. It needs to be directive and critical in the field of philosophy of education, social philosophy and political philosophy, and to look for theoretical orientations that favor universal values in the presence of the current and emergent global problems that are present in the new world scenery. In this moment, which tends to become zero hour, philosophy must prioritize ethical values with relation to human life and the planet, and to remember as Hemingway once said: "Ask not for whom the bell tolls: It tolls for thee."

Counterfactual History and its Educational Potential

Bernard Eric Jensen

My approach to the theme *History in Education* differed significantly from what turned out to be the prevailing norm at the conference. Whereas other speakers approached questions concerning history in education mainly from a starting point within philosophy, I came to such questions from a background within academic as well as public history[1].

As far as the Western world is concerned, we have never been as well-informed about history education as we are today. This is due to the fact that during the last decade there has been made several in-depth surveys about how Westerns have experienced being taught history at school. It does not mean that we are able today to answer all relevant and interesting questions about the teaching of history in schools. But it does mean that the factual knowledge about history teaching is today much more detailed and refined than it ever has been. I therefore consider it important to try to take the available knowledge into account when reflecting on how to approach history in an educational setting.

I will therefore take as my starting point a few of the more eye-opening findings from these surveys. The first of these was *Youth and History: a Comparative European Survey* (1997) in which more than 30.000 students and teachers in almost thirty countries were questioned about their views on history and history teaching. This survey did not only show that there was a major disparity between what history teachers and their students thought was taking place during history classes - this disparity was in fact so manifest that the resear-

---

1   The term ‚public history' is nowadays used as a name for a special kind of history education and research. It is concerned especially with how history is represented and used in a public setting, and it therefore focuses its attention upon how one approaches history in schools, at museums, on films etc.. There are moreover journals specifically devoted to this field of research - e.g. The Public Historian.

chers felt obliged to raise the question: do teachers and students actually attend the same history classes? The same survey also highlighted to a rather wide-spread dissatisfaction among the students about the kind of history teaching which they were taking part in. This latter finding was summarised by Susan Barschdorff in the following way:

> "Today's history teaching does not really meet student's preferences. (…) Teaching methods, the use of media and the goals of teaching history, as observed by the students, are rather traditional. Dominating this are the storage of facts, textbook use and the narrations of the teacher. Empathy, the reconstruction of past situations, project work and modern media is really seldom encountered. This is not in harmony with the students' wishes. They prefer by far audio-visual media, sources and documents, and museums to their textbooks. This gives the impression that history teaching is not up to date and has not taken account of the innovatory debates of the last decade."[2]

The other survey worth mentioning is the one carried out by Roy Rosenzweig and David Thelen; it appeared in 1998 under the title *The Presence of the Past. Popular Uses of History in American Life*. It was based on in-depth phone interviews with a sample of app. 1.500 adult Americans; they had been selected in such a way that the results could be considered to be statistically representative of contemporary American society. Through this survey Rosenzweig and Thelen were not only able to show that a history class for most adult Americans actually constituted the social setting in which they had felt the least connected with the past. History classes were in this instance compared with other settings such as: family gatherings, visits to a museum, being on holidays, reading books, watching movies or television programs. They also discovered that in the minds of adult Americans the words ,history' and ,the past' have very different connotations indeed. When asked if they were interested in history, most Americans tended to say ,no', whereas when asked if they were interest in the past, most of them tended to answer: ,yes, very much so'. Rosenzweig and Thelen sought to explain this finding of theirs in the following way:

---

2   S. Barschdorff in J. van der Leeuw-Roord (ed.), *The State of History Education in Europe: Challenges and Implications of the ,Youth and History' Survey*, 1998, p.85 & 90.

"After listening to 1500 Americans we understand how a generation has grown up to say that something is ‚history' when it is dead and gone, irrelevant, beyond any use in the present. That is how many of the people we interviewed described their classroom encounters with the past. While some praised individual teachers, their stories only underscored how deeply respondents felt alienated from the structure and content of history classes."[3]

Today there is ample evidence to show that the teaching of history in schools is not all popular in the minds of those people who are obliged to participate in such a teaching - that is to say among those who may be classified as the ‚captive audiences' of history classes. There are some exceptions to this general rule. History teaching is, for instance, less popular on a primary and lower secondary level than it is on a higher secondary level.

Yet, it should also be noted that there is some evidence indicating that we are seemingly not dealing with a problem, which is specific to contemporary Western societies. Thus, Sam Wineburg opens his book on *Historical Thinking and Other Unnatural Acts* (2001) by pointing out that throughout the 20th century American authorities have known that surveys showed that history teaching was not achieving the desired the results. When the pupils' and students' knowledge of historical facts were tested, the result was very disappointing indeed.

"Considering the vast differences between those who attended high school in 1917 and the near-universal enrollments of today, the stability of the students' ignorance is amazing. The whole world has turned on its head, but one thing has stayed the same: Kids don't know history."[4]

It can thus be said that there is a marked contrast between the fact that politicians and educational authorities consider a solid knowledge of history to be of major importance and the actual state of knowledge prevailing among pupils and students. When politicians and educational authorities have been confronted with findings such as these, they not only have tended to decry the low level of historical literacy found within their respective societies, they have also set out to amend this existing state of affairs by seeking to proscribe more of the

---

3   R. Rosenzweig & D. Thelen, *The Presence of the Past. Popular Uses of History in American Life*, 1998, p. 113.

4   S. Wineburg, *Historical Thinking and Other Unnnatural Acts. Charting the future of Teaching the Past*, 2001, p. viii.

very kind of history classes that most ordinary people find to be without much meaning or perspective. Yet, as I see it, there is no good reason to assume that such a recommendation will be able to change the present state of affairs within history teaching in any significant way.

For those scholars, whose task it is to analyse and reflect on the state of history education in Western societies, one of the central challenges consists in trying to find out why ordinary people tend to experience the prevailing forms of history teaching as a rather uninspiring and tiresome affair. But before indicating what existing research says about this issue, there is one possible misunderstanding that I would want to guard against. At the present time there is no evidence to indicate that ordinary people - young, middle-aged or old - lack an interest in what happened in the past - i.e. that they should be disinterested in issues relating to their own heritage. What the available evidence indicates is that many people are not very interested in those aspects of the past which politicians and educational authorities have been stipulating should constitute the core of a history curriculum. Thus, there exists today a significant disparity between what is presented in schools as the officially and publicly sanctioned heritage and the kind of heritages that concern ordinary people. Moreover, such a disparity can help to explain why surveys frequently show that most people remember rather little of what they had been taught during their history classes.

Rosenzweig and Thelen's survey also shed some light upon the reasons that people tend to give when asked to explain why they had felt less connected with the past during history classes than in any of the other social settings about which they were asked. Here I will limit myself to three of the reasons given. First, most people experienced their history classes as a place where they primarily were ‚forced-fed' with of series of facts which they were obliged to memorise. The appropriate section of *The Presence of the Past* (1998) was for that reason given the following sub-heading: *"It was just a giant data dump"*: *The Sad Story of History in Schools*. Second, many people experienced their history classes as a place where there was little or no room whatsoever for having an intense discussion or a heated controversy about the issues being treated during such a class. On the contrary, they saw themselves as being obliged to learn a history curriculum which they were not given any opportunity of actively shaping. Third and finally, most people found that they were unable to link their own life stories to the overarching stories which were presented to them during history classes in meaningful ways.

In light of such a set of experiences it becomes comprehensible why ordinary people by and large have viewed their history teaching as a rather uninspiring and tiresome affair. When one is considering how to approach history education, it is therefore important to remember that it is a type of teaching which very easily indeed can de-generate into forms of rote learning - that is the kind of learning processes which rest more on the memorisation of prescribed information rather than upon an active process of inquiry where one is seeking to raise interesting questions, generate some new insights and thereby try to come up with one or more plausible answers to the questions posed. One of the main challenges that history educators have to face today consists in a deliberate attempt to transform the existing forms of history teaching - to transform it from being a place of learning where one is obliged to reproduce some officially prescribed course material and to make it in stead into an active and stimulating place of learning. It is in this context that it becomes relevant to reflect on the educational potential of counterfactual history.

When I studied history at Copenhagen University in the 1960's, one of the prevailing norms stipulated that academic historians were never concern themselves with What-If-Questions - i.e. with what is known today as counterfactual history. One would, in other words, disgrace oneself in professional terms if one began to indulge in that kind of speculation. As a student it was therefore not surprising to learn that a prominent British historian such as E.H. Carr considered counterfactual history to be nothing more than ‚a parlour game‘ in *What Is History?* (1961) and later to find that E.P. Thompson classified it as outright ‚unhistorical shit‘ in *The Poverty of Theory and Other Essays* (1978).

Yet, since the 1980's things have started to change within the world of academic history. During the winter term of 1983-84 Alexander Demandt, professor of Ancient History, gave a course on counterfactual history at the University of Berlin, and he has described it retrospectively as being one of the most significant turning points (‚ein geistes Ereignis‘) in his professional career. The students were given the task of having to play through a series of realistic, yet alternative scenarios in conjunction with actual historical events in European history, but as far as the students were concerned, their participation in this course turned out to have an unforeseen and rather unfortunate consequence. After they had sat their exams, the exam commission at Berlin University ruled that it was not willing to recognise their exam papers, and they had thus to face the fact that they had partaken in a university course for which they could not be given any credits. This provoked Demandt to declare: "The first born have been sacrificed", but this set-back did not hold him back. In 1984 he published his book *Ungeschehene Geschichte. Ein Traktat über die Frage: Was wäre geschehen, wenn ...?* - i.e. History that never happened. A treatise on the question: What would have happened, if ...? - and he became subsequently the most prominent German advocate of what he himself terms: *The-What-If-School of Historical Studies*. It is worth noting that Demandt's treatise by now has appeared in a third and extended edition, and it has been followed by a whole series of books on counterfactual history written by academic historians.

How can it be explained that academic historians have begun to change their thinking about counterfactual history during the last two decades of the 20th century? Many factors play no doubt a role in such a change but I will only focus upon one such factor. Until the 1970's many academic historians and social scientists worked on the basis of the assumption that historical processes, to a significant degree, were governed by laws, and they could therefore be said to be upholding either a strong or a week variant of a historicist conception of history. It was this kind of thinking that constituted part of the background for Karl Popper writing his book on *The Poverty of Historicism* (1957). In the present context, the important point is, that as long as historians were working on the base of a historicist conception of history, it made little or no sense to start considering questions about what would have happened if this or that had been different, since a historicist conception is based on the assumption that historical processes are governed by a set of underlying regularities.

Since the 1970's many academic historians and social scientists not only have begun to question such an assumption and have started in stead to view history as a series of contingent processes - i.e. processes that only will take place if specific sets of conditions have been fulfilled. They have also become more prone to view history as the outcome of the aggregated effects of human actions - including the unintended consequences of these actions. In other word, they have become much more inclined to take the notion that people are the agents of history much more seriously than was the case during the first three-quarters of the 20th century. As soon as one begins to work on the basis of a notion of history as the aggregated effects of human actions, then it begins to make a lot of sense to ask questions about what would have happened, if specific persons or groups had opted for another of those alternative courses of action that had presented themselves at the time.

In this setting counterfactual history no longer appears to be, a mere parlour game' or a lump of ‚unhistorical shit', it will in stead be seen as an inherent and central dimensions of any historical process. As soon as one begins to stress the notion of human agency and thus start to take seriously the idea of people partaking in the making their own histories, then the working assumption will be that a historical process never will appear to be fully determined and that the future must therefore be seen as more or less open at any given point in time. Yet, it should be stressed that the degree of openness may differ from one epoch to another and from one type of situation to another.

This kind of a re-assessment of counterfactual history has opened up new possibilities when the question of how to teach history in schools comes up for consideration. If counterfactual history became an integral part of history teaching, it would become possible to move away from the type of rote learning that has predominated and to establish in stead a more creative and productive approach to history teaching. To the extent that one includes the counterfactual dimension in history teaching, there will always be a fair scope of the use of one's imagination and creativity when one seeks to generate insight into what were the actual alternative courses of action at a given place and time.

Contrary to what is sometimes assumed, counterfactual history does in no way encourage a sloppy and superficial attitude towards historical analysis. On the contrary, counterfactual analysis only becomes a stimulating intellectual challenge to the extent that one seeks to establish what constituted a set of probable alternative scenarios in a specific setting, and this will in turn demand that one has become familiar with the culture and thinking of the people in question - including of course their norms, habits, knowledge, desires, expectations, technologies, living conditions, divisions etc.

To pursue counterfactual history in a serious way will require that one starts to study in some fair detail the mental horizons of the people who were seeking to make history at a particular place and time. One of the central challenges will consist in seeking to understand how the people in question sought to establish links between their memories of the past, their understanding of the present situation and their expectation with regard to the future. Thus, it will demand generating insight into what the German historian Reinhart Koselleck has termed *Vergangene Zukunft* - i.e. the ways in which the future actually presented itself to a set of actors at specific times in the past.[5]

Working with counterfactual history thus requires that one set out to generate insight into those forms of historical consciousness that shaped the actions

---

5 Cf. R. Koselleck, *Vergangene Zukunft. Zur Semantik geschictlicher Zeiten*, 1979.

of people at the given time and place. This will only be possible to the extent that one can gain insight into the actual forms of historical consciousness that were operating in the past. Moreover, by working in such a way one will have to achieve an understanding of the temporality or historicity of historical process – i.e. the ways in which people's perception and understanding of history has undergone some very significant changes in the course of human history. In sum, one will have to seek – in Koselleck's terms – to discover the actual temporality of history (‚Zeitlichkeit der Geschichte').

History of Philosophy and Philosophy of History in the Educational Systems Today

Maija Kūle

The German philosopher W. Windelband known not only as a representative of neo-Kantianism, but also as the author of wonderful books on history of philosophy has observed the following relationship: "The more fruitless was philosophy itself, the more flourishing became history of philosophy."[1] Philosophy with its stories of the past tried to conceal its own weakness, as it were. The question is: could it be true? What is the part of history of philosophy in philosophy? Is it an indispensable part of it?

A viewpoint that history of philosophy plays the central part in philosophy is far from self-understandable and indisputable. It has had a lot of supporters up to nowadays[2], but it has opponents, too. At the turn of the 19th century the problem of historicity is in the limelight of philosophical and cultural discussions. In a way it is the question of the essence of history, the significance of historical consciousness and historicity in human self-development.

The 18th century French intellectuals started a discussion that was summed up under the title *"Querelle des Anciens et des Modernes"*. These French discussions are regarded as the starting point of historic consciousness in the history of European culture. What is more significant: the old or the new? What is the significance of the old, classical heritage in the emergence of new types of consciousness? Are "the old theories" of use to us at all? Part of the French intellectuals of the time urged: let us leave perfection to the old and secure development on the basis of our imperfection.

---

1   W. Windelband. *Die Philosophie im deutschen Geistesleben des 19. Jahrhunderts.* Verlag von J.C.B. Mohr, Tübingen, 1927, s. 87.

2   For example, K.Jaspers. *Weltgeschichte der Philosophie.* München: R.Riper & Co. Verlag, 1982; Jacques Maritain. The Philosophy of History in General.- http:www.nd.edu/departments/maritain/etext/philhist1.htm

Goethe and the German Romantics *en masse* introduce a meaningful compromise in the relations between the history of culture and creative work.

Goethe in his poetry book *God and the World* sums it up: 'That old truth, Grasp it'[3] and push it on.

Appreciating the necessity of "old truths" we follow G.W.F. Hegel's clearly expressed thought about *the inseparability of philosophy and history of philosophy that is based on the philosophy of history* standpoints[4]. Hegel writes: "The same development of thinking that is described in the history of philosophy is also described in philosophy itself."[5] The idea reveals itself in self-development. For Hegel it is important to describe the development of thought as a way to freedom, accentuating the idea and system of dialectical heredity. Hegel admits that thinking divided in time (the new, old; classical, modern times) is at variance with itself. To philosophise, according to Hegel, is to unite this variance. Philosophy is in a way "a reconciliation", a balanced calmness of thought.

Hegel's teaching admits that *thinking* is a specific form of philosophical activity because the thought is an "afterthought", in a way. That is why German classical philosophy while placing thinking in the centre sees it as a process based on its own history. Only a pure thought thinks itself and grasps ideas that everyday consciousness tries to reduce to familiar, usual notions. When philosophy is explicated in ideas created by experience, it cannot claim the status of strict thinking.

Every trend, every school of thought has a place in a system; if it does not fit in it, it does not enter the story of history of philosophy. *Philosophy* develops through *history of philosophy*, and this viewpoint is justified by *philosophy of history*. That is *the first model in the relationship of history of philosophy and philosophy of history* that has often been criticized for philosophy of history being dogmatic, metaphysical and having no right to exist in contemporary world. This model has also been criticized for only pretending to belong to historical narration, in reality excluding history because it is governed by the system [6], says P. Ricœur in his early works collected in the book "History and Truth".

---

3   Poem "Vermächtnis": Das alte Wahre, fass' es an! - *Goethes Sämmtliche Werke in Vierzig Bänden.* Zweiter Band. Stuttgart, 1869, s. 155.

4   Similar ideas developed Jacque Maritain. *The Philosophy of History in General.* - http:www.nd.edu/departments/maritain/etext/philhist1.htm;

5   Hegel G.W.F. *Enzyklopaedie der philosophischen Wissenschaften im Grundrisse.* Berlin, 1969, 14§.

6   Ricœur P. *Geschichte und Wahrheit.* List Verlag Muenchen, 1974, S.73.

The derivation of Hegel's position is Marxism that practically influenced all the standpoints of teaching philosophy in Russia, Eastern Europe, Central Europe and elsewhere. The place of philosophy of history in Marxism is taken by historical materialism. History of philosophy is acknowledged as a necessary discipline, however, mainly to the extent to which it discovers the sources of the emergence of Marxism. In Marxist philosophy teaching, for instance, a significant place is taken by the part of the history of philosophy that characterizes the development of materialist trends, thus impoverishing and criticizing the opposing – idealistic tradition. History of philosophy is only partially needed, and only in its past form. That is the *second model* of forming relations between history of philosophy and philosophy of history. Namely, philosophy of history has been turned into a part of social and political philosophy, suiting the ideological requirements to the utmost, with history of philosophy at its service.

Interestingly, in socialist countries in the 60ies –80ies there were different sentiments[7] as to the relationship between the history of philosophy and philosophy of history (meaning historical materialism). People whose field of study was history of philosophy (the more ancient, the better) regarded themselves ideologically independent, more neutral or even opposed to political power in comparison with those who taught historical materialism. While interconnected on the surface the two fields of studies - history of philosophy and philosophy of history – were in conflict because the standpoints of historical materialism used to cover instead of uncovering the multiplicity of trends and the thoroughness of viewpoints in the history of philosophy.

The certainty of the precedence of history of philosophy in philosophy was plainly visible in the universities of Latvia (and throughout the Baltic's) in the seventies-eighties of the 20th century. In Soviet Latvia times the study programmes were devised so as to cover all the ages and regions, the *classics of philosophy* placed in the forefront. In Soviet times there certainly existed obligatory study programmes worked out in Moscow, however, the question was in the way of presentation. Following Soviet ideological standpoints History of Philosophy was supposed to be concentrated on Marxism and on the works of thin-

---

7   Belief in the significance of the classics of philosophy manifested itself in Latvia in the series of editions *Works of the Thinkers of the Past* published since 1977. It must be mentioned that in those times these books were to be found in almost everybody's home as they were taken to be part of intellectual way of life. The texts of classics of philosophy attained comparatively wide circulation. Books by classics of philosophy were published in 12 to 15 thousand copies which is improbable in Latvia at the beginning of the 21st century.

kers of the Socialist camp. However, mostly it was not common practice because mastering philosophy was based on the studies of *classic authors* – Plato, Descartes, Kant, etc.

This tendency towards history of philosophy had no deeper foundation in the philosophy of history or any ideological system. The view as to who is or is not a classic stemmed from popular traditions, or books by historians of philosophy recognized in the West. The peculiarity was that history of philosophy studies displayed the epistemological, ethical, aesthetical, axiological and philosophically anthropological solutions to problems that contrasted with the prevailing standpoints of Marxism in the field. Thus, the studies of history of philosophy played the part of intellectual dissidence[8]. This could be viewed as the *third model* in which the history of philosophy besides summarizing past views undertakes the load inherent to philosophy, that of solving contemporary problems without the possibility of systemizing and basing them on the philosophy of history.

The fourth model is known as an attempt to view the history of philosophy without system, without basing it on the standpoints of the philosophy of history. The basis of the model lies in the view that what one should grasp in history is the individual, the concretely significant, not the abstractly general[9]. Thus, every significant author or school of philosophy should be viewed only in its own inherent aspect acknowledging the principle of romanticism that the particular encompasses the general. This standpoint is reflected in the metaphors: there is sea in every grain of sand, and macrocosm in every microcosm. An isolated view on history of philosophy actually excludes historicity, because it does not form the view of philosophy as the development of thought and its hereditary character. However, this model is quite often to be found in textbooks and lecture courses because it allows one to try and understand the author as much as possible irrespective of traditions whether he/she lived a thousand or a hundred years ago. It requires not only a most thorough penetration into the views of a personality, but also empathy and intellectual intuition.

---

8   The feelings were not clearly expressed or described, however, all who were engaged in philosophy studies in Soviet times understood them. The philosophers whose fields of study were, for example, Ancient Greece, Renaissance, existentialism were a sort of intellectual caste.

9   This standpoint is based on neo-Kantian philosophy concerning the problem of methodology of cultural studies although it should be taken into consideration that representatives of neo-Kantianism have themselves written outstanding books on history of philosophy illustrating traditions and the hereditary character of views.

The psychoanalytical view on the history of philosophy should be regarded as an extravagant approach.

In working out history of philosophy, system, on the one hand, and isolationism, on the other, are two extremes that seem to offer a historical aspect while actually precluding it.

The fifth model I relate to the turn to modernity in European philosophy. There appears a tendency to replace problems of the philosophy of history by some other discipline. One of the variants is sociology of knowledge, another – philosophy of culture. And still another – philosophical anthropology.

Odo Marquard writes[10] about the tendency at the beginning of the 20th century to discontinue philosophy of history and instead turn to philosophical anthropology[11]. He observes that philosophy of history was taken to mean a number of things, namely: philosophical foundations of history science, the regional ontology of the ontological sphere of "history", the fundamental ontology of human historicity, the theoretical platform of a historian's thinking.

If in the classical understanding philosophy of history is a standpoint that grasps the world processes, discerns regularities in them, purpose, sense, increase of freedom and so on, then in the age of modernity philosophy of history is regarded to be an Enlightenment myth.

One can come across ideas that philosophy of history starting point is the Apocalypse preached by the prophets and spiritual movement[12], and the 19th century philosophy of history, in its turn, is to be viewed as history of theology secularization (H. Blumenberg's ideas). Isn't philosophy of history going through the same thing that happened to modern times in the history of Europe: they just came to an end. If an end has come to philosophy of history, then is it a good end to something bad, or a bad end to something good? How can one do without philosophy of history? Interestingly, while rejecting the traditional pattern of philosophy of history there is no visible agitation as to what history of philosophy is going to be based on.

A turn towards philosophical anthropology draws philosophy nearer to the problems of culture whose solutions in a peculiar way supplant the philosophy

---

10 Marquard O. *Schwierigkeiten mit der Geschichtsphilosophie.* Suhrkamp Taschenbuch Wissenschaft, N.394, Frankfurt am Main, 1973, S.13.

11 See, for example, Max Scheler's works.

12 Loewit K.*Weltgeschichte und Heilsgeschehen. Die theologischen Voraussetzung der Geschichtsphilosophie.* W. Kohlhammer Verlag, Stuttgart, 1953.

of history niche. We shall discuss it in greater detail in the final stage of the report.

The sixth model is a reflection of the influence of phenomenology and existential philosophy on the 20th century philosophy on the whole[13]. The problems traditionally discussed in philosophy of history are turned towards the *Lebenswelt* discovered in phenomenology. That is where contemporary philosophy of history finds its anthropological bases. We do not speak of anthropology in the physical sense – what nature does to a human, but in the pragmatic sense – as an answer to the philosophical question of history: what does a human as a free, active being forms of him/herself [14]. How to combine history and time with lasting human cultural values[15]? Understanding of history is based on the understanding of human condition. M. Heidegger admits that we have to master the knowledge of the world's *historical existence*. The formation of this knowledge is the task of philosophy and the science of history. According to Heidegger, the phenomenological problem of the sense of history should be unfolded as the problem man's existence. In his Cassel lectures (1925), i.e. before publishing *Sein und Zeit*, Heidegger delves into the problems of philosophy of history and discerns three basic problems:
- what is history and the historical,
- historicity (Geschichtlichkeit) and the science of history,
- historical cognition as a possibility to be historical, that is given by history of philosophy research.

Heidegger marks a turning point when philosophy departs from concentrating on subjectivity. His style of thinking complies with the expression: We are lived by others. The battle for understanding of historicity is not a question of the world's historical image and course of development, but of the essence of historical existence itself. It is time, according to Heidegger, that makes one understand that man is historical.

K. Jaspers examines similar problems. However, if for Heidegger the theme of historicity remains in the centre of Dasein philosophy, then Jaspers, in my opinion, does not solve the question of the link of man's historicity to history;

13   Nagl-Docekal H. *Die Objektivitaet der Geschichtswissenschaft.* R.Oldenbourg, Wien, 1982.

14   M.Heidegger in his *Cassel* lectures states that contemporary philosophy of history has to thank W. Dilthey for motives, yet contemporary theories have not understood the essence of Dilthey's views and have even taken pains to "bury" it so as to leave it obscure up to our day.

15   Wendorff R. Zeit und Kultur. *Geschichte des Zeitbewusstseins in Europe.* Westdeutscher Verlag, 1985.

for him both of them remain a subject for speculation, his works accentuating either human historicity or – history.

Nowadays, philosophy of history has been so thoroughly transformed that it has lost its traditional features and is incorporated in the philosophy of being, man's existence. The task of history of philosophy is to uncover the embodiment of human historicity as an existential process that may have gone astray, too (for example, Heidegger's story of European metaphysics). It is not systemizing the predecessors' views or their unrelated description that prevails at present in history of philosophy, but rather "measuring" to the processes of existence and relation to the discovery of the truth of existence.

A great number of contemporary authors have joined the phenomenologically-Heideggerian school. The prematurely deceased Roland Rumpel writes that history should be characterized in categories of Lebenswelt, sense, structure, action, play[16]. His views have been noticeably influenced by Kant, Dilthey, Romantics, phenomenologists, and supplemented with the theme of cosmic chaos wherein human beings supply the organization of sense formation (*Sinnorganization am Chaos des Geschehens*). Rumpel believes that the subject in principle can rationally reconstruct his historicity. It is a view differing from the now popular H.G.Gadamer's hermeneutics that teaches understanding to be a historical *Ueberlieferungs* process governed by traditions and superstitions.

The seventh model is both repudiation of philosophy of history and history of philosophy as independent research subjects. Let us examine some textbooks bought and published in a number of editions in English, German and Russian. Characteristically, there are textbooks excluding the themes of history, historicity altogether. You won't find the themes in Richard Double's *Beginning Philosophy*, for instance. You will not find the entry "History" in *Glossary of Philosophical Terms*, either, the prevailing themes being knowledge, external world, mind/body, normative and metaethics, free will, existence of God, evil.

Another author, A. Anzenbacher in *Einführung in die Philosophie*[17] includes the themes Historicity (*Geschichtlichkeit*) and History in the section Man (*Mensch*), in the explanation referring to Heidegger. As to History of Philosophy, it is infiltrated into all the sections – *Seinsphilosophie, Ichphilosophie, Gott* and others. It is offered the status of *Begriffsgeschichtliche Beispiele*.

---

16 Rumpel R. *Geschichte, Freiheit und Struktur.* Verlag Karl Aller, Freiburg/München, 1990.

17 Anzenbacher A. *Einfuerung in die Philosophie.* Herder: Freiburg, Basel, Wien, 1992.

To what extent the themes of history and historicity are viewed in textbooks of philosophy is only a detail, a reflection of a wider process that is claiming its rights in the times of modernity.

After Hegel European philosophy displays tendencies that begin renouncing the importance of history of philosophy respecting, in the first place, only the potency of philosophy to solve practical problems of the life today and play "language games". The question is not of the relationships among: philosophy – history of philosophy – philosophy of history. The question is of change of understanding of the essence of philosophy itself.

F. Nietzsche is one of the most outstanding opponents who in his work *Untimely Meditations (Unzeitgemässe Betrachtungen)* once again raises the question: with history or without it? The perfect cynic animal does not live historically says Nietzsche, because it gives himself up to the present openly and without pretense. But next to him the more intelligent and educated creature - man - wastes away and perishes because the lines of his past horizon keep nervously moving towards the present. Nietzsche does not deny that only due to the power that turns the past into history does man become man. However he casts doubts on to what extent life has a need for the services of history at all. History is to man like a collar to a horse. It reins in and directs him wherever it wants. Man who surpasses himself must get rid of the collar.

Nowadays the standpoint of neo-pragmatism does not see the need for history of philosophy in philosophy. Thinking as such is not given the central place, seeing pragmatic benefit that could be based on the truth as a mode of solidarity, is what is desired instead. But that, in its turn, results from the narrative characteristic of the particular period.

R. Rorty states quite openly: "We have to see whether we can find a use for it"[18] and expresses the idea: "truth is a propery of linguistic entities, of sentences"[19]. In his understanding philosophy is "is rarely an examination of the pros and cons of a thesis. Usually it is, ... a contest between an entrenched vocabulary ... and a half-formed new vocabulary which vaguely promises great things."[20]. This way philosophy does not proceed step by step along the path of mastering history, its approach is pragmatic and at the same time all-embracing. The new style in philosophy is just trying to make the new vocabulary attractive, to arouse interest and stimulate activity.

18 Rorty R. *Contingensy, Irony, and Solidarity.* Cambridge University Press, Cambridge, 1989, p. 135.
19 Ib. p. 7.
20 Ib. p. 9.

The new standpoints denote a complete disruption with classical philosophy. German classical philosophy strictly demands philosophical thinking to look for support in understanding the borderlines and search for justifications. It denies destructively innovative activity as the only possible one, but tries to form the thought as a whole. A century later T. Adorno, K. Popper and others will reproach Hegel for pushing the idea of totality and initiation of totalitarianism, but, in my opinion, they will do it without adequate enough justification.

Hegel has viewed a situation when philosophy expresses a wish not to reflect but to act on the basis of empirical life experience. He states clearly that the reason for ignoring history of philosophy is impatience and a wish to obtain as one's own view something that is in consciousness, a concept. Our thoughts usually merge with observations, views and feelings. It is in human nature because people would rather feel than think. Philosophy, however, should not submit to the inclinations of human nature. It is necessary to cultivate oneself and to nurture a specific way of reflection that is not feasible when one gives in to experiential temptations and the wish to assert oneself in a destructive or self-descriptive activity. Hegel mocks at obtaining knowledge by way of immediate observation.

In this context let us turn to pedagogical approaches to teaching philosophy. Right in front of my eyes in Latvia there is an example of the Ministry of Education and Science demonstrating the tendency towards the "new style". It is regarded that philosophy taught at school should become a practical guideline in life. History of philosophy, its classics, in their opinion, is a superfluous collection of doctrines for life should be grasped directly, emotionally and freely. *It is an attempt to place in the centre of philosophical thought ways of arranging individual experience instead of thinking based on the history of European culture.* "We do not offer the pupil to master history of philosophy, we offer the opportunity to train oneself for an equivalent conversation with culture throughout his lifetime. This approach does not impose any concrete doctrines, its orientation is towards universal values, such as humanism, rationalism (as the fusion of the rational and the emotional) and freedom. Philosophy in this instance is not an object of research, but an instrument ...," we read in the book entitled *the Joy of Thinking. Teachers' book*[21] written by the Latvia Philosophy Education Centre authors.

---

21 Domātprieks. Skolotajnā ģramāta. – Filosofiskās izglītības centres. Riga, 2002, 10. lpp.

Without questioning the tendency towards optimizing the study process it should be recognized that this turn if put into practice under the guidance of the Ministry of Education and Science on the republican scale will mark the end of the "era of history of philosophy" in Latvia. It will signify the end of *philosophical classics as the basis of thought* "throwing" philosophy into "the playground" where all are "equal", there being neither the great, nor the foolish, just different modes of adventure. The joy of thinking is in danger of losing any connection with intellect, any feeling of intellectual gratification having been written off. Intellectual gratification cannot appear as a result of a pupil's empiric experience, in which neither ideas nor forms can be discovered. Its fountainhead has always been and will continue to be meeting with the classics of philosophy, i.e. the sphere of thinking in which within the space of thousands of years both grand ideas and subtle thinking style and forms have evolved. With the "new approach" philosophy turns into *an instrument* serving only the practical, empiric life processes.

Inhabiting "the playground" one can afford to say that the pupil will train him/herself for *an equivalent* conversation with culture. What is the meaning of *equivalent* here? Does it mean "understanding", "capable of interpreting" or having equivalent creative abilities? There are peaks in culture that can only be approached in an attempt to understand and never will all be able to possess equivalent creative abilities. This is also an evidence of a conceptual difference in the views on the nature of philosophy and history: whether to appreciate the eternal peaks (Socrates, Plato, Augustine, Thomas Aquinas, Descartes, Kant, Nietzsche, Husserl, Heidegger, Wittgenstein and a great many others that actually transcend time) or else "to democratize" philosophy drawing it into the "personality acquisition" training sessions.

Appreciating and respecting the classics of philosophy teachers teach their pupils that history of philosophy can boast of personalities of *genius* and discoveries of a scale that everyday thinking and ordinary persons' abilities cannot match up to. They are transcendent, thus raising man's view of him/herself, calling upon him/her to surpass him/herself for the sake of higher values. In the process of education the hierarchical scheme of understanding culture (acknowledging the hierarchy of values and views from the point of view of the thoroughness, profoundness and veracity of philosophical thought) will call forth consequences differing greatly from the "liberally democratic" scheme of understanding culture. The latter's attempt to make all equally alike will lay the greatest stress in one's eyes on one's own precious self.

Returning to the last, *sixth model* I'd like to characterize it in greater detail. My understanding expounded in the textbook *Philosophy* [22] (in collaboration with R. Kulis) is based on the attempts to find interconnection among the study of philosophy, history of philosophy and culture. The scheme realized in the book is as follows: history of philosophy in the context of cultural paradigms plus problems of contemporary philosophy that are "extracted" from the most outstanding patterns of the history of philosophy of the corresponding time. Linking philosophy with processes of creative cultural we come to the conclusion that the central theme of philosophy is culture. In a way that is following neo-Kantian standpoints of the turn of the 20th century interspersed with the teaching of phenomenology and existential philosophy on man and historicity.

The Latvian history of philosophy is not discussed as a detached – national thought; it is characterized against the background of the history of philosophy of the world in connection with the trends our country's authors belonged to.

I am fully aware, though, that bringing the studies of philosophy and culture together there appears a danger of diluting intellectual reflection in the description of cultural events of the past.

On the other hand, there is also a danger of drowning history of philosophy in culture research and paradigm descriptions.

How should history of philosophy and culture be written? Can it be written irrespective of the predominating narratives, paradigms or *epistemes* of the time (whatever denotation for the cultural and historic horizons one chooses to use)? Contemporary philosophy assures it is impossible. Hermeneutic interpretations remain at our disposal.

At the beginning of the 20th century the neo-Kantian W. Windelband in his work *Philosophy in the German Spiritual Life of the 19th Century* writes: "Philosophy has almost dissolved in the relativism of history of philosophy. On the other hand, the rest that has remained in connection with the tasks of the theory of cognition has become incorporated into empiric psychology"[23].

Besides, Windelband considers that the dissolution of philosophy in the philosophy of history does not proceed the way it was foreseen by Hegel. While Hegel regarded trends to be steps in the development of thought on its road to the truth, nowadays the opposite is the case: trends are considered to be falla-

---

22 The book has been published in Latvia in six repeated editions of over 30 000 copies since 1996. The work is translated into Russian and published in Latvia in 1997, though not in a great number of copies.

23 Windelband W. *Die Philosophie im deutschen Geistesleben des Jahrhundrets. Verlag von J.C.B. Mohr, Tübingen, 1927, s. 96-120.*

cies of thought. The multiplicity of different world outlooks that have emerged and their mutual opposition preclude unity in any form. Windelband cites a saying popular in the scientific circles of his time: philosophy is no more, there is only history of philosophy. We, neo-Kantians, do not agree to that because we see philosophy not as a summary of separate sciences, but as a return to idealism that sees eternal values. They are based on the highest spiritual truth while their implementation takes place in culture where values manifest themselves as significances. In this connection thanks are due to Hegel who saw values in the overall process of history and discovered their transempiric character. Philosophy, according to Windelband, has a cultural task to perform: how to reconcile a personality's inner life values with the mass culture of the outer life, how to solve the problem of personality and mass or man and society relations. This type of philosophy should be linked with philosophy of culture (*culturology*).

Philosophy of culture (culturology) as a branch of science is not widely acknowledged, however, according to Windelband, its birth at the beginning of the 20th century is as significant as the birth of natural sciences a few centuries ago[24]. I am inclined to agree with him because I am appalled at the philosophically irresponsible ease with which the modernist trends have tried to disentangle themselves from the duty to uncover and explain to the individual the manipulations with his or her life. Anthropological philosophy is capable of stimulating emancipation interest, however, it is not possible dissociating oneself from the classics of history of philosophy, but only believing in the eternity of values and discarding exaggerated fear of totalitarianism of ideas.

Claims to the part of the first fruits of cultural studies in Europe appear in another aspect, too. In quite a number of countries after the Second World War there gradually becomes apparent the dangerously dominating role of commercial pop culture. Educators are of the opinion that involving classical values of culture into education might weaken this influence. Stewart Hall[25] describes British scientists as the first discoverers[26] of cultural studies. However, this branch of science is not characterized by a wish to collaborate with philosophy. Some British scientists protest against the exaggeration of the significance of

---

24 Ib. s. 96-120.

25 Hall S. "Cultural Studies and its Theoretical Legacies". *The Cultural Studies Reader*. Ed. by Simon During. – Routledge, 2003, pp. 97-110.

26 F.R. Levis and R. Hoggart are considered to be the initiators of British cultural studies. Their main intention was to present to the wider population literary understanding of classical texts and form ethical views that were in accord with the influence of social democrats on the British political situation of the time.

theoretical and philosophical aspects in cultural studies and wish to develop critique of ideology[27]. Stewart Hall, who was head of the Centre for British Cultural Studies for a long time, remarks: "We read German idealism, we read Weber from beginning to end and the other way round, we read Hegel's idealism, we read idealistic art critique."[28] It all grew into a rather empiric trend of cultural studies of left orientation. But the British are quite quick in rejecting the left tendencies for Marxism, they maintain, cannot explain the notions "culture", "ideology", "language', "the symbolic", "our time" and others well enough. However, there was a time when they acknowledged as Marxist heritage the doctrine about historicity, hegemony, exploitation, classes, basis and superstructure adhering quite closely to the second model I mentioned.

The work of culture study specialists does not consist only in forming theories, but also in passing the knowledge over to others and that is why this discipline can be characterized by the same tendency as in Enlightenment times, namely, educate and teach. But to what extent is the knowledge ideologically tended? There was a time when British cultural study specialists tried to find the answer in the Marxist Antonio Gramsci cultural theory that characterizes culture as "engaged knowledge". It exists in a definite situation and is used to direct political and historical processes. The "alphabet" and "grammar" of culture are instruments of social power and that is why cultural processes should be linked with active and critical practice. Gramsci characterizes culture as hegemony or the concealed domination of power.[29] It lures people into a trap to make them think alike and in accordance with the interests of power.

Culture is understood through conventional consciousness.[30] Individuals are ideological constructs, ideology being understood not as belief in ideas, but as a system of images and discourses forming the most widespread totality of values and knowledge. Ideology in this sense is expressed in the words "common view, conventional consciousness". Ideology turns political, temporal and changing values into eternal and natural things, *as it were*. The initial mission of ideology is not in representing party politics, but in constructing an imaginative picture of everyday life accessible to everyone.

---

27 This tendency is well known in Germany in the works of the Frankfurt Social Research School, but every country has its own ways of implementing it.

28 Hall S. "Cultural Studies and its Theoretical Legacies." *The Cultural Studies Reader*. Routledge, 2003, p. 101.

29 With the help of this phenomenon Gramsci explains the popularity of Italian fascism because fascism is not only ideology, it is concealed in forms of culture.

30 Cultural studies in Britain in the seventies of the 20th century begin to be influenced by L. Althusser and J. Lacan.

Thus, the field of vision of cultural studies encompasses not only culture as a specific phenomenon, but also ideology as a totality of symbols and ideas. Ideology absorbs people. It may present individuals' lives to them as free and unique while in a deeper sense this symbolic order "plays its own games" with the individual. In the standpoints of the French thinker Michel Foucault culture is neither an aim in itself as a creator and keeper of positive (eternal) values, nor a product of an active autonomous subject. It is a mechanism of spreading forms of power.

Ideology acts as a glue for society (says Georgian philosopher Merab Mamardashvili), it manifests itself in cultural processes and imperceptibly even takes over philosophy.

Interestingly, in Latvia since the sixties of the 20th century cultural studies together with philosophical studies have gone through all the conceptual cycles described above although there were no direct contacts with German philosophy of culture and British literature on cultural studies was not available at the time. The problem cycles are characterized by:

(1) Marxist-tended cultural reductionism,
(2) culture as an embodiment of spiritual values and promoter of ideas of humanism, and as a basis for writing history of philosophy in Latvia,
(3) culture as understanding of symbolic forms, and philosophy explaining man's existence in culture,
(4) analysis of concrete cultural regions (Latgale, for instance) keeping in view the general impression of ideas, language, values and everyday life.

That is why culture – the basis of philosophy – can turn out to be engaged and endangered. Contemporary philosophy has uncovered a certain naiveté of neo-Kantianism in their belief in eternal values. However, to me this link of philosophy and culture[31] seems the most appropriate one in order to discover the relationships between history of philosophy and the so-called philosophy of history. The dogmatism of the philosophy of history is not being renewed. The solution of cultural themes is based on axiology and philosophical anthropology while phenomenological and hermeneutical methods guard from the system shackles. History of philosophy is not a study for its own sake, it is there to mark the problem fields and discover manifold solutions at contemporary culture.

---

31 At the XXI World Congress of Philosophy in Istanbul I noticed that philosophy of culture is widely discussed by thinkers from Eastern Europe, Russia, China and much less by philosophers from the USA and Germany.

Cultural Plurality and Education. Russian Case: Past and Present

Marietta Stepaniants

The story of teaching history in Russia proves to be very much (if not fully) depended on state ideology. It does not mean, however, that education in its turn can not indirectly be one of the main ways of striking that same ideology so much as to radically change it, or to replace by an opposite one. In this paper I shall try to reflect on teaching history of philosophy in Russia with a special attention to the approach to cultural plurality since I fully in accord with Charles Taylor who considers multicultural education as a *moral imperative* of the time.

While teaching of philosophy in Europe started in the XIII century (the University of Paris, Cambridge and Oxford), in Russia it happened much later, after the decree issued by Peter the Great (by the way, the latter followed an advice given to him by Leibniz) in 1724 to start teaching philosophy at the Academic University of Petersburg Academy of sciences. By establishing in 1855 the Moscow University teaching of philosophy firmly got a status of a secular discipline. The Russian-German academic relations of that time played the main role in raising the rank of philosophy in its opposition to the widely spread conservative public opinion, in particular, of the clerical milieu.

A favorable situation for teaching philosophy stayed for a short time, until 1811 when the Minister of Education (A.K.Razumovsky) approved a new curriculum from which philosophical disciplines were excluded. The establishment of the Ministry of religious affairs and education in 1817 promoted the shaping of the official state ideology in the long run formulated as "Provoslavie, samoderjavie, narodnost"... (that is : Orthodoxy, the czarist autocracy and nationalism).

By the czar's decree an instruction concerning a new official politics towards teaching philosophy was issued, according to which "everything that is not in accord with the Holy Scripture, is nothing but a delusion and a lie which should be without mercy to be discarded; ... only those philosophical theories are well-founded and just which are in tune with Evangelic teaching, since the truth is one, while delusions are innumerable".[1]

Starting from 1822 a term "Russian philosophy" was circulated. The latter carried on not so much an ethnic character as, using the words of Berdyaev, the character of "church nationalism", or to say more precisely, of "church isolation". A concept of "Russian philosophy" was first formulated by Prof. O. Novitsky in his speech dated 15 July 1837 in which it was declared: "The philosophy of our Fatherland will be our own creation (it would be Orthodox Christian — M.S.), it will not be borrowed from anybody".[2]

The Revolutions of 1848 in Europe had a fatal impact on the future of philosophy in Russia. Czar Nikolay the First in the beginning of 1850 ordered the minister of education "to express his views whether teaching of philosophy, which was mainly developed that time by German scholars, should take place in Russia, or it would be wise to take measures to save the students from the reasoning of the modern philosophical systems".[3] Soon after that, the decree was issued: to abolish teaching of philosophy by secular philosophers and to pass teaching of logic and practical psychology upon theologians appointed by the Ministry of Education along with the Ministry of Religion".

After the death of Nikolay the First (1855) and the abolition of the serfdom a new period of reforms took place in Russia. However the process of transformations was slow and painful. The oscillations in the political and socio-economic developments affected the spiritual life: "the thaw" of the end of 50-s – and the beginning of 60-s was replaced by "the frosts" of the 80-s. Yet, the years after the reforms marked the epoch of the cultural raise (though rather slow one) in many fields including the field of philosophy (V. Solovyev, K. Kavelin, B. Chicherin. L. Lopatin, etc.).

Teaching philosophy "blossomed" in the time of three Russian revolutions which preceded the October revolution of 1917. Philosophical life became richer, more pluralistic (though, in a European way only).

---

1   See: V.F. Pustarnakov. *Philosophy at the Russian Universities.* Moscow, 2003, p. 113, (in Russian).
2   O.Novitsky. *On Importance of Reproaches at Philosophy from Theoretical and Practical Sides.* Kiev, 1838, p. 302, (in Russian).
3   Op. cit. V.Pustarnakov, p.156.

Summing up the general trend in the history of teaching philosophy in the Russian Empire prior the October Revolution of 1917 one may say that it was characterized by the constant struggle between two opposite trends: one that was oriented to "open" Russia so that to provide its inclusion in the intellectual world of the West, to promote freedom and plurality of views, philosophical in particularly, and the other trend (mostly preferred by the authorities) which was aimed to keep Russia isolated from the impacts from the outside, to maintain and to strengthen the three "pillars" of the ideology – Orthodoxy, the czarist autocracy and nationalism.

It should be pointed up that *history* of philosophy had always stayed in the epicentre of the above mentioned struggle. It was recommended "to teach the history of philosophical systems in an accusatory sense".[4] Philosophical ideas were to be estimated from ideological and religious point of view. Yet, it does not mean that the official orders had been always strictly carried out. A number of the university professors, like P. Trubetskoy at Petersbourgh University, or P. Voznesensky at Moscow University, violated the orders and presented the history of philosophy (though only Western one) in the richness of its plurality.

Paradoxically, the October revolution, in spite of all radical changes it claimed and in fact brought, smashed the above mentioned pillars but did not them rooted out. As a result, the old pillars were replaced by the new ones which by appearance looked different but, verily, were cultivated from the former roots. Thus, Christian Orthodoxy was substituted by the orthodoxy of Marxist-Leninist ideology, the autocracy of the czars – by the dictatorship of the Communist party, nationalism – by Soviet patriotism. In the long run, the results were similar: freedom and plurality of views were limited (if not banned at all), intellectual life in the Soviet Union remained very much separated from the outside world, especially from the West.

I would not like to exaggerate and simplify the matter. The above said intellectual "separation" did not mean that the foreign writers or philosophers were not translated, published and studied. On the contrary, the Soviet Union boasted by the scope of circulation of the books translated from many languages of the world. Yet, it did not mean a genuine openness. There was a strict selection aimed to support the monopoly of the single ideology – the postulates of

---

4   N. Zagoskin. *The Educators of the Empire Kazan University for the First Century of Its Existence 1804 – 1904.* In 4 volumes. Vol. 4, 1904, p. 627. (in Russian).

Marxism-Leninism, while completely ignoring or prohibiting the views which could bring any doubts in the absolute truth of the official ideology.

Saltykov-Shchedrin, a great Russian writer, whose penetrating satire on and criticism of czarist Russia maintained its force long after the October revolution, described the mood widely spread in Russian society in the following words: "It would be most proper to make a law according to which only those sciences and humanities are capable of spreading light (in other words, of bringing enlightenment – M.S.) and that provide fulfillment of the orders given by the authorities." It seems that in the Soviet Union, this recommendation was truly followed.

Among all other disciplines philosophy was considered to be the most effective in serving the authorities and the Soviet regime as a means by which loyalty to the single ruling ideology was safeguarded.

In order to make philosophy work most effectively as a part of the ideological machine, the course on Marxist-Leninist philosophy was prescribed as compulsory for all students in the country. There were no secrets about the reasons why it had been done. Thus, it is stated very openly that the students in any field of sciences or humanities "must learn how to be right, corresponding in spirit to Marxism-Leninism in their methodological and Weltanschauung conclusions, and how to be guided in their research work by the dialectical method of knowledge."[5]

Marxist Philosophy as a part of Marxism-Leninism was declared as the only philosophy which discovered the universal laws of the development of nature, society and thinking, proved the necessity and inevitability of the socialist revolution, of the triumph of socialism and communism, thus giving to the working people valuable assistance in their struggle for the better days. Marxism had been reduced to primitive and much distorted formulas. In fact, the foundation of the Soviet teaching of philosophy had been laid by the so-called *Short Course of the History of VKPB* (abbreviation for the National Bolshevik Communist Party), part II, chapter 4. The language of that source of philosophical "wisdom" was artificial: it lacked any real meaning. It could not been understood: it could only be crammed as a kind of a spell.

The philosophical system, which was presented as the most perfect, rested on a number of basic notions: materialism as opposed to idealism, dialectics as opposed to metaphysics, rationality as opposed to irrationality, atheism as op-

---

posed to religion, and so on. The contrast between each of theses dualisms in turn was exposed in a vulgar simplified way.

Such an insistence on the recognition only materialistic, dialectical, rationalistic, and atheistic ideas as true and valuable terribly impoverished the philosophical heritage and led to a distorted presentation of the history of philosophy as such. Since history of Eastern philosophies is my field of specialization, I would like to demonstrate the above said by the referring to the *History of World Philosophy* in six volumes published in the Soviet Union.[6]

It was formulated in the introduction to the first volume that the purpose of the whole publication was to reject "Europecentrism" and "to restore the historical truth, showing the fruitful progressive development of philosophical thought, especially of materialism, in China, India, in the Arab and other countries of the East".[7] In their desire to discover at all costs the "line of Democritus and Plato" in ancient India, for example, the authors often identified with materialism any anti-Brahmanic trends of thought associated, say, with rejection of *moksa* (liberation) or with critical attitude to asceticism, etc.[8] Yet, it is well known, that the opposition to Brahmanism was not yet a proof of materialist views. Suffice it to recall that the strongest anti-Brahmanic trends were the teachings of the Buddhists and of the Jains.

A real status of and correlation between materialist and idealistic views in India were arbitrarily distorted. The role of Lokayata-Charvakas was exaggerated and pushed in to the foreground. While, say, four pages were dedicated to the Lokayata, the Vedanta darsana, the most influential of the classical Brahmanic schools in India, was mentioned only once and covered one page. Other darsanas (the Nyaya, the Vaisesika, the Yoga, the Samkhya, the Mimansa) were considered with the single purpose of finding elements of materialism in them. Since, no such elements could be discovered, say, in the Yoga, it was negatively and unequivocally defined as an extreme form of "idealism of the mystical variety".[9]

Things were about as bad in the case of philosophy of Buddhism, which was presented in a simplistic and schematic fashion. The name of the founder of

---

6   See: *History of Philosophy*. In 6 volumes. Moscow, 1957-1965, (in Russian).

7   Ibid., Vol. I, Moscow, 1957, p. 18.

8   Ibid., pp. 44-45.

9   Ibid., p. 57.

Madhyamica School Nagarjuna was merely mentioned and presented in a negative light for resorting to "logical trickery" and "speculation" on the relativity
of human knowledge.[10]

As a result, the role of idealism in the Oriental philosophical heritage was
underestimated, as was its objective significance for the development of human knowledge. In the conclusion to the chapter on "The Birth and Development of Philosophical Thought in Slave-Owning Societies of the Ancient East"
we read: "Under the dominance of slave-owning aristocracy and religious ideology, the best and most fruitful doctrines of the Ancient East were either materialist in their nature or contained materialistic elements."[11]

The chapters of *The History of Philosophy* dedicated to the East, as well as the
majority of the writings of the philosopher-orientologists of the Soviet time
were written with the aim to eradicate Europecentric approach to Eastern philosophies. The aim was solemnly declared in the beginning of the works published. However, while criticizing "bourgeois" Europecentrism, they proved to be
no less, though in their own way, europecentric. The Eastern philosophical systems were considered and evaluated solely in the frames of a vulgar, primitive-
ly understood Marxism.

The negative conditions under which history of philosophy was taught in
the Soviet Union were the consequence not only of the socio-political system
which existed for more than seven decades. Many of those conditions were
rooted much more deeply in the specific character of the Russian society as
such. The reflections by Nikolay Berdyaev on philosophy in pre-revolutionary
Russia (see for example Nikolay Berdyaev. *"Philosophical Truth and the Truth of
the Intelligentsia"*, one of his articles of 1905-1907) and his critical evaluations
could be accepted as advice for bringing the teaching of philosophy into line
with the demands of our present time.

Berdyaev points out that a Russian attitude to philosophy as well as to other
spiritual values is lacking in the culture. This negates the *independent* meaning
of philosophy, subordinating it to utilitarian, pragmatic social purposes.[12]

In Berdyaev's words, Russian intellectuals have failed "to unselfishly treat
philosophy because of their selfish attitude to the truth as such, since they
demand that truth play the role of a weapon for a social upheaval to bring

---

10   Ibid., p.188.

11   Ibid., p. 71.

12   N. Berdyaev. *Philosophical Truth and the Truth of the Intellisentia*//Vehi. Moscow, 1991, p.12, (in Russian).

fortune and happiness for the people"[13]. Due to the specific historical conditions the Russian intelligentsia's "love for equalizing justice had paralyzed the love for the truth"[14].

Thus, the first aim in teaching philosophy is to liberate truth from ideological pragmatism and revive its original status in "the quest for truth".

Secondly, Russian philosophy has always suffered from its isolation from the main trends of world philosophy. It has been too "home-bred" and sectarian. Hence, the task is to eliminate that separation, to maintain creative ties between Russian philosophy and the philosophical currents outside its borders, thus giving to the Russian people a chance to satisfy their "thirst" for truth using the rich sources of the world's philosophical heritage.

The *Perestroika* started by Gorbachev has brought radical changes in all the spheres of Russian life. One of its consequences has been the collapse of the former communist state ideology. An ideological vacuum was unusual to the people used to be guided, and resulted in painful reaction. There has been nostalgia about the lost Marxist-Leninist ideology among some while a strong wish and search for a new ideology around newly formulated "national idea" among the others. The latter trend was in particular strongly articulated during Eltsin's presidency.

For the present moment there is no officially instructed and supported search for a "national idea". However the tension between different ideological forces stays to be quite strong. As it was in the past, in the czarist Russia, there are still *slavyanifiles* and Russian *westernisers*. The former are nationalistic, with almost unconditional orientation to the Christian Orthodoxy taken as a core of the Russian identity as such, oriented to isolation from the rest world and at the same time claiming a revival of Russia as a super-power. The latter – would like to accept, even imitate, and to follow western values and institutions. There is of caurse the third trend, though much weaker than the former two: to look at Russia as Euro-Asian civilization, different from the West and the East, and at the same time in some way sharing the values of the both. The third trend has never been able to clarify its positions and has stayed to be mostly declarative one.

In my view, the new situation outside (globalization, the public reaction to it) and inside the country (the collapse of the Soviet Union, the necessity of

---

13   Ibid. p. 17.
14   Ibid.

building the Russian Federation as a democratic state which respects and gua-
rantees the rights of ethnic and religious minorities) have resulted in appearing
a new trend of thought which reflects the efforts to formulate ideological foundations of the new Russia taken into consideration multi-culturality.

Multicultural education can and should play a great role in dealing and
solving of the above said problem. Such education is of cause to be based first of
all on tolerance understood as norm of a compromise between competing cultures and as a readiness to accept those attitudes and views which promote the
conditions for preserving and maintaining cultural plurality, the right of everybody to keep one's difference from the others.

However tolerance is only a minimal ethical norm for an existence in a
multicultural society. It is not enough to tolerate, to stay out of conflict with the
otherness. It is no less important to enjoy as much as possible cultural plurality
for both individual and social perfection.

What kind of a methodology is desirable to use in shaping multicultural
education? A general answer might be − a methodology of a balanced demonstration of the general and the particular, that permits to discover an ontological commonness without which one can not start a dialogue with the other and
at the same time providing disclosure of the most principal cultural differences
(which might save from imposing any primitive, superficial homogeneity).

An intent attention to a specificity of any culture might be productive only
in case, if the former is free from the stereotypes, which result from a number of
causes, including: insufficient knowledge of a culture, measuring the latter by
one's own world-views and moral standards, arrogantly excluding or humilia-
ting even a chance for equality for different cultural values.[15] In Heidegger's
words, the global encounter or dialogues today are typically not conducted
between cultural partners, but rather on the basis of a linguistic and conceptual
framework supplied entirely by Western (or European) civilization. He called it
the "complete Europeanization [Westernization] of the earth and humankind".

The acknowledgment of a particular logically leads to making borders between that is your own and of the other. There is nothing wrong in the procedure
of such differentiation if it does not end in constructing a border similar to the
Berlin wall aimed to exclude any contacts, even more − any interaction between those who stay behind the different sides of the border. In Charles Tay-

---

15 See: Heidegger. *Dialogue on Language* // On the Way to Language. Trans. by Peter D.Hertz. San Francisco:
Harper & Row, 1971, pp. 15-16.

lor's words, the accentuation of the borders without the acknowledgment of interconnection is fraught with a danger to stifle in us an ability to respond to the deepest and the strongest human aspirations. [16]

For today the most dangerous seems to be the border-wall constructed between the Muslim and the Western (commonly identified as the Christian) worlds. That border is build up not only by the efforts of the politicians, ideologues, but, partly, of the scholars-orientologists[17], of the educators). The wall maintains and cultivates the transformation of "the other" into "the enemy", thus provoking and dictating correspondent ethical norms of relations and of behavior.

The acknowledgement of a specific, culturally particular might create premises for the respect towards "the other" and hence to promote a dialogue. However, very often it results oppositely in producing antagonistic consequences. That happens when the specific is interpreted not as value neutral but rather as a proof of the superiority of one culture over the other, which has an exclusive possession of the Truth. It is in this very way act so called Islamic fundamentalists, from one side, and those Westerners who are inclined towards arrogant and hostile attitude anything which is associated wit Islam.

The understanding of the causes which had brought cultural differences allows us to eliminate the obstacles on the way to the dialogue. The latter is possible only if the *common* features are disclosed. The people can not be absolutely different in everything. If they differ in one way, they are definitely the same in the other way. Daya Krishna, a distinguished Indian philosopher justly points out: "... if philosophy is an enterprise of the human reason, it is bound to show similarities across cultures to some extent and, similarly, as a human enterprise it is bound to be concerned with what man, in a particular culture, regards as *summum bonum* for mankind" [18].

In general, multicultural education can help to sanitize the moral climate in a society by promoting tolerance, by eliminating stereotypes which feed tension and hostility, by enlightening and enriching our knowledge, which in its

---

16 See: Charles Taylor. *Sources of the Self: The Making of Modern Identity.* Cambridge, MA: Harvard University Press, 1989, p. 520.

17 See: Edward W. Said. *Orientalism.* New York: Vintage Books, 1979.

18 Daya Krishna. *Comparative Philosophy: What It Is and What It Ought to Be* // Interpreting Across Boundaries. New Essays in Comparative Philosophy. Ed. by G.J. Larson and E. Deutsch. Princeton: Princeton University Press, 1988, p. 71.

turn enlarges opportunities for both individual and social choices, sets new ethical orientations and norms for behavior.[19]

---

19 "The crucial feature of human life is its fundamentally *dialogical* character. We became full human agents, capable of understanding ourselves, and hence of defining our identity, through our acquisition of rich human languages of expression" – where the latter include, in addition to spoken and written language, also "the languages' of art, of gesture, of love, and the like." (Charles Taylor. *The Politics of Recognition* // Multiculturalism and "The Politics of Recognition". Ed. by Amy Gutman. Princeton: Princeton University Press, 1992, pp. 31-32)

Philosophy in Bulgaria – History, Problems, Perspectives

Ivan Kaltchev

1. The Beginning of Philosophiphical Education in Bulgaria

At the beginning of his article 'A Look on the Development of the University' in the first 'Almanac of Sofia University 1888 – 1928' Prof. Ivan Georgov wrote, *'None of the Balkan nations, except for the Greeks, has ever manifested such an inclination and love for the spread of education and for intellectual development as Bulgarians do.'*

This love and inclination as well as the necessity of giving specialists the best possible training in Bulgaria for all spheres of public life have also laid the foundations of philosophical education in the country.

This was the beginning of the
"Higher School" in Sofia. In accordance with the Law on the Higher School of 20 December1894 it was divided into faculties, one of the first of which was the Faculty of History and Philology. Later, the Departments of Philosophy and History of Philosophy and Ethics were established. It was decided that the standard duration of courses of study should be 3 – 4 years.

The number of departments and their names were specified in the new Law of 1904 (which also changed the name of the Higher School to University). After this law, the Faculty of History and Philosophy comprised 16 departments, including two departments of philosophy: the Department of the History of Philosophy, which included the study of ethics, and the Department of Systematic Philosophy. These two departments existed until the academic year 1949/1950.

A Philosophy Laboratory also existed in the Faculty of History and Philosophy, which developed into an Institute of Philosophy, hosting seminars on the history of philosophy and systematic philosophy and a laboratory on experimental psychology. Ivan Georgov was the chief organiser of this institute for many years.

The specialised library of the Department of Philosophy began as a small library designed to meet the needs of lecturers, which was set up at the beginning of 1903 in the Institute of Philosophy. In 1905, it comprised 579 volumes.

During the academic year 1897/1898 the first two men specializing in philosophy and pedagogy graduated from the Higher School. In the academic years 1899/1900 and 1900/1901, their numbers grew considerably, reaching 51 men. The first five women spcializing in philosophy and pedagogy graduated in the academic year 1905/1906.

The curriculum of 1897/1898 for the study programme in Philosophy and Pedagogy featured as 'major subjects': Psychology, Logics, Ethics, Aesthetics, History of Philosophy, and Metaphysics and Pedagogy. 'Philosophical and Pedagogical Practice' and 'Auxiliary Subjects' were also included in the curriculum. The student was able to choose between teaching throughout history, philology, literature, natural sciences, mathematics and law, which were related to the major presentations in philosophy.'

Prof. Ivan Georgiev was the first specialist to offer courses in philosophy in the Higher School. During the academic year 1897/1898 he gave lectures on the History of Modern Philosophy, covering the period up to Kant (2 lectures a week + 1 practical training session), Psychology of Feeling and Will (1 lecture a week), and Logics (2 lectures a week).

In 1905 philosophy became a specialized field of study in its own right at the Faculty of History and Philosophy together with history, geography, Slavonic philology and literature. One man and one woman were the first graduates in philosophy as a new specialized field of study in 1911/1912.

Dr. Krustjo Krustev joined Prof. Georgov in the 1905/1906 academic year, conducting courses in Psychology (3 lectures a week), Problems of Metaphysics (2 lectures, plus 2 practical training sessions), Introduction to Philosophy (2 lectures) and Aesthetical Analysis (2 lectures).

Over 40 years (from 1888 to 1928) 229 men and 50 women graduated in philosophy. They received their higher education thanks to knowledgeable prominent figures including, in addition to Georgov and Krustev, Dr. Nikola Alexiev, Dimitar Mihalchev, Ivan Saruiliev, Spiridon Kazandjiev and Michail Dimitrov.

Georgov wrote in the Preface to Volume I of 'The History of Philosophy': *'It is true that not every human society devotes itself to systematic philosophical speculations but when human society reaches a certain degree of cultural development then philosophical speculation, in one form or another, appears in it out of necessity.'* Obviously, Bulgarian society in the post-liberation years needed not only economics, agronomy, medicine, history, mathematics, etc., but also to a great degree philosophy.

2. Ivan Andreev Georgov

'It seems to me that among our professors you are the one who resembles most closely Western European professors as far as your scientific activities, your manners and your private life are concerned.' These words of Ivan Saruiliev were addressed in one of his letters to Georgov, one of the founders of the University of Bulgaria and of Bulgarian academic philosophical thinking.

Georgov was born on 7 (20) January, 1862 in Veles (Macedonia). He finished his secondary education at the Civic School of Vienna and then at the teachers' college in Vienna. He started his pedagogical activities as a teacher in mathematics and geography in the school for land surveyors in Sofia in 1881. In February 1882, he was appointed Deputy Manager and Assistant Secretary of the Educational Council at the Ministry of Education. After having been awarded a scholarship from the Keremidchiev Fund in 1883, he became a student of philosophy and pedagogy in Jena. In 1885 he interrupted his training and participated in the Serbian – Bulgarian War in the Students' Legion. In 1888 he graduated and he sat for a doctor's examination in Jena. During the same year he became a teacher of philosophy and pedagogy as part of the advanced course in pedagogy and later, at a Higher School in Sofia.

Georgov was a full-time teacher, then a full-time Professor, the chair of the Department of History of Philosophy at the Higher School and at the University from 1 October 1892 to 15 September 1934; Dean of the Faculty of History and Philosophy during the 1900/1901 and 1908/1909 academic years; Rector of the Higher School and the University during the 1898/1899, 1905/1906, 1916/1917 and 1918/ 1919 academic years and a full member of Bulgarian Academy of Science beginning in 1902.

As a philosopher and scientist Georgov worked in several spheres: the history of philosophy, ethics, children's psychology, pedagogy and educational work and history, and in the public and journalistic sphere he dealt with Macedonia and Macedonian issues.

Georgov's extensive scientific studies resulted in 320 publications, 50 of which were translated into foreign languages (mainly German and French).

He died in Sofia on 13 August 1936.

3. Intellectual Resistance

During my many years of teaching philosophy, I have often speculated on the attitude towards this ancient intellectual occupation. There is hardly another sphere of human knowledge of which such opposing assessments are made – from apologetics to complete negation and even mockery. There is hardly another intellectual activity about which so many speculations have been made – religious, political, social, natural and scientific, etc. Recent years have been no exception in this respect. I have in mind the historical events in Bulgaria since 10 November 1989. I would not say that philosophy is a saint but I cannot agree that it is the miserable sinner some people think it to be and have made it to be, because during the years of totalitarianism it succumbed to political and ideological temptations, i.e. only dialectical and historical materialism were studied. Taking into account the narrow-mindedness of this form of philoso- phizing on the destructive and anti-humane role of historical materialism, we may not in the same way be incorrect and one-sided by denying that many valuable and positive ideas can be found even in the so-called Marxist philoso- phy. Not because it is Marxist but because it is philosophy. Everyone who taught dialectical and historical materialism were given, by means of the abstract language of philosophy, a unique opportunity to spread the seeds of doubt, to provoke thinking and to suggest ideas that none of their colleagues teaching other subjects would dare share and spread.

It is almost certain that during this period none of the representatives of the so-called technological and natural and scientific knowledge was aware of the potential of Marxist philosophy. They did not even consider intellectual resistance and professional dissatisfaction – especially as they often reminded us that we taught ideology and nothing else. It is logical to ask: what did these colleagues do to resist ideological guardianship? In the current situation of upheaval, philosophy is one of the focuses of negation of the totalitarian system in the name of something more reasonable and humane, i.e. democracy. Unfortunately, in the technical and technological universities today, there is scarcely room for philosophy, even though it is often spoken of as a humanizing science. Even if some generosity is shown towards philosophy, the overall policy with regard to humanitarian training cannot be said to be in favour of philosophy. Different branches of science claim to be humanities but it is extremely difficult for philosophy to win a place of its own in this struggle, even though this place belongs to it by rights and even though students at the higher schools have the opportunity of taking a second subject of specialization, for example, pedagogy or management in addition to philosophy. However, everything is reduced to private benefit, in the most mercenary sense of the word. In a developing market economy everybody defends their cushy job at the department in any one they can. One clever move that may be observed is the combination of philosophy with another science, made as if for the sake of philosophy, but made in reality, for some philosophers at least, to adapt to the new conditions. Thus, scientific hybrids sometimes originate that a respectable university would not accept. I am not against searching for a new face for philosophy and a new social role for the subject in the spirit of our time, but it must be done in accordance with academism and with competence.

4. Scepticism about Philisophy in Bulgaria?

What, then, are the reasons for the present extremely unenviable place of philosophy and philosophers in overall public life, how can this critical situation be overcome and how can progress be made in philosophical thinking and activities in Bulgaria?

Let me first of all review the reasons for the humble social status and lack of prestige of philosophy. These reasons lie beyond the contents and sphere of philosophy and beyond the behaviour of the philosophical community in Bulgaria nowadays.

The reasons reflect the attitude of society to philosophy in general, the approach of different political, social and cultural circles to deep and abstract and not always pragmatically orientated thinking, and to active participants in the process of philosophical reflection on life and on what happens in it. We might call these reasons objective or fatal because philosophy and philosophers have not participated in creating them. Instead, these reasons hav been imposed on them by historical destiny.

Among these reasons, I would rank as number one the ignorant and completely illegal identification of philosophy with Marxism and communism respectively, which the new 'democrats' make. From the existential experience I gained during the first enthusiastic years of democracy in Bulgaria as a participant in political battles and as a member, although with the status of a non-voting observer, of the Co-ordination Council of the Union of Democratic Forces, I have realised how endurable and offensive the ignorance of the major figures of this formation is as far as issues of philosophy and common ideology are concerned. With some exceptions they were people (and today's democratic leaders are neither better nor worse than them) who had never read a word by Descartes, Kierkegaard or Heidegger and had never experienced the excitement of the temptation of getting to know about life after death. At the same time, they haughtily and self-confidently said that philosophy meant Marxism and Marxism meant communism, consequently, philosophy and philosophers should be pushed into the corner because we were eradicating communism.

This extremely negative attitude to philosophy expressed by all people governing Bulgaria since 10 November 1989, was made clear in the attempts to close the Institute of Philosophy at the Bulgarian Academy of Science, to stop publications dealing with philosophy by cutting off funding and, most of all, to reduce considerably teaching of philosophy at secondary schools and universities. For example, using the Law on Higher Education as an excuse, the provisions for autonomy of higher schools and of their faculties were so freely interpreted and applied that in many places, philosophy was promptly excluded from syllabuses. Some interesting things happened. For example, philosophy was not studied by students of psychology at Sofia University, 'St. Kliment Ohridski', or by students at the Faculty of Journalism and Mass Communication. As I had conducted the philosophy course at this Faculty for many years I knew how interested students were in it because it was a special course for journalists, which gave them the minimum knowledge necessary for the elaboration of their own personal philosophical orientation with regard to the global development of social and historical processes. The course was discontinued on the initiative of one of the deputy deans, who was a former research associate at the Institute for Modern Social Theories of the Central Committee of the Bulgarian Communist Party. This action was taken without even asking the students their opinion. The response to my strong objection was that these were the conditions everywhere in Europe. This is a quite a strange argument – in all European universities teaching of philosophy is conducted in a proper manner and no European universities has a speciality, let alone a faculty, in journalism. In Europe one can become a journalist after a basic education and a post-graduate course on journalistic technique lasting several months. Such bombastic and pretentious courses like 'newspaper production' or 'newspaper architecture' are not taught there – it seems that the only missing course is 'newspaper taming'!

The negative attitude of people in governing circles to philosophy in my opinion means at least two things:

– for all of them, notwithstanding their political colours, philosophy is synonymous with Marxism and communism and now it is time for their revenge; hence, everybody who has taught philosophy before 1989 has served the communist dictatorial administration; therefore, there is no place for him in the processes of change;

– all people from governing circles hate philosophy and philosophers because, in fact, they are afraid of the idea of independent thinking and of opinions that differ from their own. They are afraid of philosophy and philosophers because they instigate differences of opinion, alternative opinions, oppositional views, and well thought out ideas and wisdom. It is not by chance that discontent against totalitarian administration has grown among professional philosophers and people close to them who like philosophising. All great world leaders behined any new beginning are people of spirit and wisdom, philosophers engaged in deep and subtle thinking and not lawyers at divorce proceedings or self-confident macroeconomists as is the case in Bulgaria.

The second reason for the unenviable circumstances of philosophy nowadays results from the objectives set by the people ruling Bulgaria. Irrespective of the demonstrated political bias it is obvious that what is called a transition to democracy is, in fact, madness for the people and an amazing opportunity for the rulers to solve their own everyday problems. Our country and our people are subject to an unprecedented robbery in the form of so-called privatisation, which has been initiated without cause and without prior analysis of how economic problems and hence, societal problems, can be solved. In their race to rob as much as they can of the national wealth of the country today because tomorrow it will be too late, the ruling circles quite deliberately avoid seeking any systematic philosophical concept for the transition from totalitarianism to democracy. Such a philosophical concept would inevitably require that the question be posed of the meaning of the transition itself, of the meaning of everything happening in Bulgaria today.

The philosopher is the only one who can ask about the meaning of things and processes. He asks questions and provides answers. Free philosophical thinking may not be allowed to overrun the public space because the first thing any smart philosopher would do is to unmask the true intentions and purposes of ruling circles. Unbridled corruption thrives at all levels of authority, as is evidenced by the confession of one Member of Parliament that he does not own a single tie that has cost less than 200 US Dollars. Corruption is the strongest protection in the ruling circles against the penetration of philosophical thinking and its quest to uncover the meaning of what is happening. The rulers do not want to be exposed for what they are (robbers) and do everything possible to keep philosophy at bay.

Philosophy and philosophers are furthermore kept at bay for another reason. This reason lies in the total amorality of both the ruling circles and the 'opposition' and this circumstance also denies the necessity of a philosophical perspective on what is being done in the country. There has hardly been such a tragicomic moment before now in the history of Bulgaria The most unscrupulous robbers talk in the quiet and singsong voice of preachers and try to resemble exhausted and hungry people. These people have neither shame nor morality and insolently compare themselves to Christ. Not only do they not feel a need philosophy, it might pose a threat to them and their work. The dishonourable person, the demagogue and hypocrite has always felt an organic hostility to philosophy because the morality it carries is a complete denial of the own amoral credo and behaviour.

The fourth and last objective reason for the lack of success of philosophy is also connected with one indicative aspect of the overall activity of the ruling circles. This aspect relates to the incredible and artificially forced admiration of pragmatic principles, of the so-called expert procedures, which inevitably will lead to poverty of mind and ideas, to the inability to make operational generalisations on the essence of current processes. Nowadays in our country the opinion is that the time of ideological statements of universal theoretical constructions, when reality could be conceptually contained, has irretrievably passed. The constant parading of the idea that we are pragmatic and do not care about ideology in our search for practical solutions to problems here and now normally leads to the alienation of those who engage themselves in long-lasting abstract conceptual schemes, which are inspired by the famous, although paradoxical, maxim that nothing is more practical than good theory. But theory is not in demand from amoral robbers and typical parvenus from the Balkans from the beginning of the century (although they live at its end). These are people who believe in immediate action, in the pragmatic approach and in the 'philosophy' of profit!

The above four reasons accounting for the status of philosophy, which are external with regard to its essence, may be summarised, in fact, into one general reason. This is the harmful quality of leaders who happen by chance to be in power at such a crucial moment from historical point of view. In fact, here the law formulated by Karl Jaspers can be seen in action, namely the law that a clique of spiritually, intellectually and morally mediocre people who are otherwise clever, calculating and fanatically persistent in their pursuit of their own mercenary motives is always in the lead in crucial moments.

The second category of reasons for the unfavourable situation of philosophy in Bulgaria today lies in the condition and behaviour of the philosophical community itself. It seems as if this community has voluntarily left the 'battlefield'

and, withdrawing into its own extremely specific problems, has given up enter-
ing the social and political market with new and efficient strategic views on the
development of Bulgaria from a long-term perspective.

On the one hand, this self-isolation might be interpreted as an expression of a
peculiar protest against undeserving treatment of philosophy in society,
against the poor conditions for development that have been imposed on it and
against the express non-commitment of philosophers whose potential is pur-
posefully ignored and whose public prestige is deliberately and constantly be-
littled. On the other hand, however, self-isolation of the philosophical community might be interpreted as an objective expression of its deep degradation
under conditions of formal servility during the course of nearly half a century.

If we accept the second interpretation as more authentic and closer to the truth,
then the conclusion could be drawn that during the totalitarian communist
regime in our country, a horde of philosophers, both novices and philosopher–
exorcists, originated. Through their activities, these people destroyed the essence of philosophising in Bulgaria, they interrupted the development of our
own philosophical thinking by reducing its previous diversity and polemical
wealth to a dogmatic and self-sufficing ideology which was meant to serve the
interests of an unscrupulous party and political clique. During this period true
philosophical errors and miserable, but at the same time awful, caricatures of
philosophers occupied the place of such leading figures like Dimitar Mihalchev
or Ivan Georgov. These caricatures of philosophers moved for quite a long time
in the great field of philosophy without being disturbed; on the contrary, they
were tolerated and established a group of loyal followers. Unfortunately, these
are the people that now deeply and, perhaps irretrievably compromise philosophy, because people with a free and independent mind, with an authentic
philosophical vocation and understanding of the great social function of philosophy belong to the minority. People like Assen Ignatov or Zhelju Zhelev, for
example, belong to this minority of Bulgarian philosophers. During the last few
years as a chairman of the Bulgarian Association of Philosophy I have travelled
abroad to congresses and conferences in philosophy. It always makes me feel
sad when I understand that Bulgarian names are not known today to the international college of philosophers.

What is the weakest point of the contemporary Bulgarian philosopher? In my opinion it is his hyper-specialisation, dealing as he does with different minor problems that presuppose sophisticated discussions on the nature of the philosopher, all of which, of course, are incomprehensible to society at large with its ideas and expectations. Is it possible for us to point out at least one name of a Bulgarian philosopher whose word as a personality, as a representative of thinking and morality carries weight in society and echoes loudly in people's consciousness? I for one cannot find such a name. The shortage of personalities in philosophy is the fundamental reason for its poor situation today! This shortage of personalities – missionaries in philosophy – 'allows' the negative objective factors to act with such great effect, working towards the complete crushing of the philosophical class and its obliteration from the spiritual map of Bulgaria.

Otherwise, we have wise and intelligent philosophers but every one of them deals with something personal and remains in isolation. For example, one of them studies in detail philosophy of the Middle Ages with its scholastic disputes, but he is unknown to society. Another devotes himself to the witty and delicate matter of classical and neo-classical logics, but society is only occasionally reminded of him by some outdated and retrograde thought. Yet another drifts along in the field of physical immensity, focusing on it in a philosophical way, but in society, he does not say a single word.

We have reached the moment when we must ask the following question: Is there any possibility of finding a brave way out of this critical situation and of making progress in philosophical activities? The answer to this question may not be simple. I would venture to say that as the situation in philosophy has resulted most of all from qualitative defects of the philosophical community itself, which has lost its individuality as a whole and from the point of view of the necessity of developed individuals, then the painful and weary way out lies in the determined mobilisation of its own internal resources, in taking a stance and in becoming actively engaged in society. All of this will increase the confidence of society in philosophers. Even though this solution will require quite a lot of time, it is possible. If it is to succeed, a national forum of Bulgarian philosophers must be summoned on the initiative of the Bulgarian Association of Philosophy; Under conditions of a painful but tolerant discussion this forum shall discuss with criticism and self-criticism the present situation and shall present a substantiated opinion on future activities of the philosophical community and on its self-entrusting with mental pursuits completely appropriate to it and shall justify in general its existence.

Education Within Theoretical and Practical Framework

Betül ÇOTUKSÖKEN

"(...) education can be reduced neither to the theory nor to the action. If it is a theory on one hand, it is an action on the other hand. Education is such a tissue that both the theory and the action are assimilated within itself. In education, both are important. It appears that the proportion of their importance varies within all educational conditions. It is this proportion of importance that determines who educates who, within what means, and from what educational view-points. From technical productivities, common to anybody, to the most abstract cultural accomplishments, education holds a meaning from the point of both knowing and doing; that is to say, from gardening to the solution of mathematical equations."[1]

Fernand Braudel appreciates the geography, the society, the economy and mentality as the constructive elements of any civilisation in his book entitled *Grammar of the Civilisations*. By this way, Braudel replies to the question as to what the conditions are in order to make up a civilisation, qua civilisation. The element playing the most major role in the given answer is the mentality that determines many situations in the context of civilisation; the human being is really indebted his existence to the cultural conditions for overcoming the nature. At this point, the most important question to be answered is how and in which way the human being constructs his relationship between civilisation (or culture) and himself. Man owing his existence to the civilisation and cultural acquisitions builds up his relationship by means of education. Man both as an educating and educated being communicates the endless forms or appearences of civilisation and culture through education. Thus, education as a milieu of communication constitutes a framework of the world concretized in civilisation and

---

1   Nermi Uygur, *Kuram-Eylem Bağlamı. Çözümleyici Bir Felsefe Denemesi* (The Context of Theory and Action. An Analytical Essay of Philosophy, First edition 1975), Yapı Kredi Yayınları, Istanbul, 1996, p. 135.

culture. The most determining element in education in which numerous views vary according to the quality of the educational environment, the instruments, attitudes and the mentality of people either educating or educated by nature appears itself in the objectives and the intentions[2] adopted. Those who consciously think about why and how they educate people in line with their intentions and goals are the acting subjects or the educators of the fact of education and they constitute the institutions in which all sorts of educational processes are realized. The fact that the individual beings gather in line with the predetermined common goals puts forward the public quality of educational acts, as it will be mentioned later. Institutions having to do with education make up the milieus which reflect the mentality either directly or indirectly. Therefore, let us focus on the elements which contribute to the fact of education; education as a kind of civilisation exists in a definite place or cultural environment that requires a society, social and public relations as well. At the same time, every fact of education is a construction with an economical dimension and owns a system of ideas, values and theories orientating all educational processes. In other words, these processes have an intellectual, conceptual or theoretical background. Moreover, it is obvious that each element taking part in the fact of education and cultural environment mutually affect each other. This is because every element is done and created by human being constructing the historical dimension of being and this area is under the impact of the interaction category as in nature.

As we consider all elements which construct education, we can clearly understand that education is an endeauvour concerning formation. As we look at what is happening around us or the flow of daily life, we can discover that each generation is in charge of forming the next. In this context, we can say that all individuals who participate in the fact of education, are in synchronic and diachronic relations taking and giving a formation. In the history of educational ideas, Plato is a philosopher who well understands that education is an activity which provides formation and because of that W. Jaeger draws attention to the parallelism between the German word "Bildung" and the essence of education as Plato mentions.[3] As we analyse the intellectual/conceptual aspect of education as the most significant element for both education in the attempt of providing formation and civilisation, we can suggest that it is the conception concerning

---

2   Intention means objective or goal. This point is very important in this context.

3   W. Jaeger, *Paideia: The Ideals of Greek Culture*, translated by G. Highet, Vol. 1, Basic Blackwell, Oxford, 1965, p. XXIII.

human being that may prove to be most important. Therefore, let us ask obviously: what is the essential role of the human conception of education acquired in any educational organisation? At this moment, we can say that this role is a determinant one in the process of formation; because the human conception in this context makes up the intellectual and conceptual appearance of education adopted as a dimension of civilisation. Here, we can ask another question: can we find a common conception on the basis of all educational approaches? At first sight, the given answer would be "no". However, when we become a little attentive, we understand that all educational activities have a common ground whatever their goals and instruments are. That is to change the human beings according to the adopted intentions and goals.

We can argue that Plato and Sophists have a common intention which aims at changing human beings with their different ways of thinking. Remembering the discourse in Plato's dialogues, we can say that the category of the change depends on the people to be educated and their intentions in accordance with the point of view represented by Socrates. While Socrates approaches to the fact of education by the *maieutics* method[4], Sophists try to educate people[5] through intervention; in addition, they aim to set up relations between educated people and democracy.[6] Nevertheless, there is a common attitude between two different approaches according to which human being can easily change. Then, adopting this approach means that there is not an unchangeable essence of human being, does it? Now that we claim there is a continuous change in the educational area, can not we say that the human being does not have an unchangeable essence? However, we insist that all educational conceptions determined by a definitive human conception aiming at providing an unchangeable formation for the individuals, at the last point. Therefore, the ultimate aim is to acquire any formation by means of some educational processes. Nonetheless, this last point to arrive is really the last target in some educational systems. Here, the last point as well as a starting point, is the definitive content, rather than the formal aspect of education. Individuals are educated in accordance with the adopted definitive content; in other words, the individual being becomes an individual who carries out the

---

4   See also *Theaithetos*, 149a-151d; and 150c-d.

5   See totally also the dialogue of *Protagoras*.

6   Philosophers take this subject as a major one from the Ancient period till now. See on this subject, Richard S. Peters, "Democracy and Education" in *Modern Philosophies of Education*, ed. By John Paul Strain, Random House, New York, 1971, pp. 341-353. See also Roger-Pol Droit, *Philosophy and Democracy in the World*, A UNESCO survey Foreword by Federico Mayor, Translation by Catherine Cullen. UNESCO Publishing, 1995.

only unchangeable content of education; in this case, the individual serves as a passive element of the fact of education; neither as the conscious doer nor the actor of the process. It is well known, in traditional education, some constructing elements are fixed and these elements are accepted as the traditions pass on from one generation to the next and thus, this sort of education labelled as "conservative" is realized by means of traditions. On the other hand, open-minded educational conception appreciates the human being as a changeable and/or changing being. However, there is a dominant conception according to which the individual follows some educational pattern and the educated person is a being of possibilites. In such an educational process, the focus is on the form rather than the unchangeable content.

In the light of these determinations, when we have looked back at the history of education, we can notice that there are a lot of educational approaches each varying in a great deal. The authors of the history of education gather some special facts of education with in different intellectual frameworks according to the qualities they have. At this point, an attentive look reveals that it is the human conception that makes each of them different. In general, religious, scientific and philosophical aspects that determine the human conception affect the educational framework as well; this impact is reflected in the institutional constructions. In the Ancient period, the individuals were educated in different communicative milieus, that is to say, in agora, Academia and Lykeion; and in the religious schools in the Middle Ages. The secularization of the school system as well as its varieties has emerged in the modern age.

Towards the end of the Ancient period, education was seen to be realized in different knowledge contexts. By the end of the Ancient p eriod, individuals were started to be educated through the systematic and classified knowledge. The most radical sample of this situation was the education realized by the seven liberal arts. <<The liberal arts denote the seven branches of knowledge that initiate the young into a life of learning. The concept is classical, but the term liberal arts and the division of the arts into the trivium and the quadrivium date from the Middle Ages.>>[7] What is the knowledge included in the context of the seven liberal arts? We can claim that all of them are the formative structures as a kind of language. Linguistic form takes place either as a natural or a symbolic

---

7   Sister Miriam Joseph, C.S.C., *The Trivium. The Liberal Arts of Logic, Grammar, and Rhetoric. Understanding the Nature and Function of Language*, ed. By Marguerite McGlinn. Paul Dry Boks, Philadelphia, 2002, p. 3.

language in the framework of the seven liberal arts. <<The trivium includes those aspects of the liberal arts that pertain to mind, and the quadrivium, those aspects of the liberal arts pertain to matter. Logic, grammar, and rhetoric constitute the trivium; and arithmetic, music, geometry, and astronomy constitute the quadrivium. Logic is the art of thinking; grammar, the art of inventing symbols and combining them to express thought; and rhetoric, the art of communicating thought from one mind to another, the adaptation of language to circumstance. Arithmetic, the theory of number, and music, an application of the theory of number (the measurement of discrete quantities in motion), are the arts of discrete quantity or number. Geometry, the theory of space, are the arts of continuous quantity or extension.>>[8] We can reply to the question concerning "what is the common function of the seven liberal arts?" as such: <<The trivium is the organon, or instrument, of all education at all levels because the arts of logic, grammar, and rhetoric are the arts of communication itself in that they govern the means of communication –namely, reading, writing, speaking, and listening.>>[9] They totally prepare the minds to acquire different knowledge; i. e. what we mean by different knowledge, we refer to the theological knowledge in the Middle Ages. However, the seven liberal arts establish a background to acquire some knowledge essential for daily life such as medicine, law, engineering etc. through understanding the value and importance of the world we live in: <<The seven liberal arts differ essentially from the many utilitarian arts (such as carpentry, masonry, plumbing, salesmanship, printing, editing, banking, law, medicine, or the care of souls) and from the seven fine arts (architecture, instrumental music, sculpture, painting, literature, the drama, and the dance), for both the utilitarian arts and fine arts are transitive activities, whereas the essential characteristic of the liberal arts is that they are immanent and intransitive activities.>>[10]

In time, education ceased to be a process serving to the upper class in the society and it became an institution including many people with a significant share of the new world images and the new communication instruments in the intellectual environment. People became aware of the world where they lived much better and its importance by the Renaissance through which the discovery of

---

8   Op. cit., p. 3.

9   Op. cit., p. 6.

10   Op. cit., p. 4.

the mind, the body and the discovery of the world in the relationship of the other as well became the propulsive power of all kinds of change. The new method created to know the entities and the new ideal of knowing aimed to change the human being through this new educational system. The first endeavours concerning education were situated in the utopian discourses which used to be dominant throughout this period. The ideal in these utopias related to education primarily focused on humanistic qualities. Humanistic educational approach contains three properties of humanism: <<1) Humanism not only describes the facts but also it assigns the things that ought to be done. 2) Humanism does not comprehend the human being by means of the unchangeable essence. 3) In accordance with the idea in which Man does not have an unchangeable essence predetermined. Man is a changeable and can be educated being, and humanism has a transformative role for creating the new human being. In this case, the essential goal is to achieve the active humanism.>>[11] We can say that humanism has not ceased to be an ideal thanks to the Renaissance utopias; in contrast, these utopias have opened ways of the active humanism. The utopias in question have appreciated human beings as a being with many possibilities clearly putting forward the ways of changing the human being by means of education. For instance, Thomas More has proposed the ideal of lifelong education in his book entitled *Utopia* as <<For it is a solemn custom there to have lectures daily early in the morning, where to be present they only be constrained that be namely chosen and appointed to learning. Howbeit a great multitude of every sort of people, both men and women, go to hear lectures, some one and some another as every man's nature is inclined.>>[12] Humanistic conception of education of the utopias considers the practical dimension of daily life important. As it is well known, the main purpose is to change the human being, society and the whole world by the power of knowledge.

The importance of the experimental world and the practical dimension of life is parallel to the idea of changing. The main goal is to learn, acquire knowledge, teach, educate and to be educated for changing the world where we live in. Doing and knowing how to do gained importance starting from the Renaissance

---

11   Betül Çotuksöken, "Çokanlamlı Bir Kavram Olarak Hümanizma", *Kavramlara Felsefe ile Bakmak*, ("Humanism as an Equivocal Concept", in *Looking at the Concepts through Philosophy*) İnsancıl Yayınları, Istanbul, 1998, p. 133.

12   Thomas More, "The Second Book, IV. Of Sciences, Crafts, and Occupations", The *Utopia of Sir Thomas More*, translated by Ralph Robinson, Macmillan and Co., Limited, London, 1937, p. 75.

period. Rabelais and Montaigne suggest some ideas by different discourses. The subject who intends to his history of the act of knowing, in Descartes's sample, attempts to account for his condition, putting a distance between his knowledge and himself. That Enlightenment and the writers of encyclopaedia endeavour to spread all sort of knowledge, especially the knowledge of daily life is very significant from the point of view of the history of knowledge.

In time, that the national dimensions have become valuable and that education is a public action letting; a lot of people share it, at the same time, the education of masses have become the most important agenda of the governments in the european geography. Becoming a nation and adopting the vernacular language as a national language, reorganizing the public area as a nationalistic one, have led to reform the educational acts in the nationalistic quality. Communities with an experience in the processes of nationalisation in different periods and interactive relations as well have tried to lay a foundation for the changes that they have realized in their political conditions by means of the scientific and philosophic concepts. The processes of nationalisation have become concretized within national language and in a nationally qualifed education as well. Especially, the West and the North European countries have started to establish the public order with an understanding of the "social welfare state" that has well appeared in organizing education. Schools, universities and lifelong education taking place only through the pages of utopian texts once upon a time have been seriously appreciated by socialist governments and people. In Denmark, for instance, Nikolai Frederik Severin Grundtvik's endeavours concerning the establishment of the public schools and high schools for young people and adults were the most significant ones in the first half of the nineteenth century. From this point of view, one of the European Union educational projects has been recently given the name of Grundtvik; this is quite a meaningful and an important act; since this project in question is very broad and has been considered for adults only.

A similar educational program was realized in the early years of the Republican period in Turkey. The Republican government that aimed to educate every citizen according to their own needs for all ages established "Public Houses" (Halk Evleri) in 1932 on one hand, it developed, on the other hand, a new educational model developed particularly for children from rural areas with limited resources based on humanistic foundation under the name of "Village Institutes"

(Köy Enstitüleri) in 1936. This educational project was considered and organized according to a conception taking human being as a total being from a theoretical and practical point of view. Organized by the minister of that period, Hasan Ali Yücel, and the general manager of primary teaching, there were some principles on determining the curricula in these institutions. We can enumerate these principles as such:

- Half of the schedule includes the cultural studies and the other part covers agricultural and technical studies.
- Instead of the courses, issues and knowledge with no functions at all the courses and knowledge provided to meet needs, takes part in school program.
- The choice of the teaching issues and courses should be applicable in daily life.
- To teach in the areas of production and work. The implementation of the cultural studies in the field of work and production in integration and unity with each other is of high importance as well as ending all courses and studies in practice and production. The implementation of such a Project protected the individuals' educational rights as a basic human right as well.>>[13]

Clearly, education is a basic human need and a basic human right as well. *The Universal Declaration of Human Rights* in Article 26 declares on this issue as such: <<

(1) Everyone has the right to education. Education shall be free, at least in the elementary and fundamental stages. Elementary education shall be compulsory. Technical and professional education shall be made generally available and higher education shall be equally accessible to all on the basis of merit.

(2) Education shall be directed to the full development of the human personality and to the stregthening of respect for human rights and fundamental freedoms. It shall promote understanding, tolerance and friendship among all nations, racial or religious groups, and shall further the activities of the United Nations for the maintenance of peace.

(3) Parents have a prior right to choose the kind of education that shall be given to their children.>>[14] Although this third item of the Article is open to discussion at some points, it is clearly seen that, education is an important need

---

13   Pakize Türkoğlu, *Tonguç ve Enstitüleri* (Tonguç and his Institutes, First edition 1999), Türkiye İş Bankası Yayınları, Istanbul, 2000, p. 212.

and a basic right in human life. What is the thesis proposing that "Education is a basic right" based on? <<What could be used as a criterion in revising our lists of human rights and also for determining "new" rights, a criterion which would not leave too much ground for dispute concerning the fundamentality of some rights? The systematic knowledge of Man's potentialities of the conditions securing the ground for the actualisation of these potentialities, affords us the criterion.>>[15] It depends on the use of educational rights as a foundation to see what we have succeeded as a human being. <<There is also another group of rights in which all human beings are equal, fundamental rights that belong to each individual, as human individual, i. e. which are not given, but neither can be respected nor violated. They are demands related to the pre-conditions affording each individual the possibility to develop his human potentialities. Rights such as the right to a standart of living adequate for one's health, the right to education etc. The difficulty with such rights is that their fulfillment is dependent on rights of another kind, that they can be protected only indirectly, through other rights given to individuals by a State –through social-economic-(and some) political- and through public institutions and organized founded, not always but mostly, by political decisions>>[16] As it is clearly seen, the provision of education as a basic right, by nature, requires a milieu of public and institutional communication and therefore it must be protected by the public order.

At the beginning of the 21st century where we are in, education is an important fact especially in globalization which is a new communicative position. The globalization has obviously showed that there are great differences between individuals. At this point, it is well understood that education is a basic need. The circulation of productions and services have increased the significant role of education. If we focus on this issue, the humanistic educational notion specifically outlined has gained a great importance. However, we have a lot of troubles in this context. The most controversial issue has to do with the question on how to overcome these inequalities around us. The public dimension of education has been ignored by some people or states. In fact, education with a theoretical and practical framework is a public and institutional affair and should be

---

14 *Universal Human Rights Declarations*, Article: 26.

15 Ioanna Kuçuradi, "Philosophy and Human Rights", *Philosophical Foundation of Human Rights*, Hacettepe University, Ankara, 1982, p. 48.

16 *Op. cit.*, p. 50.

protected by the public institutions. This action has been realized in different levels. For instance, European Union Education Programs is one of the sample programs concerning this issue. The dominant aspect of the projects practised and works realized in the context of education is of humanistic quality. This sort of education, as mentioned before, appreciates the human being as a being of possibilities and aims to promote the human potentialities and abilities including such skills as reading, writing, building up true communication, creative, innovative and critical thinking, solving problems and knowing himself and so on. The humanistic education has a principle as to approaching to educational processes from humanistic view-point and is of a secular quality from this perspective. In a nutshell, the humanistic education is an education taking human world as a whole and binding the theoretical and practical qualities together; as human life is a totality of both aspects.

Contributors

Agazzi, Evandro, Professor, Department of Philosophy, University of Genova, Italy, president of Academie internationale de philosophie des sciences (AIPS); agazzi@nous.unige.it

Çotuksöken, Betül, Professor, Maltepe University, Faculty of Science and Letters, Istanbul, Turkey Vice-President of the Philosophical Society of Turkey; betulc@maltepe.edu.tr

Evans, David, Professor, School of Philosophical Studies, Queen's University, Belfast, UK; jdg.evans@qub.ac.uk

Ferrari, Jean, professeur émérite et associé, Centre Bachelard de l'Université de Bourgogne, Dijon, France; fax: +33-(0)3-80662206

Jensen, Bernard Eric, Associate Professor, Department of Curriculum Research, Danish University of Education, Copenhagen, Denmark; bernard@dpu.dk

Kaltchev, Ivan, Professor, Sofia University, Bulgaria Chairman of the Bulgarian Philosophical Association, President of Association of Philosophers from South-Eastern Europe; ivan_kaltchev@yahoo.com

Kemp, Peter, Professor, Head, Department of Philosophy of Education, Danish University of Education, Copenhagen, Denmark, President of FISP; kemp@dpu.dk

Korsgaard, Ove, Associate Professor, Department of Philosophy of Education, Danish University of Education, Copenhagen, Denmark; ove@dpu.dk

Ku d, Maija, Professor, Institute of Philosophy and Sociology, University of Latvia, Riga, Latvia; FSI@ac.lza.lv

McBride, William L., Professor, Department of Philosophy, Purdue University, West Lafayette, Indiana, USA; wmcbride@purdue.edu

Moran, Dermot, Professor, Department of Philosophy, University College Dublin, Ireland, dermot.moran@ucd.ie

Poser, Hans, Professor, Institute for Philosophy and History of Science and Technology, Technical University Berlin, Germany; Hans.Poser@tu-berlin.de

Riverón, Thalia Fung, Dra. Sc., profesa, Universidad de la Habana, Cuba;
thf@ffh.uh.cu, thaliafung@yahoo.com, fung@infomed.sld.cu

Rojo, Basilio, Professor, University of the Americas, Cholula, Puebla, Mexico;
brojo@mail.udlap.mx

Schmidt, Lars-Henrik, Professor, Rector, Danish University of Education, Copenhagen, Denmark; rektor@dpu.dk

Stepaniants, Marietta, Head, Department of the Oriental Philosophies, Director,
Center for Oriental Philosophies' Studies at the Institute of Philosophy, Russian
Academy of Sciences, Moscow; Professor and Head, Chair of Philosophy and
Political Thought of the East of the Russian State University of Humanities,
Moscow, Russian Federation; editor_iei@iicas.org

Sweet, William, Professor and Chair, Department of Philosophy, Director of Centre
for Philosophy, Theology and Cultural Traditions, St. Francis Xavier University,
Nova Scotia, Canada, Secretary General, World Union of Catholic Philosophical
Societies; wsweet@stfx.ca

Yao, Jiehou, Professor, Institute of Philosophy Chinese Academy of Social Sciences,
Institute of Philosophy, Chinese Academy of Social Sciences, Beijing, China;
yaojiehou@hotmail.com

All contributors except David Evans, Bernard Eric Jensen, Ove Korsgaard and
Lars-Henrik Schmidt are members of the Steering Committee of FISP - the Inter-
national Federation of Philosophical Societies / Fédération Internationale des
Sociétés de Philosophie